Urban Castles

THE COLUMBIA HISTORY OF URBAN LIFE

Kenneth T. Jackson, General Editor

THE COLUMBIA HISTORY OF URBAN LIFE
Kenneth T. Jackson, General Editor

Deborah Dash Moore, *At Home in America: Second Generation New York Jews*   1981

Edward K. Spann, *The New Metropolis: New York City, 1840–1857*   1981

Matthew Edel, Elliott D. Sclar, and Daniel Luria, *Shaky Palaces: Homeownership and Social Mobility in Boston's Suburbanization*   1984

Steven J. Ross, *Workers on the Edge: Work, Leisure, and Politics in Industrializing Cincinnati, 1788–1890*   1985

Andrew Lees, *Cities Perceived: Urban Society in European and American Thought, 1820–1940*   1985

R. J. R. Kirkby, *Urbanization in China: Town and Country in a Developing Economy, 1949–2000 A.D.*   1985

Judith Ann Trolander, *Professionalism and Social Change: From the Settlement House Movement to Neighborhood Centers, 1886 to the Present*   1987

Marc A. Weiss, *The Rise of the Community Builders: The American Real Estate Industry and Urban Land Planning*   1987

Jacqueline Leavitt and Susan Saegert, *From Abandonment to Hope: Community-Households in Harlem*   1990

Richard Plunz, *A History of Housing in New York City: Dwelling Type and Social Change in the American Metropolis*   1990

David Hamer, *New Towns in the New World: Images and Perceptions of the Nineteenth-Century Urban Frontier*   1990

Andrew Heinze, *Adapting to Abundance: Jewish Immigrants, Mass Consumption, and the Search for American Identity*   1990

Chris McNickle, *To Be Mayor of New York: Ethnic Politics in the City*   1993

Clay McShane, *Down the Asphalt Path: The Automobile and the American City*   1994

Clarence Taylor, *The Black Churches of Brooklyn*   1994

Frederick Binder and David Reimers, *"All the Nations Under Heaven": A Racial and Ethnic History of New York City*   1995

Clarence Taylor, *Knocking at Our Own Door: Milton A. Galamison and the Struggle to Integrate New York City Schools*   1997

Andrew S. Dolkart, *Morningside Heights: A History of Its Architecture and Developement*   1998

Urban Castles

Tenement Housing and Landlord Activism in
New York City, 1890—1943

Jared N. Day

NEW YORK   COLUMBIA UNIVERSITY PRESS

Columbia University Press
Publishers Since 1893
New York Chichester, West Sussex
Copyright © 1999 Columbia University Press
All rights reserved
Library of Congress Cataloging-in-Publication Data
Day, Jared N., 1963–
  Urban castles : tenement housing and landlord
  activism in New York City, 1890–1943 / Jared N. Day
    p. cm. – (Columbia history of urban life)
    Includes bibliographical references and index.
    ISBN 0–231–11402–8 (cloth)
    ISBN 0–231–11403–6 (pbk.)
    1. Tenement houses–New York (State)–New York
–History. 2. Apartment houses–New York (State)–
New York –History. 3. Landlord and tenant–New York
(State)–New York–History. 4. City and town life–New
York (State)–New York–History. 5. New
York (N.Y.)–Social conditions. I. Title. II. Series.
HD7287.6.U52N73   1999
333.33'8–dc21   99–25052
                                                         CIP

Casebound editions of Columbia University Press
books are printed on permanent and durable acid-free
paper.
Printed in the United States of America
c 10 9 8 7 6 5 4 3 2 1
p 10 9 8 7 6 5 4 3 2 1

*Dedicated to my parents,
Jon W. Day and
Dorothy R. Day*

CONTENTS

Acknowledgments ix

Introduction 1

1. The Growth of Tenement Districts in the Tenement Owner's City 7
2. Tenement Ownership and Ethnic Enterprise in New York City 31
3. Landlord Activism in the Early Twentieth Century 57
4. Rent Strikes and the Landlord's "Reign of Terror" 93
5. Shades of Activism During the Red Scare 119
6. Landlords in the Tenants' Court 143
7. The Depression and the Decline of Amateur Tenement Operators 169

Conclusion: The Tenant City 191

Notes 195

Selected Bibliography 243

Index 255

ACKNOWLEDGMENTS

From my earliest thoughts of studying real estate associations, I have had the assistance of many good colleagues and friends. Foremost among them are Joel Tarr and Steven Schlossman, who have given their time, expertise, and unstinting support to this project. To both of them, I am deeply grateful.

The following people have all helped to shape this project, sometimes indirectly and often in ways that they themselves might not fully appreciate. I happily thank those who first encouraged my earliest examinations of tenement ownership in New York in the nineteenth century. They helped convince me that the topic had real possibilities. At Bard College, I would like to thank Mark Lytle, Dick Wiles, John Fout, Alice Stroup, Carol Karlsen, and especially Myra Young-Armstead.

At Carnegie Mellon University, a number of professors, graduate students, and library staff gave me invaluable assistance in shaping this topic for my dissertation. Thanks go to Peter Stearns, Kate Lynch, Mary Lindemann, Sue Collins, and especially to David Miller, Eugene Levy, and Joe Trotter, who gave very generously of their time and expertise. Two colleagues I would especially like to thank for their unwavering support are Joseph Spillane of Florida State University and Steven Corey of Worcester College. I would also like to thank Lisa Sigel, Matthew Weiss, Jennifer Trost, Sherie Mershon, Steven Hoffman, Marilyn Zoidis, Bob Gleeson, Matthew Hawkins, and particularly Timothy Haggerty.

In the greater New York area, I would like to thank various faculty at Columbia University, City University, Queens College, and elsewhere who assisted me in shaping this research and gathering material for what has proven to be an elusive topic requiring (as Elizabeth Blackmar predicted) an "eclectic approach" to sources. Particular thanks to Marc Weiss, Elizabeth Blackmar, Joel Schwartz, Arlene Newman, Ronald Lawson, and Kenneth Jackson who each gave me what I needed when I had no clue as to where to go next. Thomas Kessner's National Endowment for the Humanities 1995 Summer Seminar on the History of New York City reactivated my enthusiasm for this project and began the manuscript's transformation from a dissertation into a book. A Loewenstein-Weiner Fellowship from the Jacob R. Marcus Archives at Hebrew Union College provided me critical assistance in rewriting several chapters. Thanks to Kevin Profitt and the Archives staff.

I would also like to thank Ruth Carr and Mark Andres of the New York Public Library, as well as the librarians, archivists, and staff at Avery Library at Columbia, the New York Historical Society, the Municipal Library, Babbage Library at the University of Connecticut, and particularly the New York State Library in Albany and the Library of Congress. For their invaluable assistance gathering and organizing a huge amount of material, I would also like to thank Silk Kaya and Katie Barry. Special thanks as always to Ruth and Marjorie Maher who, for thirteen years, have allowed me to share their wonderful home on my numerous trips to New York.

Finally, I would like to thank my family. They have all contributed to my success, and, without them, this study would never have been made. Thanks and much love to my parents, Jon and Dorothy Day; and my brother and his family, Jon, Pam, Jonnie, Sydney, and Sammy.

Urban Castles

INTRODUCTION

Tenement landlords designed and shaped the urban landscapes of nineteenth- and twentieth-century America. They built the homes for the nation's growing industrial workforce and then managed those homes in ways that, in many cities, created some of the most haunting and lasting images of urban life—images that challenged generations of social reformers and mocked prevailing views of America as a nation of limitless promise and economic opportunity. Left with the task of housing *everyone* who could not afford to buy their own homes, urban landlords routinely undermined the grand schemes of urban reform and transformed so-called "model" homes and communities into scornful tributes to the reformers' faltering commitment. As much as politicians, designers, architects, developers, and city planners, landlords were central to the city-building process.

Despite their critical importance, very little is known about exactly how tenement landlords operated, who they were, or how they influenced public policy, and this lack of understanding is due largely to scholars failure to tell the landlord's story on so many *basic historical levels*. The landlord's shadow drifts through every history of tenement housing, through every empirical analysis of inner-city slums, and through every journal and newspaper broadside directed against rental housing conditions, in New York City and elsewhere—even those explicitly targeting landlords! And yet, their social, political, and economic history remains largely unknown, the political influence and tactics of landlord leaders and activists remains obscure, and the changing business practices of landlords (and others in the real estate business) have been treated by scholars as an arcane field largely divorced from the main forces that have built America's cities in the twentieth century.

Exploring the landlord's role in this process requires a marriage of two fields of historical inquiry: real estate history and social history. Still a young field by any measure, real estate history explores the interrelationships between people and the land on which they live, how land is organized and used, and what social, institutional, and economic forces create new forms of usage. This approach has yielded many outstanding works. Such studies are at their best when they explore the competing interests in government and within the real estate industry, showing how different laws, policies, and programs affect the shape of the urban terrain. Works such as Marc Weiss's *The Rise of the Community Builders* and Richard Plunz's *A History of Housing in New York City* have shown the critical role of the state in interceding in the city-building process with often unpredictable results. With their emphasis on the state's role as mediator, these works provide a very useful framework for examining urban realtors and developers. Unfortunately, scholars of real estate history have focused largely on the role of innovative upper-class developers, realtors, architects, politicians, and planners. Tenement landlords, whose clientele are for the most part the working poor, have received no attention at all. As a group, landlords *cannot* be understood without recognizing the vital economic and cultural barriers that divided this class of real estate owner.[1]

More than any other group of property owners, tenement landlords stood directly on the social fault lines of class, ethnicity, and race. For tenement landlords, there was no disguising the mistrust and antipathy underlying their relationship with their primary customers — urban, working-class tenants. In general, social historians have done better at capturing these social divisions and long-term changes in patterns of behavior and public perception. Works such as Thomas Kessner's *The Golden Door: Italian and Jewish Immigrant Mobility in New York City, 1880–1915*; Edel, Sclar, and Luria's *Shaky Palaces: Homeownership and Social Mobility in Boston's Suburbanization*, and Bodnar, Simon and Weber's *Lives of Their Own: Blacks, Italians, and Poles in Pittsburgh, 1900–1960* demonstrate this approach for New York and comparable cities.[2] With their larger emphasis on racial, ethnic and class divisions, these studies tend to overlook the internal dynamics of the real estate industry, particularly in regard to rental housing, areas in which real estate historians have excelled.

For real estate history and social history, a few studies have already bridged these two disciplines, and their findings speak directly to the broader history of landlords and tenants. Elizabeth Blackmar, most notably, has demonstrated that industrial capitalism transformed patterns of land use in New York and brought differentiation and conflict along the lines of class, gender, and ethnicity. In *Manhattan for Rent*, Blackmar examines the formation of the real estate and housing markets in New York from 1785 to 1850. She shows how the changing relations of production and the increasing separation of home and work ultimately led to greater economic inequality and concentration of property ownership. Blackmar's work is central for understanding how the economic organization of real estate influences social relations between owners and renters. However, in noting the growing diversification of labor within the working class, she continues, for the most part, to treat landowners as a monolith. Blackmar's study does not account for the "division of labor" that existed among owners and managers. Moreover, *Manhattan for Rent* fails to capture the intense conflict that existed within the real estate industry between property owners of all classifications.

In contrast, Donna Gabaccia, in her essay "Little Italy's Decline; Immigrant Realtors and Investors in a Changing City" explores both the social and economic role of landlords in New York's Little Italy. The author examines family relationships and friendship networks among the area's residents and shows how these relationships were shaped, in part, by the investment strategies of neighborhood insiders who built new tenements—insiders who were gradually displaced by more powerful corporate developers.[3] Both Blackmar and Gabaccia provide fundamental theoretical and factual underpinnings for a more thorough examination of tenement landlords in the late nineteenth and early twentieth centuries.

Therefore, by building on their work and others, my aim is to approach the process of city building and the growth of tenement districts as the products of class-based competing agendas brought forward by rental consumers, on the one hand, and class-based internal conflicts within rental housing providers on the other—conflicts that transformed patterns of land use, the legal framework governing urban real estate, and the entire economic and political fabric of property relations. I hope to shed some light into all of these areas.

I propose the cross-threading of two fields not simply for the sake of tracing a new course for the history of housing policy in New York, but rather to put forth a case study that provides an invaluable glimpse into the broader historical world of corporate advocacy. This inquiry explores those organizations, individuals, and social movements which have represented the institutional brains and muscle that lay behind so-called "corporate influence." Through a broad array of social and political groups and associations, business people mold public policy and ultimately shape the urban landscape. They do so, however, not necessarily from within the plush, well-ordered boardrooms of executives but rather in the more chaotic world of small-scale entrepreneurs—a world that, in the nineteenth century, was filled with modest stores, offices, and pushcarts. This analysis of tenement operators can be likened to the work of new labor historians in chronicling the struggle between large corporations and organized labor. In this case, however, the "corporations" are small-scale real estate providers, and their antagonists are working-class consumers. More broadly, such an approach requires that scholars of the twentieth century examine the dark underside of America's emerging welfare state in the last hundred years and to take seriously those individuals and organizations that have bitterly opposed these efforts to expand the rights of workers and consumers. Largely marginalized as obstructionists in these struggles, corporate advocates and the small-scale business people they often represented nonetheless exercised a decisive influence over public policy, urban reform, labor activism, and the environment, and their decisions helped shape the twentieth-century city as we know it.

Such an approach also requires a more detailed examination of business people and a broader application of many of the methodologies developed in social and labor history. In general, social historians, with their theoretical dichotomy between the study of wealthy and middle-class elites, on the one side, and larger society on the other have avoided systematic examinations of the gray areas in-between, particularly in regard to lower-middle-class and the upper-working-class business people. Indeed, the history of these small-scale entrepreneurs begins with us, as historians, taking the day-to-day business persons' *world*, their activities, politics, and outlook, more seriously. Just as studies of the working class have benefited from a fuller analysis of work processes, so an examination of lower-middle-class business people should begin with a clearer understanding of their activities and their "work world."

Some caveats must be stated from the outset. While one of my goals is to explore the social dynamics of tenement management, I have consciously chosen not to examine in detail two critical aspects—race and gender. I made this choice in the belief that the scope and time range of this study are too broad to do justice to such vital topics.

While the organization of this study is fundamentally chronological, each chapter also touches on certain central themes of tenement management in New York and the city's changing landlord-tenant relations. Chapter 1 examines the historical development of tenement districts from the colonial period up to the late nineteenth century. Building on the works of Blackmar and others, it describes the changing patterns of land use that led to a concentration of property ownership into the hands of a small group of large land owners. Chapter 2 explores the different types of tenement landlords that existed in the city at the turn of the twentieth century. It examines who they were, how they financed tenement construction, and how many of them interacted with the community at large. It describes the critical, social, and economic divisions that existed among the wealthy loan operators, the middle- and lower-middle-class tenement owners, and the relatively poor building lessees. While a wide range of socioeconomic groups gradually gained access to tenement property ownership, it came at a terrible price, as the only way many of these landlords could sustain themselves was by deliberately neglecting their properties—properties in which members of their own ethnic community often resided.

Chapter 3 examines the political emergence of landlord lobbying organizations as the growing discontent of tenants in the Lower East Side finally drove landlords into action. Assisted by landlord leaders and a larger public sympathetic to the landlord's rights, these nascent tenant movements were crushed. Chapter 4 explores the growth of New York's middle-class tenant population and their emerging sympathy for the plight of working-class tenants. Moreover, this chapter charts how middle-class New Yorkers became drawn into one of the most contentious landlord-tenant battles of the twentieth century, New York's rent strikes of 1918–1920. Chapter 5 explores the increasing involvement of state and local authorities in regulating central aspects of the landlord-tenant relationship even as the tenant movement itself became co-opted into a middle-class reform agenda. Chapter 6 describes the growing role of civil courts in regulating landlord behavior and their effect on basic tenement management practices. Finally, Chapter 7 explores the impact of the Depression on old-style tenement landlords, and the influence of a resurgent tenant movement that not only spelled the end to nineteenth-century styles of tenement operation but also closed out the first era of landlord organizations in New York as they gradually lost their relevance in a new political environment shaped by federally sponsored rent control.

General Tenement Views

Top Left

Entrance to Fisher's Court - 22 to 26 Oak Street. View From Street looking into alley-way circa 1890–1900. Building over 40 years old. Observers noted that this type of tenement "deteriorated through bad management." SOURCE: This illustration, and the others except when otherwise noted, are courtesy of the New York City Tenement House Collection, United States History, Local History & Genealogy Division, The New York Public Library, Astor, Lenox, and Tilden Foundations.

Bottom Left

Rear tenements, 246–254 Mott Street. View showing front and rear buildings. Between the years 1890–1896, 58 orders were made against these buildings by the Board of Health. Between the year 1890–1896 the death rate was 32.59 per 1,000; the city death rate in 1896 was 21.52 per 1,000. These buildings were torn down by order of the Board of Health.

Above

Push carts in tenement back yards, circa 1914.

According to the Tenement House Department, the conditions here were the "fault of the tenant."

CHAPTER 1

The Growth of Tenement Districts in the Tenement Owner's City

In December 1894, Colonel Stephen Van Rensselaer Cruger stood before a state-appointed committee investigating tenement housing conditions in New York. Cruger represented the Trinity Church, the largest owner of tenement houses in the city, many of which, the committee discovered, were dilapidated firetraps rife with disease. One member of the committee criticized Cruger for not abiding by some of the state's health laws as they applied to Trinity's tenement houses. Cruger replied that he considered the law "a very extreme exercise of power to require all the modern improvements to be placed in many of these old houses. . . . We determined that the question had better be determined [in the courts]." Cruger's boss, Morgan Dix, Rector of Trinity, stated more broadly his view on the health laws (and all laws affecting tenant conditions) when he stated in defense of Trinity's policy, "It might be said that much more might have been done and ought to have been expended in such improvements; but that is the easy remark of persons who have no responsibility in the matter; *the corporation must be the judge of its ability to do all that might be done* [my italics]."[1] Such was the view of Dix, Cruger, and virtually every other tenement manager in the city. In nineteenth-century New York, from the lofty board rooms of the Trinity Corporation to the run-down living rooms of small-scale building lessees, tenement operators demanded this authority to run their properties as they saw fit—and to a large extent they got it.

Who lived in these dilapidated structures? The center of the factory district on the Lower East Side, the Tenth Ward, was the most crowded tenement neighborhood in the city, with 523.6 inhabitants per acre. Manhattan as a whole averaged 114 per acre. As Milton Meltzer has noted, by 1914, the streets below Fourteenth Street, an area amounting to one eighty-second of New York's total land area, contained one sixth of the city's population. In 1881, Manhattan's 22,000 slum tenements held 500,000 people. By 1895, around the time of Cruger's testimony, the number of tenements had almost doubled, to 40,000, but the population they contained had risen far higher proportionately—to 1.3 million. More than 95 percent of those slum dwellers were immigrants and their children.[2] For Trinity and thousands of other tenement operators, these were their tenants.

In forming their management policies, Cruger and Trinity Church both drew upon long years of experience in the tenement business. Cruger, with his familial ties to the Van Rensselaers, one of the state's most prominent land-owning families, and Trinity, one of Manhattan's most affluent and prestigious land-owning institutions, both could trace their pedigrees back through generations of privileged land owners whose powers were largely unregulated by the state. Large-scale tenement owners built on long-established patterns of land use based on the region's system of land tenure, a system that had emerged out of early Dutch and English colonial practices.

I. The Origins of the Land Tenure System in New York City

In New York, as in other colonies, European settlers relied on land grants to promote quick settlement and to reward investors. In the early seventeenth century, the Dutch West Indies Company established settlements on Manhattan. Company officials wanted to create both a farming community and an independent port on the island which would provide the basic survival needs of the port's colonists as well as those of the settlers in other Dutch colonies in Albany to the north and along the Delaware River to the south.

The new port, Nieuw Amsterdam or New Amsterdam, was ideally located for both military and commercial purposes, and it served as the gathering point for the primary business of the Dutch—the fur trade.[3] Like Charleston and Boston and other colonial ports established along the Atlantic Coast, it was an island-peninsula, protected from bad winter weather and the sea. It was accessible to major waterways, and it was strategically located between the Dutch outposts in Delaware and in Albany. By September 1626, Fort Amsterdam, thirty houses, and a counting house had been established, and settlers were already clearing fields for company farms called boweries.[4]

Dutch officials had hoped to establish a well-populated port before settling the interior. However, throughout the seventeenth century New Amsterdam had trouble attracting permanent colonists, particularly artisans and laborers. The fur trade drew settlers away to the north and west. People who settled in the colony at their own expense or in the service of others might be granted as much land as they could cultivate. However, as Michael Kammen has noted, the company's terms were comparatively stingy and unattractive, and they did not entice many Dutch to settle in Manhattan in large numbers.[5] Moreover, the fur trade and tenant farming to the north proved more alluring for enterprising settlers. Throughout the seventeenth century, Albany and the upper Hudson Valley overshadowed Manhattan as a point of settlement.[6]

Because of these settlement problems on Manhattan, roughly three distinct patterns of land use emerged on the island, patterns in which the Dutch West Indies Company granted waterfront acreage on Manhattan's southern tip to mercantile interests involved in shipping. For property north of the port (or just north of Wall Street), the Dutch distributed town lots (or lots designed for the construction of a house with a small amount of land) to settlers, including tradesmen and tavern keepers as well as company officials and various churches.[7] For the remaining land on Manhattan, the Company granted large tracts north of settled areas to important company investors such as Peter Stuyvesant.[8]

Large property owners in the Hudson Valley and on Manhattan used their land grants in ways that reflected the two regions' unique economic uncertainties. Hudson Valley landowners relied upon the value of tenants' crops, the payment of milling fees, and ground rents. In these and other ways, land generated wealth. In Manhattan, in contrast, company investors could not copy the tenant-farming system that had developed in the Hudson Valley because large portions of northern and central Manhattan were too swampy, rocky, and uneven. As Elizabeth Blackmar has argued, the island's large property owners viewed land primarily as a resource that stored, displayed, and transferred wealth rather than generated it—a pattern copied largely from European precedents. Investment in speculative merchandise was risky. Land represented an investment that could not be lost or destroyed. It also remained a respected form of transferable capital to the other landed elites in the port and in the Hudson Valley with whom property owners usually did business. For colonial merchants and magnates in New Amsterdam, their use of land may have diminished their possible return, but it also helped minimize their potential risk.[9]

The Dutch and the Dutch West India Company began to lose control of land distribution as other nationalities came to dominate the colony. The company had faced severe problems regarding the recruitment of labor. It had to choose suitable immigrants, entice them to go, motivate them to work, and induce them to stay after their term of service had expired. This was especially problematic since, in general, the working hours were long and the wages low. To solve the problem, company officials attracted immigrants from all over northern and western Europe. As a result, as Michael Kamman has noted, the whole colony of New Netherland developed as the most socially heterogeneous of all the North American colonies.[10] The English came in particularly large numbers, both from their colonies in New England and from Britain. By the 1660s, the English settlers to the north and south of Manhattan were tenfold more numerous than the Dutch, and, even in New Amsterdam, the Dutch were close to being a minority.

The migration of English settlers had long-term political consequences for New Amsterdam and its Dutch masters. For years, England's King Charles II had been eager to challenge the Dutch commercial and maritime strength in the Atlantic. The Anglo-Dutch trade rivalry had been festering for years, and many English officials believed that the presence of a Dutch colony midway between New England and Maryland threatened England's Atlantic possessions. As a result, the British Council for

Foreign Plantations asked Charles to claim New Netherland by whatever means they could contrive. In 1664, the King used John Cabot's voyage to America in 1497 as a pretense for assuming control of the entire area. Shortly thereafter, he gave the colony to his brother, the Duke of York, later King James II, who rechristened the colony New York, and New Amsterdam became New York City.[11]

In Manhattan, to buttress their political support, the new British authorities made land grants for speculative investment. Officials turned one-hundred to two-hundred-acre tracts located four to eight miles from the port settlement over to private owners. These land grants, like earlier ones, tended to favor those who had already acquired wealth. The English takeover of the colony did little to alter Dutch patterns of property distribution. Along the Hudson, the English left the feudal system intact and adopted it for British landowners. The Livingstons and the Morrises joined the Van Rensselaers, Beekmans, and Bayards, owning what were thereafter referred to as manors. After many years, the Dutch and British landed magnates coalesced into a strong regional elite.[12]

By the mid-eighteenth century, the port of New York was experiencing significant growth. In 1743, New York was the third largest American City, and by 1760 it was second only to Philadelphia. Between 1783 and 1786, the population of the city more than doubled. The city's growth stunned observers. According to on English observer in 1756, "I had no idea of finding a place in America, consisting of nearly 2,000 houses elegantly built of brick, raised on an eminence and the streets paved and spacious, furnished with commodious keys [quays] and warehouses, and employing some hundreds of vessels in foreign trade and fisheries . . . but such is this city that few in England can rival it in its show."[13]

As the port grew, Manhattan upland became part of the city proper and became accessible to landowners and artisans. The municipal corporations owned much of the land north of the port, and as population increased, the corporation put that land up for leases whenever it needed revenue. By 1762, the corporation surveyed lots between the Boston Road and the East River and offered them up for four pounds a year on twenty-one leases. In 1763, it added 31 five-acre lots in the Murray Hill area for farms and homes.[14]

As the value of land increased, landowners began changing the way they used it. With property on the island's southern tip controlled by merchants, land farther north rose in value. Tradesmen and laborers, finding it increasingly difficult to live and work near the city's commercial district, began to look to the periphery to buy property for their shops and homes. However, as they moved northward, as Blackmar has shown, they encountered the large landowners who were holding land as an investment and as a secure repository for wealth. These landowners began subdividing their large tracts into small lots, not for tenant farming—as was the case in the Hudson Valley, but for renting at low rates to workers and tradesmen who were becoming an important element in the city's population. The large property owners negotiated contracts with the tradesmen for the use of the subdivided land, and the owners began to see a steady profit from their tracts. Increased population and New York's growing importance as a port transformed the large tracts of land from simple repositories of wealth into capital-generating resources.[15]

For urban artisans and laborers, this new system of lease holding offered some advantages over similar tenant farming leases. Long-term ground leases allowed artisans to rent land at fairly modest rates, leaving them with enough capital to construct homes and shops. Property owners allowed ground lease holders to use their interest in this land like a title and sell it for the remaining term of the lease. As the city expanded, ground leases replaced small independent ownerships or freeholds as the tradesman's primary means of access to property and housing. The lease-holding system encouraged broad access to land and allowed skilled workers a greater degree of individual control over the home and the workplace.[16] Lease holding also allowed large proprietors to promote settlement and urban expansion without selling their land. Moreover, as land values increased through improvement and other factors, landowners and lease holders were both able to use their interest in the land to make a profit. Lease holders retained the "use value" of the land over time, while landowners received ground rents and future capital gains.[17]

By organizing land in this fashion, large proprietors, such as Henry Rutgers, Peter Stuyvesant, James DeLancey, Peter Warren, and institutions like Trinity Church, significantly limited access to Manhattan land. In the eighteenth century, they each subdivided their estates into lots, adopting long- and short-term agricultural leases. Short-term leases with terms from seven to twenty-one years, were available to artisans while long-term leases ran for up to ninety-nine years. Proprietorship became more concentrated in the hands of a small group of landowners, a trend that was particularly evident on the city's northern fringe where three of five proprietors owned more than one house and two out of five held three or more. By the time of the Revolution, as the number of property owners decreased relative to the population, tradesmen and laborers found it more difficult to gain access to land. Between 1790 and 1814, the percentage of property-owning voters in the city declined by almost one quarter from 46.9 to 22.7.[18]

Following the Revolution, the system of lease holding remained intact, and it became the foundation for the fortunes of many of New York's most prominent families in the nineteenth and twentieth centuries. Between 1785 and 1800, land values in Manhattan skyrocketed in a frenzy of speculation. Improved lands near the town that had sold for $50 an acre following the Revolution rose to $250 by 1800. The assessed valuation of personal and real property in the city increased nearly fourfold in the first decade of the century. While some loyalist families, such as the DeLanceys and the Bayards, lost their property through confiscation, other New Yorkers exploited these new conditions including the Roosevelts, the Janeways, and most notably John Jacob Astor, the so-called "Landlord of New York," whose real estate interests contributed to one of the largest fortunes in the young United States.[19]

II: The Emergence of Tenement Landlords

During the late eighteenth and early nineteenth centuries, New York experienced an economic expansion that transformed the quality and character of artisanal labor. Unlike many urban centers, such as Lynn, Massachusetts, where large manufacturing complexes dominated, New York City developed a diverse economy based on the proliferation of many different kinds of working environments. As Sean Wilentz has noted, manufacturing was centered in small shops and factories, large lofts, as well as garret and cellar sweatshops. By 1840, significant innovation in textiles, printing, the building trades and other industries helped New York to become the preeminent manufacturing and commercial center of the country.

As the city expanded, however, metropolitan industrialization also transformed master-worker relations in many trades through subcontracting, piece work, and especially the division of labor. In the needle trades, workers performed many handicraft tasks in strictly subdivided routines based on piece rates. Often, jobbers contracted out special tasks to independent producers who, in turn, reduced rates and wages even further to make a profit. Business people who succeeded through these methods pressured competitors to follow suit. In most industries where these dynamics took hold, brutal competition led to successive wage reductions and a decline in worker independence.[20] As these practices took hold in the building trades, market forces began to devalue the work of skilled artisans and laborers in trades associated with home construction. This devaluation, furthermore, transformed the quality and character of the homes that builders constructed by shifting their focus from simple but sturdy structures to poorly built firetraps packed to capacity.[21]

These economic changes brought a dramatic influx of immigration. As manufacturing expanded, the demand for unskilled and semi-skilled labor increased. European immigrants came in growing numbers, putting pressure on the city's construction industry to provide homes. As the immigrant population increased, so did the number of tenements and the percentage of New Yorkers living in them. By 1861, fifty percent or 401,376 inhabitants of the city lived in 12,374 tenements and thousands more lived in shacks and shanties.[22] In the seven wards south of Canal Street, the average population density per acre went from 157.5 persons in 1820 to 272.5 in 1850. The gross population density per acre went from 94.5 to 163.5 during the same years.[23]

The demand for working-class housing combined with the changes in work processes helped to transform the building trades. In the colonial era, home construction agreements were usually very personal transactions between landowners and master builders whereby the builder, guided by the owner's detailed specifications, constructed a house using skilled journeymen. However, in the early nineteenth century, small-scale speculative builders began pressuring master builders to reduce costs. Following the depression of 1819–1822, the number of small-scale contractors and builders mushroomed. Speculators used the glutted market to drive construction prices down and to encourage broad-based underbidding. In this environment, master builders subdivided work on a given project into dozens of smaller tasks. In turn, contractors often further subcontracted out part of their work to others. The division of labor in the building trades became intense, and thus, as in the needle trades, had the effect of driving wages down for skilled workers.[24] For a commission, the contractor arranged agreements with builders who, for a fixed price and according to a set schedule, supplied materials and labor and arranged subcontracts with tradesmen. As speculative building became more common and the importance of quality workmanship declined, speculators pushed master builders out of the low-income housing market to be replaced by contractors who had little time, experience, or interest in hiring, purchasing, and other tasks associated with actual construction.[25]

As tenement management became more profitable, tenement owners began contracting out the management responsibilities. Owners began leasing individual structures or groups of buildings to landlord entrepreneurs and former tenants willing to take risks. These entrepreneurs rented blocks, or purchased them on time, or managed them for a percentage. In turn, they held the buildings for subletting to applicants with few resources and only a precarious livelihood. In 1859, investigators described these subletters.

The lessee becomes, by his lease, the agent, middle-man or sub-landlord; he is responsible for the aggregate rent, and must, for self-protection, underlet the premises to the best advantage. He, therefore calculates, to the smallest fraction, all that the speculation is capable of producing him as reimbursement and interest upon his invested risk. He measures the rooms, and estimates—not their capacities for accommodating human life to pay the rent. For a room twelve feet square and scarcely high enough to permit one's standing upright in it he estimates that from 75 cents to $1.25 per week should be charged. On this basis, . . . the calculation of aggregate rental is made, and the premises offered to all comers on the sub-landlord's terms.[26]

Owners and landlords subdivided thousands of apartments in this fashion. They established rental rates, schedules, and modes of payment, which secured enough profit for landlords and sub-landlords to pay weekly dues, while leaving for property owners an aggregate profit from the whole block twice and three times the amount of a normal lease of the building to one occupant. Profits covered not only all risks and secured exorbitant interest on investment, but also allowed a wide margin for damage and abuse. The margin allowed owners, landlords, and subletters to let their buildings deteriorate as quickly as continual occupancy permitted.[27]

These new pressures altered routine construction methods and led to a noticeable decline in construction standards. In many working-class neighborhoods, monotonous, ornate edifices of questionable quality

Figure 1.1.
A typical New York tenement, circa. 1850. Housing reformers attacked the small back yard and rear building.
SOURCE: New York State Assembly, Tenement House Committee, *Report of 1895*, p. 13.

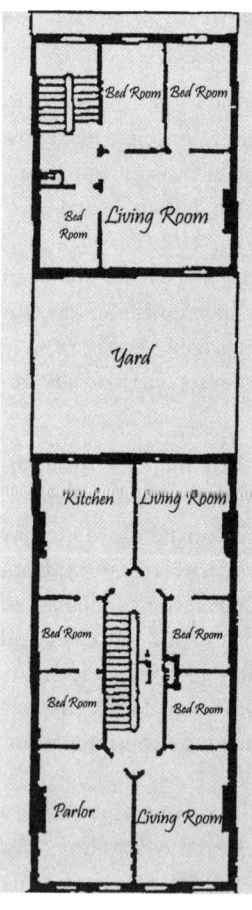

replaced the generally simpler, more robust structures of the colonial era. In 1850, former Mayor Philip Hone described the "shameful manner of constructing houses for renting ... [and] I have noticed especially in the eastern section of the city, blocks of new buildings so tightly built that they could not stand alone, and, like drunken men, require the support of each other to keep from falling." In some cases multi-family dwellings collapsed upon themselves due to a lack of mortar or because the walls were the thickness of one brick.[28] Following the great fire of 1835 in lower Manhattan, these so-called "gimcrack" builders accomplished as much as nine-tenths of the rebuilding.[29]

One reason these speculative builders were so successful was the unrelenting demand for cheap rental housing created by immigration. Dense ethnic enclaves began to form in the Five Points, the Lower East Side, and elsewhere. Dutch, German, and Polish Jews began to settle in Bayard, Baxter, Catherine, and Mott Streets. Irish and, later in the 1860s, Italian immigrants settled on Mulberry and Centre Streets. As Carol Groneman has shown in her study of the sixth ward, one of the city's poorest areas in the nineteenth century, the foreign-born population increased from 15.7 percent of the ward's population in 1810 to 25.3 percent in 1825, and 50.9 percent in 1855.[30]

By 1850, standard types of tenements began to proliferate based on the narrow parameters allowed by speculators' profit margins and New York's gridiron street pattern. A sanitary inspector described these structures in 1865 (See Figure 1.1).

On a lot of ordinary size, 25 x 100 feet, will be erected a front house 25 x 50, and a rear house 25 x 25 with a court 25 x 25, and frequently less, in which are usually located hydrant, cesspool, and privy. These houses are commonly five and frequently six stories in height above the basement. The principal rooms, of which there are four to each floor, occupy the width of the building, front and rear, with small bedrooms between one to each main room. The arrangement gives accommodation to four families on each floor, making in a six-story building twenty-four families. Each family averages five members and frequently more, as it is common for the occupants of these houses to take lodgers.[31]

Increasingly, landlords adopted practices that maximized the sheer number of renters in each tenement. To house as many families as possible, builders and landlords reduced the width of hallways and passages often to the extent that two people had trouble passing.[32] Landlords and owners routinely subdivided living rooms and bedroom into closet-sized, windowless compartments. They often reduced to almost nothing the size of back yards, and, at times, they even added floors onto already shaky structures. In 1834, a city inspector noted, "we have serious cause to regret that there are in our city so many mercenary landlords who only contrive in what manner they can [to] shove the greatest number of human beings in the smallest place."[33] In 1856, a committee investigating a standard tenement on Hester Street noted that there was "no provision for ventilation; drainage was insufficient; the sinks in wretched condition, and the entire structure thick with nauseating smells."[34]

III: Landlords, Tenants, and the Law

Working-class tenants had little choice but to accept tenements as they were. They had no means to seriously challenge prevailing practices. While the economic structure of lease holding encouraged neglect and overcrowding, landlord-tenant laws placed significant limitations on tenants' ability to address these problems in the courts. Laws governing urban renting were mediated by two distinct legal traditions—agricultural landlord-tenant law, and contract law—both of which heavily favored the landlords.

New York's landed magnates had transported legal and political institutions from the Netherlands and England. In seventeenth-century England, the common law strongly favored the landed gentry. The codes governing real estate's transfer, succession, and use helped sustain their monopoly on property. Lawmakers viewed land as a special form of real property, and the law granted landlords special jurisdiction over tenants, giving them unilateral power to collect rents.[35] Since the Middle Ages, agricultural landlords and tenants had each assumed certain obligations. The landlord's primary obligation was to turn over "possession" of the land to the tenant farmer and to leave the tenant in "peaceful possession." In other words, the law did not expect the landlord to assist in the farming of the land, and he was not legally responsible in any way for the farm's success or failure. In fact, the participants expected the landlord to stay away since, for the term of the lease, the land was subject to the tenant's care. In principle, if the landlord interfered, he risked violating the law. In an agricultural economy, the best landlord was the one who did the least.

Possession of the land was the tenant's part of the agreement, and his own economic well being was linked to the property. The land yielded grain from the field, heat and lumber from the woods, and so forth. Once the tenant took possession, the agreement obligated him to pay rent. If, by chance, the land flooded, destroying the tenant's crops, or the tenant experienced some other misfortune, there was no disruption in the tenant's obligations to pay rent.

If either party did not meet his obligations, the penalties were well established. If the tenant failed to pay the rent, standard agreements required that the courts deprive him of possession. Conversely, if the landlord tried to evict a tenant in good standing before the expiration of the lease, the tenant could sue for damages and recover possession. Once the tenant recovered possession, the laws reinstituted his obligation to pay rent. The ancient law's paramount concern was adjusting for imbalances in the possession-rent relationship.[36]

In the early modern period, the obligations of agricultural leases were contractual in nature. Equal parties assumed mutual obligations, and either party could, in theory, seek redress from the state if the obligations were not met. In eighteenth- and nineteenth-century New York, however, as commerce expanded, new practices emerged to facilitate the rental of business property. The urban property lease became a conveyance of an interest in land subject to conditions, and its contractual aspects (with their connotations of mutual obligations) declined. Urban landlord-tenant leases lost basic principles of contract law such as mutuality of covenants and mitigation of damages. Courts presumed that tenants had inspected the premises for any defects, and, if problems existed or the tenant wanted specific services from the landlord, the rent payer could not force the landlord to address these issues. *Caveat emptor*—"let the buyer beware"—controlled the landlord's obligations.[37]

In colonial New York, landed magnates could not fully replicate the feudal model of agricultural production, even in the Hudson Valley. The abundance of land and the anti-feudal sentiment of settlers undermined proprietors' efforts to tie tenants to the land. However, colonial lawmakers readily transferred the legal doctrines of landlord-tenant obligation to New York's growing urban environment. In New York City, landlords and tenants had obvious differences compared to their agricultural counterparts. First, the land was no longer the object of the lease but rather a part of a building, i.e., the flat, which lacked the productive capacity of agricultural land. Also, in contrast with the self-sufficient farmer, urban tenants were in a dependent relationship with their landlords concerning the furnishing of essential services such as heat, water, and the maintenance of the flat. The laws, however, made only minor adjustments for these new circumstances. The possession-rent relationship remained intact, and all rights concerning heat, water, light, safety, and maintenance constituted a *separate* agreement wherein a tenant could sue for redress if the landlord did not provide services. These services, however, had to be explicitly enumerated in the rental agreement. If the leasing agreement did not contain such covenants for maintenance or heat, then the tenant could make no claim. As Thomas Quinn and Earl Phillips have noted, "The result was a . . . two-level relationship. . . . A failure to perform on one level generated a remedy on that level, but in no way affected the other level. In technical terms, the covenants on one level were not reciprocal with the covenants on the other." Thus, as long as the tenant lived in the apartment, he had to pay rent (level one), even if the landlord failed to provide services (level two). If the tenant refused to pay rent to force his landlord to provide services, the tenant had violated the principles of the possession-rent relationship, and the landlord could promptly evict the tenant. In theory, the tenant could explore the avenues of redress appropriate for level two—he could sue the landlord. However, in practice, this route was exceedingly time-consuming and costly, and it exposed the tenant to the landlord's retribution, often leading to further reductions in services. As tenants waited for court action, their flats remained unheated or unrepaired. Abandoning the apartment was not a legal option. The fact that an apartment was deteriorating had no bearing on the possession-rent relationship. If the tenant chose to leave, he could do so, but his obligation to pay rent lasted for the full term of the lease.

The courts curbed the landlords' power under certain circumstances. They allowed for "constructive" eviction where, due to the neglect or harassment of landlords, the tenants' only option was to leave the apartment. In effect, indirect means deprived the tenant of "peaceful possession." As a legal remedy in such cases, the courts allowed rental abatement. However, this remedy was possession-oriented. No matter how bad the conditions, tenants had to pay rent as long as they remained in the apartment. Abandonment itself was necessary in order for tenants to claim constructive eviction. As they sought legal redress, tenants had to seek other accommodations. Often these were no better than the first. Even if they found better accommodations, the law still obligated them to pay rent on the older apartment until a judge reviewed their case. All the while, landlords used legal delays or, on occasion, made perfunctory repairs that undermined the tenant's case.[38] Furthermore, the periodic nature of common tenant problems further complicated legal action. When tenants lacked heat or water, the problem might persist for days or weeks but suddenly service would return once the tenant threatened legal action. In turn, landlords often used the periodic deprivation of services to harass tenants or to save money. In such instances when basic services came and went, tenants found it difficult to claim constructive eviction.

Civil Court justices who processed dispossess cases had virtually no latitude to allow tenants to stay in their homes. Justices routinely pleaded with landlords for extra time in especially desperate cases. At times, they even asked for donations from the court room gallery so that the tenant might avoid eviction. However, if the landlord insisted on it, the judge had no option but to put out the tenant. As one judge noted in 1893, "The odds are too much in favor of the landlords, who can fix the rents to suit themselves. . . . The courts must see that the rent is paid or that the tenant goes into the street. What becomes of the tenant afterwards is nobody's business, unless the police have occasion to look after him or the morgue keeper fixes him in a deal box for interment in the home of the desolate on Harte's Island—Potter's Field."[39] Landlords decided (largely through their own initiatives) how well maintained their properties were; they also determined the rents: and if they really wanted their tenants out, the tenants were *out*.

The courts rarely protected tenants from eviction, and tenants had little recourse in the courts if they were injured because of the landlord's neglect. Tort law governed the relations between landlord and tenant, and the courts interpreted it on the basis of common law (in contrast to written or statute law). The common law did not require that landlords do anything to fix or repair their buildings. Since the landlords were not responsible for maintaining the interiors of their apartments, tenants could not hold them responsible for injuries that were a direct result of the landlords' neglect. As Arlene Newman has concluded in her review of landlord liability in the late nineteenth century, "Where there is no responsibility to act, there is no responsibility deriving from the failure to act."[40]

The laws allowed some minor exceptions. The landlord was responsible, to some degree, for the common areas of the property such as staircases, hallways, entranceways, and the sidewalks that everyone used and yet were still in the possession of the landlord. However, even here, not until 1898 in *Trustees of Canandaigua v. Foster* did a court actually hold a landlord liable. As one authority noted in 1928, "in the absence of a statute, the owner or occupier of real property is responsible only to insure that members of the public shall not run upon hidden peril and that they shall not be wantonly or freely harmed."[41] Thus, for landlords to be held liable there had to be statutes regulating tenement housing, and between 1867 and 1900, these laws either did not exist, or they were weak, unenforced, and largely ignored by landlords, inspectors, and the courts alike.

IV: The Limits of Tenement House Reform

By the mid-nineteenth century, New York's landlord-tenant laws and the city's system of leasing and subleasing produced horrific living conditions for many urban workers and their families. Neglected and overcrowded tenements proliferated in the city's dense, ethnic enclaves, producing some of the most stunning images of nineteenth-century urban poverty. Many New Yorkers viewed these images with growing alarm and, prompted by a wide range of motives, began pressuring civic and political leaders to take some action. Religious leaders and architectural reformers became particularly active in the second half of the century. However, despite tremendous effort and publicity, these early housing activists failed to produce meaningful reform.

Beginning with the first "model tenement" experiments in the 1850s to the passage of the Tenement House laws of 1894, housing advocates tried to combine moral suasion, education, and mild regulatory measures to motivate landlords to voluntarily improve their tenements. Initially, they tried to educate landlords and tenants about healthier standards and practices. Reformers considered well-publicized model tenements ideal projects for this kind of instruction. In theory, they demonstrated new design principles that emphasized health, cleanliness, and limitations on overcrowding. Moreover, reformers felt that such projects lifted the tenants morally and spiritually as well as the communities in which they were located. Housing activists also began exploring new, more pragmatic types of tenements that were healthier but still profitable for landlords. Experiments with model tenements became important testing grounds for structural innovations but, through the end of the century, they failed to significantly improve living conditions in the slums. Indirectly, such experiments may even have made conditions worse.

While "model tenements" began to appear as early as the 1820s, the first large-scale project for the poor, Gotham Court, was built in 1850 (see Figure 1.2).

The project consisted of two rows of six tenements back-to-back, each six stories in height, arranged in two narrow alleys intersecting Cherry Street on the Lower East Side. Reformers hailed Gotham Court as an improvement because of both its orderly design and its ventilated water closets and basement sinks. The Association for Improving the Conditions of the Poor constructed the first real "philanthropic" model tenement, the massive Workingmen's Home, between Mott and Elizabeth Streets in 1855. Superintendents offered concerts and religious services in the top floor, and tenants had to abide by a rigid moral and sanitary code. Observers considered the project to be particularly revolutionary because it provided each apartment with water and a water closet while gas lamps lighted the main halls.

Both experiments failed because of their owners' unwillingness to subordinate economic profits to critical philanthropic goals such as providing

Figure 1.2.
Gotham Court, a "model tenement" built in 1850 by Silas Wood on Cherry Street, eventually became one of New York's most notorious tenements. Originally designed for 140 families, by 1879 the building housed 240. The apartments were small, dark, and poorly ventilated. Gotham Court became a favorite target for Jacob Riis and other critics. It was eventually demolished in 1895.
SOURCE: Citizens Association of New York, *Report of the Council of Hygiene and Public Health Upon the Sanitary Condition of the City* (NEW YORK: D. APPLETON & CO., 1866), p. lxxxi.

decent housing for the poor. Even for the well-maintained and monitored model tenements, the most serious limitation was reformers' inability to get more than five percent return on investment at a time when landlords expected ten to thirty percent. Philanthropists eventually sold Gotham Court and the Workingmen's Home (later called the "Big Flat") to private investors who increased the number of tenants while ignoring maintenance. Gotham Court proved to be especially lucrative for private landlords; it was designed to house 140 families but, by 1879, it was alleged to hold 240. Eventually, they became two of New York's most notorious tenements. In keeping with conventional business practices, landlords were unwilling to monitor tenement maintenance and limit congestion at the expense of profits.[42]

While model tenements remained popular vehicles for reform well into the twentieth century, many average New Yorkers viewed such experiments with disfavor. Middle-class stereotypes about the character of the poor and the benefits of single-family homes seriously undermined reformers' efforts to generate wider public support. As Elizabeth Collins Cromley has argued, many New Yorkers expressed antipathy toward the proliferation of multifamily dwellings, viewing them as a moral threat that undermined the family unit. Many still expressed a profound faith in the redemptive qualities of single-family homes.[43] The failure of model tenements also stemmed from the conflicting attitudes of most middle-class reformers, which combined a rather paternalistic concern for tenants with genuine fear of the consequences of neglecting the slums.[44] Most reformers understood only vaguely the economic and social problems facing the poor. Often their understanding was shaped by the works of contemporary writers who expressed a morbid fascination for tenement dwellers and used fictional archetypes like "Little Nell" and "Wicked Quilp" in describing the poor.[45] Such descriptions reflected the profound social and economic gulf between reformers and tenants, a distance that complicated serious reform efforts.

Growing concern over sanitary conditions in tenement districts raised middle-class fears even further. Cholera epidemics in 1832, 1849, and 1866 claimed more than 7,000 lives, mostly from New York's tenement districts.[46] Many community leaders blamed these upheavals on the congested conditions that existed in New York's poorer districts. Civic organizations such as the Citizen Association of New York began pressing for regulations to improve sanitary conditions in tenements. Using standards developed in model tenements to design restrictive legislation, the state legislature passed a law in 1866 defining standards for building construction in New York City. A year later, the first comprehensive housing law, the Tenement House Act of 1867, marked the beginning of the state's long involvement in regulating low-cost housing design. These two laws required one water closet for every twenty tenants, while school sinks and many types of cellar dwellings were outlawed. They also created mandatory provisions for fire escapes for nonfireproof structures. For the most part, these laws proved ineffective.[47]

Proponents of model tenements tried new ways to influence private builders and tenement owners, hoping for wider adoption and more universal application of housing principles. Charles Wingate, Charles F. Chandler, and other reformers argued that, as an inducement to landlords, sanitary housing construction should be combined with sound business practices. Thus, in 1879, *The Plumber and Sanitary Engineer* sponsored a contest that reviewed designs for tenements which (a) could be used on a 25 x 100 foot lot, (b) would incorporate more sanitation, ventilation, light, and fireproofing than the average flat, and (c) would accommodate enough families to pay as an investment. Of the 209 plans submitted, the final winner, a design by architect James Ware, offered only minimal modification of existing practices, calling for ninety percent coverage of the lot with four apartments on each floor surrounding a central stairway. Vertical air shafts located near the center, in theory, supplied light and fresh air (see figure 1.3).[48]

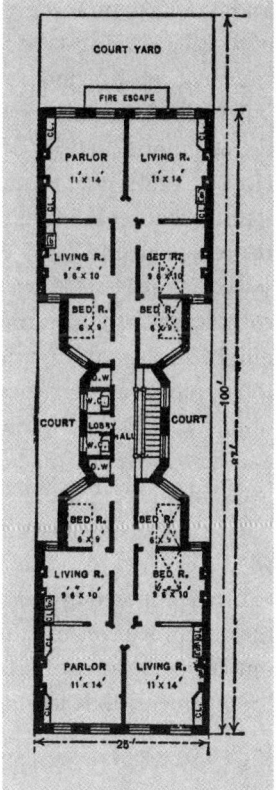

Figure 1.3.
Tenement landlords and builders quickly adopted James Ware's winning design for the *Plumber and Sanitary Engineer* Contest in 1879. Architects and housing reformers vilified the design because of its lot coverage, lack of natural light and ventilation, and its numerous fire hazards.

SOURCE: ROBERT DEFOREST and LAWRENCE VEILLER, eds. *THE TENEMENT HOUSE PROBLEM* (New York: Macmillan, 1903) 1: 101.

As an occasion to couple philanthropy and publicity, the contest became a public relations debacle. Critics immediately noted that the plan contained many fire hazards, particularly with the design of the air shafts and the central stairwell. Ware's plan also failed to provide any windows for interior rooms, and the lot coverage, reviewers argued, encouraged congestion. Dejectedly, the judges declared that, "it is impossible to secure the requirements of physical and moral health within these narrow and arbitrary lines."[49]

While lauded by many architects, the press and even the contest judges vilified the winning design (along with most of the other entries), prompting some contest organizers to form the New York Sanitary Reform Society, which pressed for more legislation. Their efforts led to the passage of the Tenement House Act of 1879. New requirements set building lot coverage at 65 percent, set minimum distances between front and rear buildings, and set minimum standards concerning windows and cubic feet per occupant.[50] Ironically, the provisions mandating bedroom windows facilitated the adoption of Ware's design as it included these features. Thus, the act rather than prompting better conditions, encouraged the construction of so-called "dumb-bell" tenements which became characteristic of new tenement construction between 1879 and the turn of the century.

In their efforts to improve housing conditions, reformers often ignored the economic realities of urban poverty. For example, the Tenement House Committee, formed in 1894, stressed the strict enforcement of statutes that set minimum space requirements for each person living in the tenements. Richard Watson Gilder and others felt that this would solve the problem of overcrowding. The committee, however, did not consider the problem from the immigrant's perspective. By limiting the number of tenants, immigrant families could no longer take in borders to supplement their meager incomes. While conditions might have improved as a result, most tenants were unable to afford the rent. In addition, those tenants pushed out by the space restrictions also had to live somewhere. Since there was no provision for building houses or for relocation, dispossessed tenants simply crowded into tenements elsewhere. The net gain was negligible. None of the sanitary or structural reforms proposed by the Committee seriously affected the 25 x 100 lot or the dumb-bell construction design. As Roy Lubove has noted, the Committee, like its predecessors, tried to abolish the terrible byproducts of the tenement while leaving it fundamentally intact.[51]

For Gilder's Committee, however, there was one important exception to the reformers' reluctance to challenge traditional property rights. Influenced by English slum clearance laws, the committee urged that "power be given to the Board of Health to institute condemnation proceedings for the destruction of buildings which are so unsanitary as to be unfit for human habitation; with provision for reasonable compensation to the owners in case of such destruction."[52] The New York Legislature passed the slum clearance measure in 1895, and in less than a year the Board of Health condemned eighty-seven buildings. As Roy Lubove has argued, this law was less important in itself than as a premonition of things to come. If the conservative legislature was prepared to recommend these limitations of landlords' property rights to protect the health of the community, it was only a matter of time before reformers limited them again in response to other inequalities inherent in the landlord-tenant relationship.

These early housing laws contained many flaws, and they faced many obstacles to their enforcement. Many of the laws' provisions were vague. The Tenement House Act of 1867, for example, left too much discretionary authority in the hands of the newly created Board of Health. In reference to fire escapes, for example, all tenements had to have them *or some other means of egress* approved by the inspector of public buildings. Thus, wooden ladders were acceptable. Water closets for tenants could be located in the yard. Cesspools were outlawed—*except when unavoidable*. Privies had to connect with sewers—*where they existed*. Such language allowed landlords and builders ample latitude to circumvent the law.[53] Disputes over jurisdiction between the various agencies responsible further complicated tenement law enforcement. In the 1860s and 1870s, for example, the city's Buildings Department approved tenement plans but did not bother to inspect the structures. The Board of Health often discovered violations after construction was complete. However, because of the preapproved plans, the courts refused to order substantive changes.[54]

Individual property owners felt justified in opposing reform. Landlords and builders deeply resented even the limited interference provided for in these early housing and sanitation laws. They had little understanding of the complex problems created by urbanization and the new demands that it made upon municipal government to preserve public welfare. Raised in an age when the public lionized entrepreneurs, the right of one type of business person to pursue his destiny was the same as any other. This precluded any control of land use.⁵⁵

The fact that many reformers sympathized with the general principles of property owners helped buttress landlords' views. Most housing activists refused to attack landlords' property rights or advocate more radical proposals to improve tenement conditions. For example, the *New York Sun*, an important organ for nineteenth-century housing activists, proclaimed in 1856 its unwillingness to completely condemn the tenement house system since in many cases tenants were "comfortably situated . . . in multi-dwellings . . . properly built, and adopted to the comfort and safety of the occupants."⁵⁶ Even the organizers for the Association for Improving the Conditions of the Poor took a more pragmatic view, arguing in 1857 that more radical government intervention would only alienate potential supporters.⁵⁷

Conclusion

In the nineteenth century, landlords had little to fear from housing advocates because of social and political realities that undermined housing reform in three ways. First, housing advocates' agenda for reform often placed undue emphasis on innovations in tenement design and philanthropic experiments in "model tenements." Through minimum standards, improved tenements could save poor children, educate immigrants about American values and citizenship, and protect workers' families from disintegration. By focusing so strongly upon the tenement environment and its structural and sanitary defects, reformers failed to perceive that the structures themselves did not necessarily create overcrowding, exorbitant rents, or run-down conditions. Landlords and, to a lesser extent, tenants made these choices based on market conditions and on the legal and social dynamics of the landlord-tenant relationship.

The reform movement's second weakness stemmed from the philosophical orientation of most reformers. Even the most ardent advocates of change viewed property rights as sacrosanct. Reformers never pushed for changes in landlord-tenant law (as they would in the twentieth century), and even when they succeeded in passing limited building, health, and safety codes, reformers failed to establish appropriate levels of funding, staffing, authority, and oversight.

The third weakness was reformers' attitudes toward tenants. Without any real advocates in Albany or at City Hall, tenants relied instead on middle-class reformers whose attitudes toward the poor usually reflected paternalistic concern combined with fear of working-class differences and social unrest. As a result of this relationship, radical housing reform, which would have challenged tenement management practices and traditional landlord-tenant laws and customs, never really materialized. Many tenants actually found themselves under attack by housing reformers who viewed tenants themselves as the major cause of poor housing conditions.

In essence, tenants faced a property owner's city. The tenants, viewed as they were, through the prism of class and ethnicity, found little sympathy or understanding of their plight from middle-class New Yorkers. While the middle-class was swiftly moving into rented quarters in the late nineteenth century, in general, their ideological and social sympathies were much more with the entrepreneurial property owners than the Jewish or Italian working-class renters, and political outcomes reflected this larger truth.

Political inaction on tenant reform, however, occurred within a much broader economic and legal environment, one that pitted landlord against landlord. More than any political or legal initiatives, it was this competition that shaped the blighted tenant districts of turn-of-the-century New York. The relationship between landlords and other property owners significantly expanded and accelerated the growth of run-down, overcrowded disease-ridden dwellings. This will be the focus of chapter 2.

Building Tenements

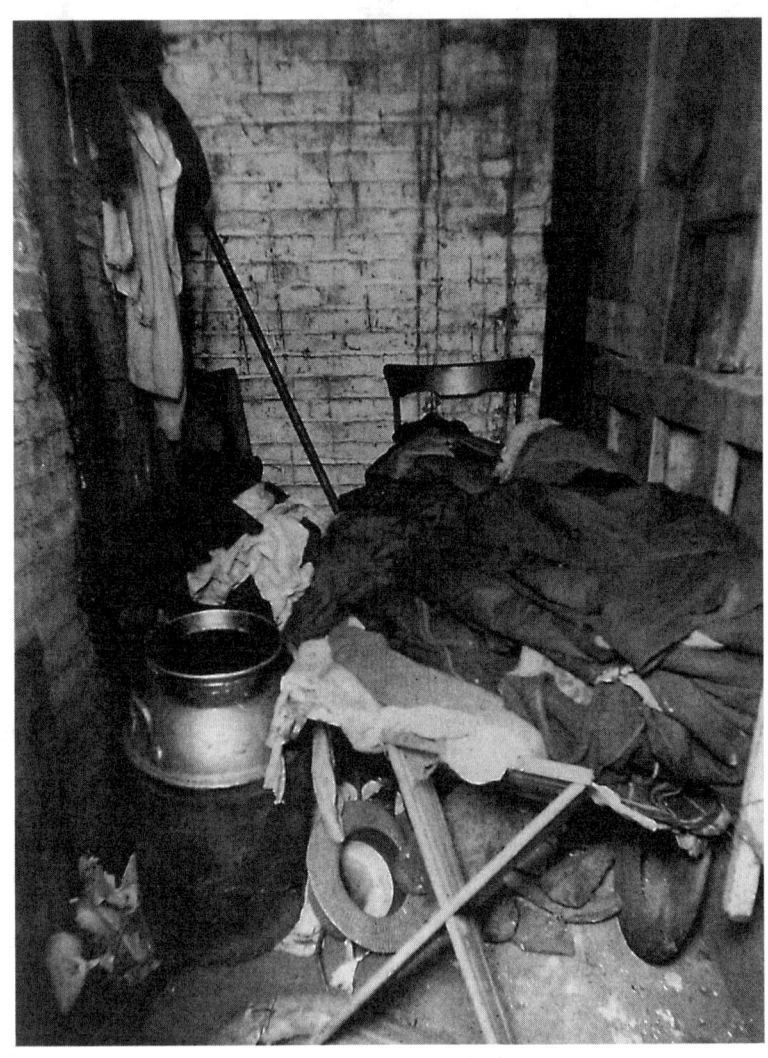

The owner of this Brooklyn tenement lived in this cellar bedroom 4 & 1/2 feet wide, 8 feet long, 7 feet high, circa 1915–1916. Between 1880 and 1920, landlords and leasing agents often lived in the same rundown tenements they managed.

Real estate brokers, immigrant banks and other types of unlicensed lenders, such as this one circa 1907, acted as buyers, sellers and financiers of tenements.

A tenement under construction circa 1907. Tenement "builders" acted as general contractors. They would hire skilled groups of framers, bricklayers, and carpenters and would engage in "skinning," "lumping," and other methods which reduced both the quality of the craftsmanship and the construction materials.

A true "cross section" of an old-law tenement at a demolition site circa 1903–1904 provides a rare view of the central stairwell, the sinks, and plumbing and gives some scale as to the size of the small rooms facing the front and back.

House partly destroyed by fire but still occupied circa 1904–1905. Standard building methods created fire hazards, both obvious and hidden. Builders often applied "three months" paint. The mixture was inexpensive, and it made the apartments look good for about three months, long enough for the builder to sell the tenement. Unfortunately, not only did the paint deteriorate quickly but, as with many of the cheap materials used, it was a fire hazard. A reporter for *McClure's Magazine* noted in 1911 that "let a lamp or a candle near enough to it while it is still damp, and fire would go around the room or down the tenement hall as fast as a man could run."

Demolition site circa 1906. Even with walls missing, tenants still live here. Landlords had little to fear from injured tenants because successful lawsuits against landlords were rare.

Above Left
Fat boiling in a tenement cellar, circa 1915–1916.

Below Left
A tannery in a tenement house cellar, circa 1914, ordered out by the Tenement House Department.

Above
A macaroni factory in cellar, circa 1904–1905.

Above Left

Probably staged photograph of Tenement House Inspector ordering a resident to remove garbage, circa 1914. While they often inconvenienced tenants, their effect on landlords was substantial as tenants used inspectors to pressure or get back at landlords, and, in the 1920s and 1930s, the growing number of violations by owners of old-law tenements forced many landlords out of the market.

Below Left

This new-law tenement, circa 1912–1913, showcases both the new building standards mandated by the Tenement House Law of 1901 and some of the changes it forced landlords to make. The sign at center advertises "steam heat" and "owner on premises," costly investments in both money and time.

Above

A row of new-law tenements, early twentieth century. Rather than constructing tenements in groups of 1 to 5, builders found they could only make a profit by building them in groups of 3 to 12 or higher, a scale of building that eliminated many small-scale builders from the market.

CHAPTER 2

Tenement Ownership and Ethic Enterprise in New York City

In the late nineteenth century, before the days of urban planning and wholesale redevelopment, the growth of the city's tenement districts had a distinctly organic quality, prompted in large measure by the small-scale entrepreneurism of tenement developers and landlords. While in many of New York's more affluent areas a select set of developers adopted a wide range of opulent architectural styles and formulas, tenement districts saw, in contrast, thousands of small-scale developers and investors use, for all intents and purposes, one or two patterns to build incrementally the housing infrastructure of New York's burgeoning working-class neighborhoods. In the process, many of these investors amassed modest fortunes and moved up the economic ladder. Simply constructed and loosely maintained, the city's tenements beckoned as business opportunities to lower-middle-class, and even working-class immigrants anxiously seeking a fast route out of urban squalor and up to the secure and independent living which was, for so many, at the core of their "American dream."

Managing tenement property in late-nineteenth-century New York was a perilous avenue to economic advancement. Building, buying, selling, and leasing tenements was a notoriously risky and cut-throat business. Landlords competed with each other, with builders, as well as with other property owners. Tenement operators routinely poached on neighboring property managers, luring away tenants, lowering rents, and constantly crafting new advantages over their tenement-owning competitors. Many undercapitalized entrepreneurs invested everything into tenements, counting on high profits while ignoring the ever present danger of economic downturns and bankruptcy. In addition, landlords tended to view their tenants with a mixture of contempt, suspicion, and indifference, a factor that further amplified their anxiety.

This environment of mistrust among tenement lenders, builders, purchasers, and lessees, however, stood in marked contrast to the more complex relations that routinely existed among the investors that capitalized each of these groups and between landlords and the broader community. Often drawing upon familial ties, business relations, and formal and informal community institutions, small-scale ethnic investors formed distinct credit networks to finance the contractors who built the tenements and to capitalize the shopkeepers and other small-scale business people who bought and managed the finished structures. Barred from the city's institutionalized sources of credit, tenement builders and buyers looked to those in the real estate business and to their own communities for the needed capital.

I. The Social Outlines of Tenement Ownership

Who were these investors in tenements? While it is impossible to account for the patterns in all of New York's tenement districts, glimpses into the Lower East Side, Little Italy, and Harlem provide several benchmarks. An examination of land transfers between 1860 and 1920 in the Lower East Side, for example, shows a clear movement toward ethnic ownership. In working-class neighborhoods of Manhattan at the turn of the century, Slavs, Poles, Italians, Jews, and other ethnic groups were the primary spurs for local tenement development within their own respective communities. Because this study relies on the treasure trove of tenement house data from the Lower East Side where, between 1880 and 1920, the population was overwhelmingly Jewish, most of the cited illustrations deal with Jews. An analysis of property ownership and leasing in three of the most densely populated sections of the Lower East Side, for instance, reveals the growing dominance of Jewish tenement owners around the turn of the century. Of the 218 lots examined, only 9.2 percent were owned by individuals with Jewish first and last names in 1860.[1] However, by 1900 the number had leaped to 62.8 percent. Furthermore, not only was tenement ownership in these areas passing to Jewish interests, but also evidence suggests that Jewish property owners were, in turn, leasing the properties to Jewish lessees as well. In the three samples, between 1880 and 1937, 633 tenement owners registered their leasing agreements with the city. Of those agreements, more than fifty percent were between individuals who both had Jewish surnames. In his large study of the Lower East Side, Leo Grebler noted a similar transfer of tenement property from non-Jewish ownership to Jewish ownership during these decades.[2]

Contemporaries often suggested that, in some areas, Jewish entrepreneurs tended to dominate certain aspects of the tenement construction business between 1890 and 1910 and perhaps later. In fact, many observers believed that tenement construction and ownership were almost exclusively Jewish ventures. For example, George Cohen stated with pride that the

> purchase of real estate and the building of new homes has become a Jewish business in New York, . . . Whole stretches of hitherto uninhabited territory, like the Bronx, Borough Park and Bensonhurst in New York City . . . have been converted into veritable cities. . . . A perusal of the real estate columns of the daily newspapers bring out the fact that the overwhelming majority of buyers of real estate are German and Russian Jews. The vast heterogeneous population of New York City are sheltered in Jewish houses. The *Real Estate Record and Guide* might be mistaken for a Jewish directory of the city.[3]

However, despite this Jewish presence, other immigrant groups were also involved. As Donna Gabaccia has stated in her study of Italian landlords,

> Most early builders of tenements were modest investors. In the 1870's barracks could be built in the 14th Ward for $11,000 to $12,000, and most builders were local German or Irish residents. About half were building craftsmen; most of the rest were grocers and saloon keepers building to accommodate business ventures and acquire income. Most builders erected only one tenement.[4]

In sum, between 1880 and 1920, tenement owning flourished as an ethnic enterprise in both Jewish neighborhoods and elsewhere.

While professional real estate developers constituted an important segment of tenement investors, sources suggest that business people with non-real estate backgrounds did most of the lending, building, buying, and leasing of tenements in New York City. Other historians have indicated the importance of small-scale entrepreneurs in the development of Jewish immigrant communities. Speaking broadly about Jewish entrepreneurism in America, Jacob Rader Marcus observed that, "After the peddler became a storekeeper, one of the first things he did when business began to flourish, was to buy a house. Many Jews owned their homes; they believed in property. As the nineteenth century advanced Jews with capital and of speculative bent began to deal in real estate. . . . [and] most Jewish real estate ventures were comparatively modest."[5] Neil Cowan and Ruth Schwartz Cowan expand on this point, arguing that

> Entrepreneurial skills can be used in many ways. Some members of the immigrant generation took risks not in their primary business but in pursuit of profits from real estate. With the money they had saved from their salaries, they bought perhaps a multiple dwelling that had an apartment for themselves, then another—perhaps with a store underneath; then another, all the while continuing to work as painters or carpenters or managers of hardware stores.[6]

In the hazardous world of tenement real estate, having a secure shopkeeping profession helped small-scale owners to reduce the risks inherent in local tenement investment.

As a practical matter, how did small-scale shopowners and peddlers become tenement owners? Between 1860 and 1920, several significant obstacles hindered these small-scale investors' access to tenement real estate. Tenements routinely cost between $20,000 and $40,000, and observers noted at the time that rates of failure were extremely high. In fact, many established businessmen considered tenement investment nothing short of gambling. For the vast majority of ethnic investors with modest amounts of capital, the issue was fundamentally one of access to credit and other pools of capital.

Mainstream banks were not an option because, as Shelly Tenenbaum has shown in her study of Jewish loan societies, in New York City and elsewhere banks provided loans only to borrowers with tangible, secure assets.[7] According to Leon Henderson, Director of the Division of Reme-

34

dial Loans of the Russell Sage Foundation, approximately 85 percent of the population were "beyond the pale of bank credit."[8] In addition, representatives of New York City's established banks and credit agencies including Dun and Bradstreet routinely viewed Jews as fundamentally dishonest. They made no efforts to overcome barriers of language or culture; they placed no branches in immigrant neighborhoods; and, to the extent that they accepted the deposits of immigrants, they usually did so through intermediaries.[9] In the Lower East Side and other Jewish neighborhoods where an estimated 80 percent of heads of household engaged in some entrepreneurial activity, the lack of access to established sources of credit forced real estate investors and other business people to look for capital elsewhere.[10]

Other institutional lenders also refused to advance credit to tenement builders and investors. For example, an examination of the mortgage records of the sample of Lower East Side tenement properties noted earlier reveals that building and loan associations and life insurance companies, major investors in real estate in New York and elsewhere, avoided tenement property until the 1890s, and even then only a few appear in the records. Not until the twentieth century do they appear in significantly greater numbers to advance credit for tenement construction and purchase.[11] The major providers of capital were large estates and unlicensed lenders. These institutions and individuals offered various types of vertical housing loans. These sources supplied ample capital (and ample incentive) for any ethnic entrepreneur enticed by the tenement's alluring promise of easy profits.

II. Vertical Housing Loans

In the nineteenth century, the lack of capital by such small-scale retailers as shopkeepers and peddlers had forced many manufacturers to offer them loans to keep their product moving. In the garment industry, for example, manufacturers of cheap clothing routinely provided credit to wholesalers who, in turn, offered it to retailers and peddlers.[12] In many ways, a similar system of within-the-industry vertical lending existed for tenement construction. In place of the manufacturer-wholesaler-retailer triad there existed the loan operator, the builder, and the purchaser. The first served as the major source of credit for the latter two who built and rented the final products to the public.

In a 1903 study of speculative building, Lawrence Veiller described the system of lending that dominated the construction and sale of tenements in New York.[13] Building loan operators (or simply loan operators) were the central players in transforming older, residential sections of New York into tenement districts. They generally bought, sold, and controlled the land upon which tenements were built. In addition, they were usually the capitalists who financed most of the construction either with their own money or with funds obtained from groups, institutions, or other credit sources. As a rule, they initiated and oversaw tenement-building projects from site selection and clearance to eventual sale, and their profits came from property sales, leasing, and the lending of money to other parties in the building process.

Loan operators required a significant amount of real estate expertise, and large and small real estate firms, institutional lenders, and wealthy New Yorkers often engaged in this kind of speculation. Many of the most famous loan operators were managers of large estates, and these individuals controlled a crucial segment of the real estate in tenement districts, particularly when transactions involved short-term leases.[14] However, evidence suggests that the large estates controlled only a small percentage of tenement property. In his detailed analysis of historical patterns of tenement ownership in the Lower East Side, Leo Grebler found that large ground-leasing property owners, such as the Astors and Trinity Church, accounted for only about ten percent of the ownership in the Lower East Side at the end of the nineteenth century, a figure that would remain relatively constant through the 1920s.[15]

Instead, as Leo Grebler and many contemporaries noted, at the end of the nineteenth century individuals and groups of investors of modest means tended to dominate all phases of tenement construction, from lending and construction to purchasing and leasing.[16] These entrepreneurs frequently sought out one or two inexpensive lots covered by old, two- or three-story single-family houses, the once-sturdy, fashionable homes of the middle class.[17] Who were these more modest lenders, and how did they gain access to enough capital to finance tenement construction? As lenders and as managers of tenement property, the most important figures in immigrant communities were unlicensed lenders and operators of so-called "immigrant banks." Despite the name, immigrant bankers bear only a passing relationship to their more widely known immigrant savings and loan operators that prospered briefly in the early twentieth century. Operating under a wide variety of titles, these largely unstudied business people provided a host of services to newly arrived groups of immigrants, including Jews, Italians, Hungarians, Poles, Russians, Slovaks, and Greeks. The unchartered immigrant banks of the late nineteenth century were far more common, even though they were more discretely located within the visual, social, and economic fabric of New York's ethnic tenement neighborhoods.[18] Furthermore, many of these capitalists served much broader economic roles within their communities. For the new immigrants that made up most of their clientele, they often acted as notary publics, rudimentary postmen, lawyers or bankers, employment and steamship agents, and, of course, locators of residential housing. These bankers routinely performed a wide range of social functions, and, in the process, as Frederick Binder and David Reimers have suggested, they emerged as central actors in the social networks that coordinated the process of the immigrants' relocation to the new world.[19]

Nascent immigrant bankers of all nationalities shared two common characteristics: they were widely trusted within their communities; and they had access to a large pool of customers, workers, or tenants. Small-scale entrepreneurs such as shopkeepers, butchers, peddlers, boarding-house keepers, and, in Italian and other non-Jewish neighborhoods, saloon keepers figured prominently. "Immigrant banks" were, to a large extent, phantom institutions in that they operated within the economic folds of other business enterprises. For example, in a 1911 federal study of 86 immigrant banks in several urban cities, investigators noted that almost all of the operators carried on some other enterprise, sometimes two or three, which were their primary businesses. The study found, for example, that 24 ran real estate, rental, insurance, or collection agencies, and 21 were saloon keepers. In addition, there were 14 grocers, butchers, and fruit vendors, 12 book, jewelry, and foreign novelty stores, 11 postal substations, 9 general merchants, 8 boarding house keepers, 7 wholesalers and importers, 2 barbers, 2 printers, and 2 pool-room keepers. In all of these various businesses, proprietors routinely provided credit to their patrons. In so doing, they naturally took on certain characteristics of established bankers.[20]

Over time, these informal credit providers became adept at managing installment plans, calculating interest, and working with more established financial institutions that tended to eschew immigrant neighborhoods. For example, many immigrant bankers acted as correspondents for steamship companies. For a bond of between $250 to $1,000 an entrepreneur could become an agent for one of the three associations of steamship companies: the Continental, the North Atlantic, or the Mediterranean Conference. Workers purchased steamship tickets from these established agents for ten to fifteen dollars down and a dollar or more a week until the balance was paid.[21]

While there were only a handful of agents authorized to sell tickets, hundreds of unauthorized people in the Lower East Side, Brooklyn, and elsewhere were involved in this lucrative business. In 1909, according to one agent, there were about twenty-three authorized sellers on the East Side while there were "probably five thousand to six thousand, and certainly three thousand runners or peddlers in New York City who sell tickets outside of offices." Investigators concluded that "for two or three hundred authorized agents for whom the companies stood sponsors, there are probably three thousand peddlers or runners who sell tickets for cash on the installment plan, on push carts, or tenements or shops."[22] The linkage between steamship ticket agents and immigrant bankers was very strong. According to one study of 107 steamship agencies, 101 also ran immigrant banks. As federal investigators observed, "Nothing is more natural than that the immigrant should take his savings to the agent and ask that the agent should send them home for them. . . . It is not long before the agent has a nucleus for a banking business."[23]

Storefront and newspaper advertising were their primary method of attracting patrons, and their prevalence in the city's dailies attests to their larger presence in immigrant neighborhoods. For example, according to a study by Louis Robinson and Rolf Nugent, the *New York World* in 1885 had between two and thirteen immigrant bank advertisements each day for the whole month of February. During a week in October 1890, the number of advertisements varied from 14 to 38, and during a week in 1900, 24 were inserted regularly, and for several days there were 27.[24] In the early twentieth century, the *New York Globe* devoted several columns daily to these advertisements while the *New York World* routinely contained four full columns.[25] This heightened advertising reflected the intense competition that existed among immigrant bankers for patrons. Federal investigators noted that in "every center of alien population there is a very keen competition among the banks conducted by men of the different immigrant races. Far from being united in a community of interest, a spirit of acrimonious rivalry is prevalent."[26]

While many bankers simply kept deposits in a safe or other secure location, most took the money to established banking houses and placed the money in their own personal accounts. As investigators noted, "It is a common practice with immigrant bankers to redeposit the funds with some regular bank. Many bankers are deriving from 2 to 4 per cent interest on thousands of dollars which have been entrusted to them but on which they make no return. They usually made no effort to separate their banking deposits from their normal business receipts. Indeed, as investigators noted, "The most objectionable use to which deposits are usually put is that of direct investment in the proprietor's own business." For example, one grocer, who was also a contractor, received deposits from the patrons of his store and from the laborers who worked for him. The grocer routinely borrowed from the deposits without interest to complete various contracting jobs and used them indiscriminately in the operation of his store. He also drew three and a half percent interest on the remaining deposits, which he had redeposited in an established bank.[27]

Immigrant banks were wholly unregulated. As a result, business people of all kinds could become bankers. As investigators of New York immigrant banks noted in 1909, "It is easier to become a banker than to open a saloon or barber shop, or to run a push-cart, or to enter other less responsible occupations which are subject to regulation of some kind."[28] Due to the lack of oversight, individual bankers frequently exercised broad discretion over how deposits were used. Also, bankers ordinarily did not offer interest. Patrons usually left their deposits for temporary safekeeping rather than in interest-bearing accounts. As far as most depositors were concerned, immigrant bankers were free to use the funds as they pleased. Others did provide nominal rates of interest. As one Polish banker noted, "A number of my friends who have confidence in me have brought me their savings, with the understanding that, for a stipulated interest return, I would have the right to invest these deposits for my own purpose as I saw fit." In his own case, deposits were either loaned out or used in real estate operations to which his banking functions were merely contributory.[29]

In the 1911 study of immigrant banks, researchers found that these capitalists quickly amassed tens of thousands of dollars in bank assets, usually split between investments in interest-bearing savings accounts (in their own names) and real estate ventures. While data specific to New York City bankers is not available, statistics on individual bankers from New York State and elsewhere clearly show this capability. A 1907 survey of twenty-two immigrant banks in the state found that their cumulative deposits amounted to more than $2,364,000. One banker stated that he had between three to four hundred accounts and that their total deposits amounted to more than $125,000 of which only thirty to forty received interest. In other parts of the country, the results could be equally astonishing. For example, in St. Louis, a Greek saloon keeper and immigrant banker kept the deposits of his Macedonian workmen. The deposits ranged from $50 to $300. In five years, the banker was able to accumulate more than $5,000 in deposits, and he was able to loan out approximately $15,000. He was able to amass this much capital even though he had only about twenty-three *depositors*. In another case, a Magyar banker kept the deposits of his patrons for safekeeping and then made regular, large transfers of cash to established banks. After twenty years of operation, he had invested over $55,000 in local real estate and $25,000 in real estate outside his community. Moreover, he had $21,300 in other assets, including $4,000 in stocks and bonds. While the scale of his success was unusual, it demonstrates what was possible for immigrant bankers given the right conditions.[30]

At the turn of the century, immigrant banks were exceedingly common in New York's ethnic, working-class communities, and they acted as reservoirs for local investment capital. In 1908, state authorities had records of more than 500 immigrant bankers in New York City, a number they readily admitted fell far short of the actual figure. When federal authorities studied the prevalence of immigrant banks, they noted that in New York City "these concerns flourish as they do nowhere else."[31] A head of an established banking house noted that his bank alone had more than 1,000 correspondents in the state who forwarded money to him for transmission, most of whom, he implied, were immigrant bankers.[32]

The two most significant features of immigrant banks were that they provided many simple shopkeepers and small-scale entrepreneurs ready access to large pools of capital, and that they overwhelmingly invested these funds in local real estate either as unlicensed lenders or as direct builders and purchasers. As federal investigators observed, "It was found

40

that real estate, first and second mortgages, and speculative securities were favored forms of investment. Such holdings are almost uniformly the heaviest assets of the banker." Furthermore, they noted, "As regards the tendency among immigrant bankers to invest funds entrusted to them in real estate and stocks, it is only necessary to state here that many of these bankers who receive deposits are property holders to an extent not warranted by the legitimate profits they would derive from their steamship, foreign exchange, or other business. But rarely is a banker found with any considerable amount of unencumbered property."[33]

While immigrant banks served as critical sources of capital for local real estate investment, they were simply part of a much larger body of ethnic capitalists who operated as unlicensed lenders. Immigrant bankers stood at the center of a broad continuum of unregulated lenders that embraced loansharks and pawnbrokers, on the one hand, and unlicensed bankers whose operations, in all other regards, resembled those of established, chartered banking houses, on the other.[34] Several immigrant bankers who began as peddlers or shopkeepers went on to establish large brokerage houses. For example, Semon Bache, founder of Bache and Company, Philip Heidelbach of Heidelbach, Ickelheimer and Company, and Henry, Emanuel, and Mayer Lehman, the founders of Lehman Brothers, all had their start as peddlers, grocers, or shopkeepers.[35] While it is not clear to what extent these other lenders invested in real estate, evidence suggests that the overall volume of their economic activity may have been staggering. For example, analysts from the Russell Sage Foundation, perennially interested in the small loan business, estimated that unlicensed lenders controlled roughly $750 million in assets nationally, a number they suggested that was incomplete.[36]

III. The Builder

If they had specific lots they wanted developed, loan operators sought out willing and suitable builders to construct tenements. In the 1840s, builders had constructed houses usually in groups of between one and five at a time. By 1900, they built in groups of between three and twelve tenements, usually using set patterns. Construction on this scale required access to more capital than most entrepreneurial builders had on hand. This need for capital drew most builders into elaborate networks of credit involving landowners or lending institutions who offered short-term mortgages both to purchase property and to raise money for improvements.[37]

In many ways, builders were very similar to the loan operators. At the turn of the century, they were usually ethnic investors, often Jewish in areas such as the Lower East Side and Harlem, and they usually had small-scale business backgrounds. Jeffrey Gurrock, in his study of Harlem in the 1890s, found that Jewish investment embraced all aspects of tenement construction, sale, and management. In Harlem, however, differences between ethnic investors with capital and those without created significantly different approaches to property development. For example, many German Jews with capital opened up Harlem by negotiating with the landed estates and old Knickerbocker families to purchase undeveloped lands strategically located along proposed subway routes through the area. These capitalists then subdivided these properties and sold to small contractors who, in turn, contracted them out to builders. Gurrock states that many of these builders were Russian Jews themselves, and, around the turn of the century, they constructed tenements in central Harlem.[38]

Because a majority of so-called "builders" lacked both essential knowledge of building construction and easy access to capital, the resulting structures were generally substandard. Tenement investors themselves usually took on for themselves the role of general contractor. Elgin R. L. Gould, in his study of speculative building, summarized the builders' basic approach.

> The owner, who is the builder, personally superintends the work of construction, buying the bricks, sand, lime, cement, lumber, etc. The laying of the brick is given by him to a "lumper" at so much per thousand, the owner furnishing all the materials. So also with the rough framing. The owner buys the timber, and the framer sets the beams and partitions. The trim, doors, closets, etc., are set the same way. . . . There are no general contractor's commissions or architect's fees to pay. The owner generally deals directly with the supply people. When the work is completed, the final bills of all the contractors are shaved in order to make quick settlements.[39]

Builders were usually nonprofessional business people who organized the work crews to perform the various construction tasks. Reflecting back on the growth of tenement districts, Clarence Stein stated in 1920 that "most of New York's miles of apartments were erected by butchers, by bakers, by anyone who could borrow enough money to get material and labor."[40] The *New York Times* corroborated this observation in 1903 when it noted that most builders were tailors, cloak makers, peddlers and professional men.[41] Donna Gabaccia also noted the prevalence of nonprofessional builders in her study of Little Italy.[42]

At this point, according to Lawrence Veiller, builders usually returned to the loan operator for capital, and they often agreed to burdensome terms that left builders vulnerable to economic downturns or other financial crises. At the start, the loan operator usually marked up the price of the property by 10 percent and then advanced to the builder the necessary capital to buy the property in the form of a loan agreement or mortgage at 5.5 to 6 percent interest. The loan operator then lent the builder enough capital to cover part of the expense for constructing the tenement and required payments when the builder completed each stage of construction. Along with the builder's initial debt (the first mortgage) to the loan operator, builders often had to secure second mortgages to fully cover the costs of the materials. In this way, Veiller argued, loan operators acted both as real estate brokers and as lending institutions, and they made their profit from the initial sale of the property and through the interest collected on the mortgage and advance granted to the builder.

The builders made their profits only if they completed the tenements and sold them quickly. Given these overriding concerns, most builders viewed rental profits as largely incidental. The monthly rates charged to tenants acted simply as a lure for prospective buyers. This emphasis on speed reduced the value of quality construction and, combined with the builder's already meager resources, led to many infamous building practices designed to reduce costs and construction time. Two of the most notorious were "skinning" and "lumping." "Skinning" involved buying the most inexpensive building materials available, while "lumping" cheapened the skill and quality of work of the average construction workers. A leading builder described how the two interacted in 1903.

The average speculator who erects a tenement house knows practically nothing of building. He purchases the raw materials, in the case of brickwork, and awards the contract for putting up the masonry to what is termed a "lumper" who furnishes him the labor at a certain price per thousand for laying the brick. A similar system prevails in some of the finishing trades. . . . The various lumpers in doing this class of work are often irresponsible men who have no interest in the building, beyond forcing their employees to do the greatest amount of work possible, irrespective of the principles of mechanics or the building laws.... The product is a miserably built structure, often without any mortar in the interior of the wall, and one that will deteriorate very rapidly.[43]

Builders routinely cheapened other materials, leading to the creation of dangerous fire and safety hazards. For example, they often used what they called "three months" paint. The mixture was inexpensive, and it made the apartments look good for about three months, long enough for the builder to sell the tenement. Unfortunately, not only did the paint deteriorate quickly but also, as with many of the cheap materials used, it was a fire hazard. A reporter for *McClure's Magazine* noted in 1911 that "let a lamp or a candle near enough to it while it is still damp, and fire would go around the room or down the tenement hall as fast as a man could run." Builders applied these principles even to fire escapes where, according to the reporter, "the bar iron could be brought to the legal thickness by successive coats of 'black wash.' "[44]

Before 1901, according to studies conducted by the Charity Organization Society and other groups, the vast majority of New York's tenements built each year routinely had structural problems, and they did not comply with the city's limited building and safety codes.[45] Stories of construction site accidents and collapsed tenements appeared in newspapers regularly throughout the second half of the nineteenth century. In 1885, for example, a tenement on the West Side collapsed during construction. Investigators found that the builder, trying to cut costs, had used loam excavated from the cellar instead of sand to make the mortar. In an infamous episode from the 1840s, investigators found a building with retaining walls of one brick thick with a wash of plaster on the interior, a total density of about three inches.[46]

While loan operators and builders depended on each other, common business practices often bred a predatory relationship between the two. Due to builders' general lack of experience and good repute in construction, loan operators usually monitored their activities very closely. If problems emerged during the construction process, loan operators frequently foreclosed, thus wiping out the builder's small equity.[47] A tenement architect described the tense relations that existed between builder and loan operator in 1907.

The loan man owns a lot worth $20,000. The speculator has $2,000 cash and proposes to erect a house costing $25,000. Because the speculator wants a loan and has so little cash, he pays $3,000 for his lot; and the loan man takes a purchase money mortgage for $28,000—$8,000 more than the lot's real value. If the operation is successful and a quick sale is made, the loan man gets all his legitimate interest and an additional interest on the inflated value. If the speculator fails in any of his engagements, the property is foreclosed, the loan man's mortgage taking precedence over all other claims and liens to the extent of its inflation it wipes them out; and the loan man exchanges $8,000 of inflated value for $8,000 of real estate. The loan man then completes the house and begins his operations with $8,000 on the right side of the ledger.[48]

These and many other practices made tenement construction extremely risky for builders. However, most builders devised various methods for passing much of this risk on to the tenement purchasers.

IV. The Purchaser

Once builders completed construction, they immediately looked for purchasers. Again, small-scale business people were usually the buyers of finished tenements. Because of installment plans, the purchase price was within the means of modestly successful entrepreneurs. Furthermore, tenement buyers often pooled their resources, making it possible for groups of investors to buy more than one building. To buy a completed tenement on installments usually cost between $1,000 and $3,000 down with monthly payments, sometimes as small as $5. At such prices, becoming a tenement landlord appeared enticingly easy and well within the means of modestly successful entrepreneurs.[49]

To minimize their risks, tenement buyers often pooled their resources into investment syndicates, partnerships, or combinations of investors. In many ways during these early decades of the twentieth century, purchasers amassed the requisite capital for tenement construction using methods outlined by Hugo Rotheschild in his examination of real estate syndicates in the 1950s and 1960s. As Rotheschild noted, the real estate syndicate was "a pooling of resources of many investors to buy either a building or a long-term leasehold.... When you buy an interest or a participation in a real estate interest, you buy a part of a building or a part of a leasehold and you buy the strengths and weaknesses of the managing partners. In other words, you are buying both physical assets (real estate) and people (the management)."[50] Within the context of the early twentieth century, investors were middle-class and upper-working-class ethnic entrepreneurs. Leo Grebler, in his study of the Lower East Side, noted a discernible decline in ownership by non-immigrant owners between 1900 and 1910, and a corresponding increase in ownership by Jewish immigrants. Grebler goes on to note that, in general, these new investors had to pool their resources to acquire tenement property.[51] Jeffrey Gurrock has also found that in East Harlem small-scale Jewish investors with little capital often pooled their limited resources to purchase or lease tenements.[52] My survey of the Lower East Side property ownership, like any review of Manhattan land transfer records for the city's tenement districts, reveals the names of thousands of ethnic, syndicate investors.

While the primary considerations for builders were low cost and speed of construction, purchasers usually looked more at the overall value of the tenement, costs, and the rate of return based on rentals. Traditionally, tenement buyers used the gross rent multiplier (or gross rents per month multiplied by a customary figure) and the agreement the builder had with the loan operator as primary indicators of the tenement's overall value. According to Louis Winnick, tenement purchasers usually used a figure between 8.0 and 10.5 to calculate the tenement's overall value in the period from 1890 to 1925.[53] Builders devised selling strategies that exploited these customs. In relying so heavily upon the gross rent multiplier, purchasers became vulnerable to common forms of fraud as builders used inflated appraisals to misrepresent the actual value of tenement property. To qualify for loans, builders often obtained inflated appraisals from willing real estate brokers, and, on this basis, loan operators granted large loans. In turn, purchasers used these appraisals and the loans as misleading evidence of a tenement's overall value.[54] Not surprisingly, builders also routinely did not tell the purchasers if the tenement needed repairs.[55]

Builders manipulated the gross rent multiplier in other ways. For example, they packed tenements full of tenants through dubious means to create the illusion of high rental returns. While the fresh appearance of a new apartment was often inducement enough for many tenants, many builders frequently canvassed the surrounding neighborhood to lure the tenants of other landlords into breaking their existing leases to move to new accommodations. Depending on rental market conditions, builders often offered one- to three-months free rent, a ton of coal, or even moving expenses as additional expenses. A Bronx real estate broker noted in 1900 that,

> One does not really know whom to trust, and, although a house may be filled with tenants, a buyer cannot tell whether or not every floor will be vacant the following month. The free rent and inducement system is one of the worst things that could be devised to our business but I do not see any way of abolishing it, for builders and owners will persist in filling up their flats at any cost in order to get them off their hands.[56]

At times, builders found themselves competing with other builders to fill their houses.[57] Some even wrote fraudulent leases that misrepresented the actual rentals being charged to the tenants. All of these devices, as Veiller noted, were "purely for the purpose of impressing the purchaser or investor of the property with the idea of the large rentals to be secured from it."[58] When they completed the sale, purchasers usually assumed the builder's mortgages and other loans taken out during the construction process, all of which the builder included in the asking price. Whatever remained above and beyond these obligations was the builder's profit.

For purchasers, tenement owning had the reputation of providing a steady return while requiring little commitment in terms of maintenance or supervision.[59] One advocate of tenement ownership stated in 1921 that "the tenement presents ideal possibilities in so far as ease of management is concerned.... Renting low, running on a low expense with comparatively small cash invested, the tenement shows a low but steady return."[60] Experts agreed that tenement construction was a good investment returning between 10 and 12 percent annually. Dumb-bell tenements proved particularly profitable since they had more rooms per floor, and thus guaranteed bigger rental incomes.[61] Trumpeted by the press, tenement ownership became the investment of choice for capitalists seeking high, steady returns but who wanted to take no part in day-to-day operations. These responsibilities were left to lessees.

V. The Lessee

Rather than building or operating tenements, many property owners and estate managers chose to abdicate almost all responsibility for running tenements. They did this through a complex system of subleasing that created a distinct type of landlord, the building leaseholder, commonly called a lessee, agent, or "leaster." Fully three-quarters of all tenements had absentee owners; they, in turn, relied on lessees or agents to collect rents.⁶² Building leaseholders received a small allowance from the property or building owner out of the gross rents, and they received the balance of their income by increasing monthly rents, usually from fifty cents to a dollar a month although, when conditions were favorable, the lessee routinely demanded much higher increases.

Lessees frequently lived in tenements themselves and, while operators, builders, and purchasers were usually businessmen, evidence suggests that lessees were often simply ambitious tenants with a small amount of capital.⁶³ For many landlords of this class, marginal, high-risk leasing became a critical avenue out of poverty. An investigator described how immigrants from eastern Europe became property owners.

First, they become lessees. By constantly saving, the East Sider gets together $200 or $300, as security, he gets a four or five-year lease of a house. He moves his own family into the least expensive apartment. He himself acts as a janitor, his wife and daughters as scrubwomen and housekeepers. He is his own agent, his own painter, carpenter, plumber, and repairman. Thus he reduces expenses to a minimum. He lets out apartments by the week, always calling promptly himself for the rent. By thus giving constant attention to his work he has perhaps a few hundred dollars every year as profit. By the time his lease expires, it has swollen to a few thousand. With this he buys a tenement outright. He puts down from $3,000 to $5,000 on a $45,000 building, giving one, two, three, sometimes four mortgages in payment . . . then he repeats his old operation. . . . When the third or fourth mortgage comes due, he has invariably made enough out of the building to pay it off. He keeps on at hard work and likewise pays off the third and second. Then, as his rents still come in, he invests them in more tenements.⁶⁴

One observer noted in 1904 that, when tenement owning was especially profitable,

[S]ome men hitherto very poor [come into possession of] a few thousand dollars, and he loses no time in investing it, choosing real estate with astonishing frequency. If he has little money he leases a few houses for two or three years and proceeds to collect the rent. He is now a "cockroach" landlord. He passes from working in a tailor shop or factory to a business more remunerative. . . . It is . . . not a business to attract men of good feelings, and the "cockroach" landlords, who in most cases are East Siders, are of a low type. They lease houses from someone who may perhaps have leased them from yet another.... With every new lease, with every extra middleman, rent must go up. The three or four investors concerned in the transaction must all make money, and the tenant at the bottom of the heap pays for it all.[65]

Owners and lessees further complicated matters through the extensive use of tenement basements for both residential and commercial use. During most of the 1800s, tenants lived in the cellars of old, dilapidated multifamily dwellings in such areas as the Five Points and the Fifth Ward.

The completion of the Croton Aqueduct in 1842 elevated the city's water table and, over time, flooded many cellar dwellings. At mid-century, city health officials such as John Griscom attacked the use of cellars for their dampness and other unhealthy conditions, and reformers increasingly described them as the worst housing in the city. Between 1850 and 1859, the number of New Yorkers living in cellars dropped from 29,000 to 20,000, and landlords' use of them for residential space gradually declined.[66] However, tenement managers routinely replaced residential renters with commercial tenants. By the late nineteenth century, property owners regularly rented out tenement basements for rag pickers, bone boilers, bakeries, candy and macaroni makers and many other types of manufacturer.[67] Within overcrowded tenements, the co-existence of families and commercial businesses and their communal use of sinks, toilets, and other facilities remained a central concern for housing reformers well into the twentieth century.

Often illiterate, unable to speak English, and with little knowledge of building and safety laws, lessees were extremely vulnerable as tenement managers. They also tended to come from the same class or ethnic background as the tenants from whom they collected rent. As Donna Gabaccia noted in her sample of Italian tenement lessees, "For Italian immigrants, . . . work as an agent was a first step into ethnic real estate; every twentieth century Italian builder, realtor, and owner of multiple tenements in the 14th Ward had worked previously as a building agent."[68]

With an exceedingly narrow profit margin and lacking the needed resources to make repairs, building leaseholders developed the reputation for being the worst landlords in the city. They usually ignored maintenance and focused exclusively on the regular collecting of rents. For example, one observer looked at these lessees when rents skyrocketed in 1904.

The custom of the actual landlord to lease the whole house to one party and allow him to make what he can out of the tenement is a fruitful surface cause of the increase. In many cases the lessee is absolutely ignorant and grasping. . . . Lessees have heard of increases elsewhere and want to come in for their share and have asked for a larger increase than is justifiable. . . . It seems to be true that the large estates and realty companies are not demanding abnormal increases . . . . [T]hese lessees do less for the property, and yet demand higher rents.[69]

Lessees had few incentives to maintain the property. They customarily adopted the view, "You pay the money, we don't care what you do to the rooms."[70] This neglect stemmed largely from the lessees' dependence upon rents for their incomes. Lessees ran the risk of losing their small security if the rental market declined, if tenants were late in paying, if they refused to pay outright, or if they vacated unannounced. During times of economic downturn, such as during the years 1910–1916, these lessees often experienced real hardship.[71] When the rental market improved, as it did in 1907–8 and 1918–21, they routinely boosted rents significantly, overcompensating for the years of privation.[72] For this reason, many New Yorkers referred to lessees as "leasters": they were penurious and unwilling to make repairs, lower the rents, or accept excuses for late payment or nonpayment. On occasion, this led to significant tension between tenants and "leasters" and, in extreme cases, resulted in rent strikes, an exceedingly effective strategy for tenants since the lessee rarely had the financial reserves to withstand a prolonged holdout.[73]

What of the lessor? While lessees faced very narrow profit margins, the leasing of land and buildings proved particularly lucrative for the large-scale property owners and landed estates. Most estate managers leased and managed tenement property without any public scrutiny. They projected an aloof, "business is business" image that helped to distance themselves mentally, physically, and publicly from the grimy, dilapidated, overcrowded structures that were their stock and trade. One of the few large-scale lessors to drop this veil of anonymity was the Trinity Corporation, which managed the revenues and assets of the Trinity Church, one of the wealthiest landholding institutions in New York. While public officials and reporters often attacked Trinity for the moral incongruity of a church leasing tenements, it is of greater interest to historians due to the unprecedented exposure their investigations provided of Trinity's management strategies. Moreover, unlike other large estate managers, church officials often felt it necessary to disclose and justify their policies. Such was the case in 1894 and 1895 when Richard Watson Gilder's state-appointed Tenement House Committee investigated Trinity's tenement holdings. Gilder's findings combined with investigations by some of the city's dailies provide a rare portrait of one of the city's major tenement lessors.

Beginning in the eighteenth century, the Trinity Corporation slowly gathered property in lower Manhattan until it controlled land containing more than a thousand city lots. In 1705, England's Queen Anne granted Trinity Church a patent for 32 acres of land west of Broadway between Fulton and Duane Streets. The Church added onto its holdings through the acquisition of farmland between Duane and Christopher Streets. Through further purchases, grants, and gifts, the Corporation became one of the city's largest land-owning institutions. As Elizabeth Blackmar has noted, guided by the vestrymen of the Church (many of them wealthy landowners in their own right) the Corporation pursued a distribution policy that promoted settlement without the sale of land. Corporation officials leased out rather than sold their subdivided properties.[74]

In 1894, Trinity owned more than 300 tenement houses in the city. Corporation officials negotiated directly with lessees who collected the rents. A majority of the Trinity's tenement holdings were located in a fourteen-block stretch of lower Manhattan bounded on Christopher Street to the north and Vestry Street to the south (See Figure 2.1). Technically, most of these buildings were not tenements (such as the notorious double-decker or dumb-bell) but were rather smaller two or three-family homes sixty to eighty years old. As such, existing tenement house laws did not generally apply to them.[75]

In the 1890s, Colonel Stephen Van Rensselaer Cruger, the Corporation's controller, managed Trinity's tenement holdings. Born in 1844 into two of New York's most prominent families, the Crugers and the Van Rensselaers, Cruger became one of the city's most influential loan operators, managing not just Trinity's assets but also the properties of many other estates as well. Cruger's pedigree and business acumen propelled him toward a life in New York real estate and investment. After serving as a Union officer in the Civil War, Cruger returned to New York to enter a career in business. His executive and managing abilities soon became well known, and, as a partner in the firm of McVickar and Cruger, he became the manager of numerous estates, the largest being Trinity.

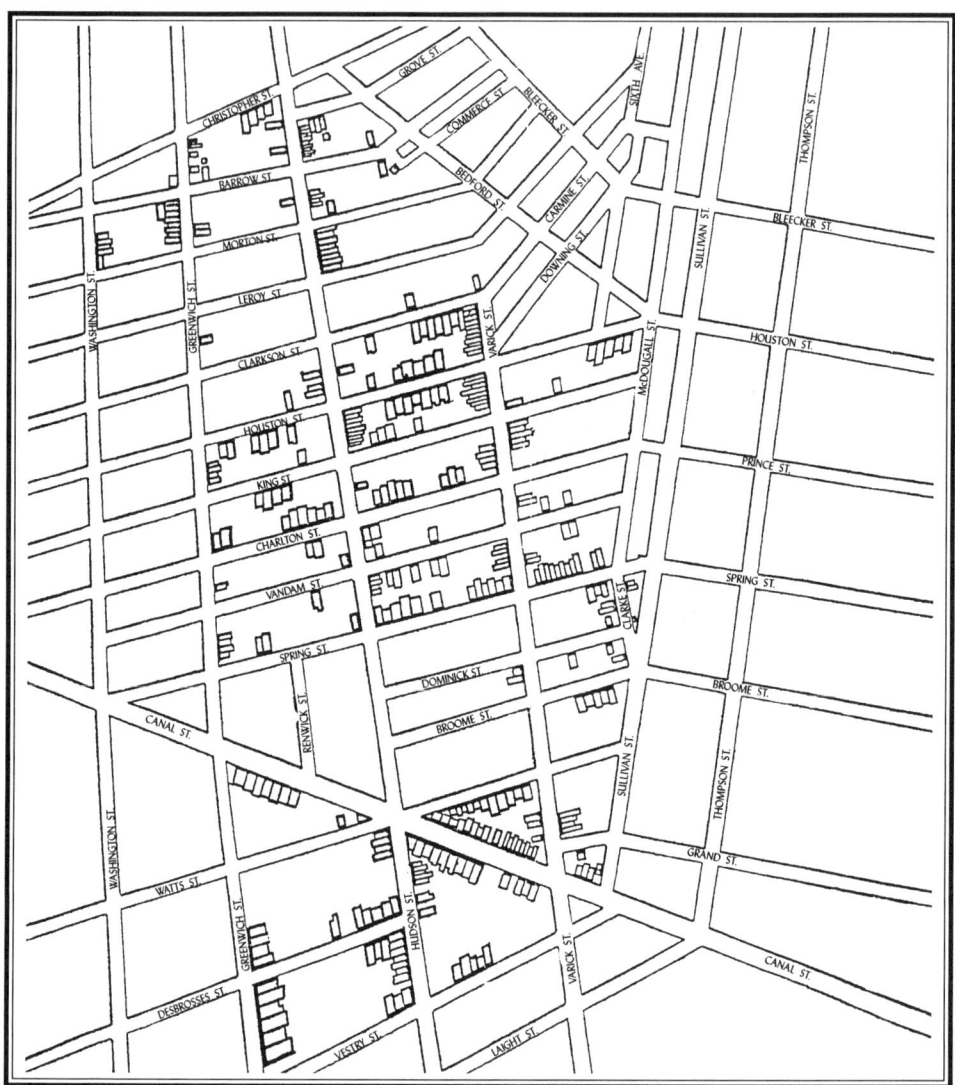

MAP OF TRINITY CORPORATION PROPERTY

Figure 2.1.

Trinity Church, one of the city's most prominent landholders, owned over 300 tenements in the 1890s, most of them between Thompson and Christopher Streets in lower Manhattan. The Church's activities became the focus of a state investigators and numerous newspaper exposes in 1894. The *New York Times* published the map above showing many of the properties owned by Trinity.

SOURCE: *New York Times*, December 21, 1894.

Cruger was steeped in the world of capital investment. He was a Trustee of some of New York's largest corporations including the Mutual Life Insurance Company, the New York Life Insurance and Trust Company, the Union Insurance Company, and he was a Director for the Illinois Central Railroad. In addition, Cruger was also politically active in the state Republican Party. He was, at one time, the Chairman of the Republican County Committee, and, in 1888, the state GOP nominated him to run for the post of lieutenant governor. In 1894, the Republicans of the fourteenth Assembly district even nominated Cruger to run for Mayor of New York.[76]

Cruger's main client was the Trinity Corporation. He served the vestrymen of Trinity Church, who included influential New Yorkers such as William W. Astor and real estate broker David Ogden. Even before Cruger's appointment and dating back to 1873 (if not much earlier), Trinity officials had committed themselves to a program of neglect concerning their tenement properties. Cruger and his predecessors refused to invest money into repairing the old structures, looking instead for suitable builders to demolish them and build new ones. Cruger hoped that the city's growing commercial districts would overtake the tenement property and transform it into suitable business real estate. As a result, he resisted any pressures from the city to improve Trinity's properties. For example, when the Board of Health began in the early 1890s to pressure the Trinity Corporation to install sinks and running water on each floor of its tenements, Cruger adamantly refused. He argued that the tenants would not know how to use the sinks and that they were better off using pumps in the yard. He stated that "In many of the old houses the tenants are dirty and careless, and if there is water through the house they will throw all their slops in their sinks if they had the water there, and the whole place would be nasty and dirty. . . . they are first-class houses, but you can not expect to have all the modern improvements for $7 per month."

Cruger viewed his role not as a tenement builder or a "landlord" but as a financier, capitalist, and manager of assets. Cruger argued that, "anyone who comes along and wants to lease lots and put up some modern buildings, we are only too glad to give them all the lots they want for a long term."[77] The *New York Times* blasted church officials' use of short-term leases, noting that "Trinity has been giving leases for short periods, sometimes from year to year. This has the effect of preventing lessees from improving because of the shortness of the terms."[78] When pressed about the short-term leases, Cruger stated, "It is a better policy for all concerned, for the good of the city and all, that these leases should not be long, thereby insuring the retention of these old buildings for years to come." Cruger's policies, designed to entice investors, often led to further neglect of Trinity houses. Indeed, in Gilder's investigation and in the studies by local newspapers, Trinity tenements suffered most from neglect.[79]

Due to its size and religious affiliations, the Trinity Corporation's management style doubtless created certain anomalies. However, at their core, the views of the Corporation and Cruger represented the conventional wisdom of most tenement owners. As Elizabeth Blackmar has argued, the wealthy men who made up the vestry board (as they had dating back to the early 1700s) wanted the church's land managed as they would manage their own property.[80] Every decision was measured by whether it was good business and secured a profit for investors (in this case the vestrymen of Trinity Church). It was all that concerned Cruger; it was all that concerned the vestrymen; and it was all that concerned most tenement investors.

In reviewing the spectrum of tenement owners, the loan operators, the speculative builders, the purchasers, and the lessees, recall that *all of them* were, depending on time and circumstance, landlords. Moreover, their investment strategies, whether by chance or design, all influenced the shape and condition of New York's tenements. Despite this central truth, their diverse interests, their arcane relationship one to the other, and the general lack of social accountability to which they were held allowed responsibility for tenement conditions to be diluted or deflected onto the tenants.

Conclusion

Who, then, were these investors in tenement property, these lenders, builders, purchasers, and lessees at the end of the nineteenth century? Evidence suggests that for the most part they were the people who lived or worked in the tenements themselves. They were the tenants who scraped together small sums to buy leases; they were the grocers, butchers, boarding house keepers, and barbers who pooled their resources to buy or build tenements; and they were the immigrant bankers, often the most trusted business people in their communities, who took the savings of average ethnic workers and invested them in local housing. To be sure, wealthy land owners and estates such as the Astors and the Trinity Corporation controlled an important segment of the city's tenement real estate. However, as a practical matter, ethnic New Yorkers themselves supported through their investment dollars the activities of tenement builders, buyers, and lessees, and they did so within their own communities.

The case of Edward Rafter, a grocer and tenement owner, graphically illustrates many of the internal and external tensions created by managing tenements in the community where you live, work, or have ethnic ties. Between 1872 and 1894, he operated several groceries and built or purchased tenements. At two of his buildings, 343 and 345 East Eleventh Street, a baker and fish seller worked in two of the three stores on the first floor, and they shared the sink in the basement. The baker used water from the sink for his bread; the fish seller washed his fish in the sink; and the sixteen families in the two buildings used the sink as a urinal. When investigators pressed Rafter, under threat of indictment, to correct the situation, he stated that he could not. He said, "I can't take any steps [to address the problem]—what steps can I take? . . . I would have to leave [a housekeeper] down there all day long. . . . It is a very hard matter to take charge of all the tenants in the house." Rafter refused to take any concrete measures even though *his grocery* was the third store in 345 East Eleventh. Rafter, the owner of eight tenements and twelve groceries, chose to work and run a store in this building, despite the health hazards posed by the sink.[81]

Unlike the solidly middle-class reformers like Gilder, who voiced shock and dismay at conditions in the tenements, Rafter's views of these buildings were more complex. Like so many other ethnic shopkeepers and petty entrepreneurs in New York's tenement districts, he looked past the conditions and considered primarily his own economic condition, his resources, and his obligations both as a property owner and a breadwinner. Rafter's tale exposes a darker, more vexing dynamic for tenement managers. Despite their presence at all levels of tenement construction and ownership, ethnic New Yorkers lacked the economic leeway to alter significantly their business methods or, in any way, remedy the ills of urban tenements. Given the relationship between loan operators, builders, purchasers, and lessees and the general market conditions for tenement property, neglect and evasion of the law were not merely common practices; they were *essential strategies* for marginal property managers trying to make a living. These small-scale professionals had access to tenement property only for so long as they could remain, for all intents and purposes, "passive" investors. Laws and customs encouraged them to view tenement property in this fashion. As described in Chapter 1, legal precedents discouraged landlords from getting more involved, holding it as a form of "interference" in the tenant's "peaceful possession."[82] To some extent, this attitude permeated the entire real estate industry. In 1913, *The Real Estate Record and Builders Guide* noted that 65 percent of the buildings in Manhattan, both residential and commercial properties, were neglected "as a matter of custom and regular business practice."[83]

As a central management principle, neglect—the avoidance of routine maintenance and health and safety precautions—offered a complex set of opportunities and hazards to small-scale ethnic business people largely unversed in the intricacies of tenement construction and urban real estate markets. On the one hand, the lack of regulation and accountability made it possible for these unschooled, ethnic investors to enter the business in the first place and make a profit. On the other hand, however, this easy access came at a price. Due to the systematic neglect of New York's tenements and the laws that strongly favored landlords, these housing structures were volatile social, political, and physical tinderboxes. By the early twentieth century, tenants and housing reformers began separate campaigns against these small-scale tenement owners and the basic foundations of the business which allowed them access to the market. The first major assault came with the passage of the Tenement House Law of 1901 and was quickly followed by large-scale, tenant-initiated rent strikes in 1904 and 1907 and 1908. These conflicts and their origins will be the focus of chapter 3.

Landlord Leaders and Activists

Above Left

Colonel Stephen Van Rensselaer Cruger (1844–1898), comptroller of the Trinity Corporation, managed and leased more than 300 tenement properties in the city at the end of the nineteenth century. SOURCE: From the Portrait File, Miriam and Ira D. Wallach Division of Art, Prints and Photographs, The New York Public Library, Astor, Lenox, and Tilden Foundations.

Above Right

Ignatz Reich (1867-1941), President of the Greater New York Taxpayers Association. Reich and other GNYTA officials bitterly opposed tenant activists during the rent strikes of 1919-1920. Along with other lanlord leaders, they hired thugs to protect their members' properties, assault tenant leaders, and break up protest meetings. SOURCE: *Real Estate News* (February, 1924), p. 7.

Above

Isador Berger (1872–1952), General Manager and President of the Greater New York Taxpayers Association, the largest real estate association in New York City devoted almost exclusively to tenement house owners. SOURCE: *Real Estate News* (December 1921), p. 12.

Left

Stewart Browne (1854–1938), President of the United Real Estate Owners Association, one of the most outspoken, caustic, and mercurial landlord lobbyists in the 1920s and 1930s. His vocal support of the "iron-clad" lease and other controversial devices caused significant conflict and debate within real estate circles. However, by the 1930s, many of these devices had become standard practice for tenement managers. SOURCE: Library of Congress *New York Globe Collection*, LC-US262-11251.

The legal team of the Greater New York Taxpayers Association, including Harold Phillips, front left, a founder of the GNYTA and a master of the real estate "spin off" organization, and Max Kahn, back right, chief of GNYTA's investigation of accident claims against landlords. At times, GNYTA officials used intimidation to keep tenants from filing law suits. The *Real Estate News* lauded the organization's legal team for the "sheer aggressiveness of its attack in every case whether small or large coming within its auspices." SOURCE: *Real Estate News* (December 1921), p. 13.

CHAPTER 3

Landlord Activism in the Early Twentieth Century

In reviewing the activities of reformers in the nineteenth century, one might suspect that landlords' organized efforts were very instrumental in defeating housing reform both in its political creation and in its practical application. However, in general, there is little evidence of their direct involvement. Certainly landlords strongly defended their construction and management practices from proposed housing and sanitary reforms. However, they did so largely on an individual basis or through brief flurries of concerted lobbying from landlord coalitions. Landlord groups began to emerge but they usually had small memberships, a shadowy public image, and they usually addressed specific issues on an ad hoc basis. Moreover, as a group, landlords were extremely divided along the lines of class and ethnicity, so that their influence on lawmakers was rather sporadic; there is little evidence that any particular group significantly shaped city or state housing policy. In general, tenement owners did not need such organizations on a regular basis since individual landlords had little to fear from New

York's nineteenth-century reformers. The reasons lie both in the weaknesses and orientation of the reform movement (as discussed in chapter 1), and the ease of access owners had both to politicians and, just as important, to officials charged with the implementation of health, building, and safety policies.

Tenement landlords tended to avoid permanent lobbying organizations in favor of political alliances with trade organizations in related businesses, most notably the building trades, and other groups that exerted significant power over the shape of housing policy. Although landlords as a group relied on these alliances to kill any harmful legislation, individual landlords directly shaped the way housing policies were implemented. Landlords focused their resources on those officials assigned to enforce the city's relatively mild health and safety codes. Rather than encouraging collective lobbying, tenement landlords tended to favor a more individualistic style of "micro-lobbying." These measures were adequate so long as landlords only had to fend off idealistic, politically ineffective reformers. However, with the new century came a new adversary, the tenants themselves.

I. Landlord Political Influence in the Nineteenth-Century City

In critical ways, New York City's corrupt political structure greatly favored landlords in the nineteenth century. Tenement owners found important allies in ward politicians and city officials who were indifferent to the need for better housing. Between 1844 and 1866, for example, corrupt officials staffed the City Inspector's department with incompetents who obtained their jobs through political patronage. Municipal authorities charged nonmedical personnel with health and sanitary inspection in New York's tenement districts. These same officials and inspectors consistently threw their support to whichever political machine was in power; they misappropriated funds, and special interests employed some inspectors to lobby *against* housing reform in Albany.[1] Following the passage of the Tenement House Law of 1867, the *New York Sun* charged in 1870 that,

for the last three years not one tenement house has been built in the city of New York in conformity with the law. That nearly every man building a tenement house within that time has paid from one to five hundred dollars a home for the privilege of violating the law. That within the past three years over 5000 . . . tenement houses have been built, and that for the unlawful privilege accorded the builders[,] over one million two hundred and fifty thousand dollars have been paid.[2]

Corrupt political leaders, lobbyists, and landlords easily persuaded such individuals to ignore building and safety codes. In a mocking parody of the system as practiced, *Harper's Weekly* described the inspection process from the *tenement's* perspective.

> Well, I was about built . . . when an inspector from the Department of Buildings came to look at me. He was about to measure something, when the contracting mechanic and my agent invited him "across the street" to drink a toast to my health. The agent said that I would be "all right," and that . . . he would become sponsor for me. . . . The insurance agent came to have a look at me. My sponsor gave him an open hand with friendly invitation "across the street," and that is the last I have seen of him.[3]

Property owners in New York's worst tenement districts were often well connected with the city's political machines through political patronage. In my examination of 117 properties in the Five Points district between 1837 and 1853, for example, thirteen out of fifty-seven owners had clearly discernible ties with political officials or had patronage jobs. Tenement owners ranged from aldermen, assemblymen, and inspectors, to deputy sheriffs, fire wardens, and municipal hearse drivers.[4]

With such close ties with local political figures, even honest administrators of the law worried about the influence of local landlords and property owners. In 1879, for example, the President of the Board of Health, according to the *New York Times*, "no doubt feared the political influence which the landlords could bring to bear on the legislature."[5] In some ways, small-scale landlords benefited from the influence frequently exercised by wealthy, large-scale landlords and property owners who mobilized on an *ad hoc* basis. In 1901, D. B. Ogden, Vice President of the Lawyers' Title Insurance Company noted frankly that "some of the large property owners have men stationed at Albany on the watch for harmful legislation, who immediately notify them, and in case a bad law is proposed the owners affected combine to fight it." As a result, Ogden added, small-scale property owners did not require more sophisticated lobbying methods.[6]

While landlords lacked lobbying organizations dedicated explicitly to their interests in the nineteenth century, they had a powerful, well-organized ally in the city's building trades. Through a score of builders associations and allied interests, New York's construction industry was a powerful force in City Hall and in Albany. The building trades associations represented plumbers, bricklayers, masons, and carpenters—the skilled craftsmen that depended for most of their business on the builders described in Chapter 2. They made up the crews that builders hired, and they, and their associations, were very dependent upon tenement investors. Through the nineteenth century, their opposition to tenement reform usually proved decisive. One critical reason for their success was that, like the municipal government, the building trades were rife with corruption and were often the main beneficiaries of municipal largess.

Ethnic animosities also precluded large-scale landlord lobbying. While many tenement owners probably felt they could rest easy as long as they could rely on their political allies in the building trades, sources suggest a more conflicted reason for their lack of mobilization. Ethnic tensions between Jewish and non-Jewish landlords; between Jews of the Lower East Side and those that lived uptown (the *Yahudin*); and German Jews and Russian Jews routinely undermined any broad-based organization. For example, in her study of tenement landlords, Arlene Newman has noted that, in 1896, a handful of tenement landlords in the Lower East Side began meeting to voice their growing concern about the costs of tenement reform. At one point, some members of the group tried to join with other real estate interests to present their case to the state legislature. However, according to Newman, Lower East Side landlords, owners of one or two homes, never felt welcomed by the uptown Jews and the established real estate interests.[7]

There are other more long-term reasons why tenement landlords failed to form professional associations or lobbies. In terms of occupation and identity, when business people begin creating advocacy organizations, this tends to indicate a broader shift toward professionalization. In many critical respects, most tenement landlords at the end of the nineteenth century were *not* "professionals" but were "amateurs" in the field of real estate. The use of these terms here corresponds, to some extent, with the common usage employed by late-twentieth-century scholars of urban housing. Housing policy analysts such as John Gilderbloom and Richard P. Applebaum speak of professional landlords as "relatively sophisticated investors who approach rental housing much as they would any business investment."[8] Furthermore, as Michael Stegman has noted, landlords become professionals when their holdings reach a point where they have to cease being part-time landlords and concentrate full-time on their holdings, lest they lose control of their operations.[9] In addition, Gilderbloom and Applebaum also note that most professional landlords belong to local apartment owners associations, and that such organizations provide informal and formal networks that are important in promoting cooperation.[10] While Stegman, Applebaum, and Gilderbloom describe landlord management patterns for the late twentieth century, in those features noted above, they also described the late nineteenth century.[11]

These characteristics are all lacking in amateur landlords who, in contrast, tend to control a small number of buildings and often seek steady, long-term income over short-term profits. Moreover, they routinely adopt less formal renting arrangements with tenants, and they tend to eschew local property owners associations or networks. In this study, amateurs are considered those landlords who, in general, continued to treat tenement management largely as a "passive investment" rather than as a business. Professionals, in contrast, not only devoted significant time to property management, but also formed professional associations, sought greater rationalization of laws, regulations, and business practices, and, in general, treated their properties as commodities and viewed themselves, to some extent, as commodity brokers rather than long-term investors. The shift from amateur to professional began to occur at the end of the nineteenth century, and it would have important consequences for the ethnic, tenement builders, buyers, and lessees.

Even in the 1890s, not all realtors and property managers left political advocacy to their allies in the building trades. Small real estate groups had already begun to emerge. However, these associations tended to have small memberships, no programs or services, and usually focused on social activities and local boosterism in small neighborhoods or districts; and they usually did not include tenement operators. They also often engaged in lobbying but only when the need clearly existed. For example, the Washington Heights Taxpayers Association founded in 1891 had about 100 members by 1901, and its organizers focused primarily on local improvements like having the 155th Street viaduct or the Harlem Ship Canal built. The association charged annual dues of two dollars and held meetings when the need arose. This organization had close ties with the Washington Heights Progressive Association which had 200 to 300 members and engaged largely in social activities for its members.

Together, according to one observer, the two organizations "exerted a very powerful influence in improving and beautifying [the Washington Heights,]" and that "this association has seldom failed to land a needed improvement." Boosterism of this sort reflected the strong local orientation of these early real estate groups.

According to a study done by the *Real Estate Record and Builders Guide* in 1901, similar local organizations represented most of Manhattan's neighborhoods (see figure 3.1). Most of these groups focused on the needs of realtors, builders, and brokers working in the city's burgeoning suburban periphery. Indirectly, the map shows this. Note that the oldest tenement districts, like the Lower East Side and areas west of the Bowery, are not represented by nearly as many groups as newer sections of the city experiencing greater development, like the Upper West Side and Washington Heights. In fact, no real estate organizations worked at all on the southern tip of Manhattan.[12]

In the nineteenth century, New York lacked a city-wide association. Some real estate leaders expressed serious doubt about the utility of such an organization, fearing that the organization's leaders would be corrupted by New York's political environment. A president of one of New York's realty trust companies noted that "[such a city-wide organization] has been tried before and failed because it was used eventually to forward the political aspirations of one or two men. They were offered positions under the city government. Such would likely be the fate of a similar organization at present." When pressed about the possible need for such an organization, Ogden of the Lawyers' Title Insurance Company stated that "I am of the opinion that no results could be obtained by the organization which are not obtainable now by the individual or by a temporary association of individuals." John A. Ely of Horace S. Ely and Company, a large real estate firm, noted that "I should say that individual property owners could receive better attention from local organizations working independently. When matters affecting the entire city, such as legislative enactments, come up there would be time for the local organizations to get together and work in unison."[13] To the extent that property owners were organized in New York, they tended to be realtors and brokers; they retained a strong local orientation, and they mobilized only when there was a clear need. In contrast, landlords tended to avoid organized advocacy, preferring instead to rely on institutional inertia, corruption, and their influence with a politically powerful ally.

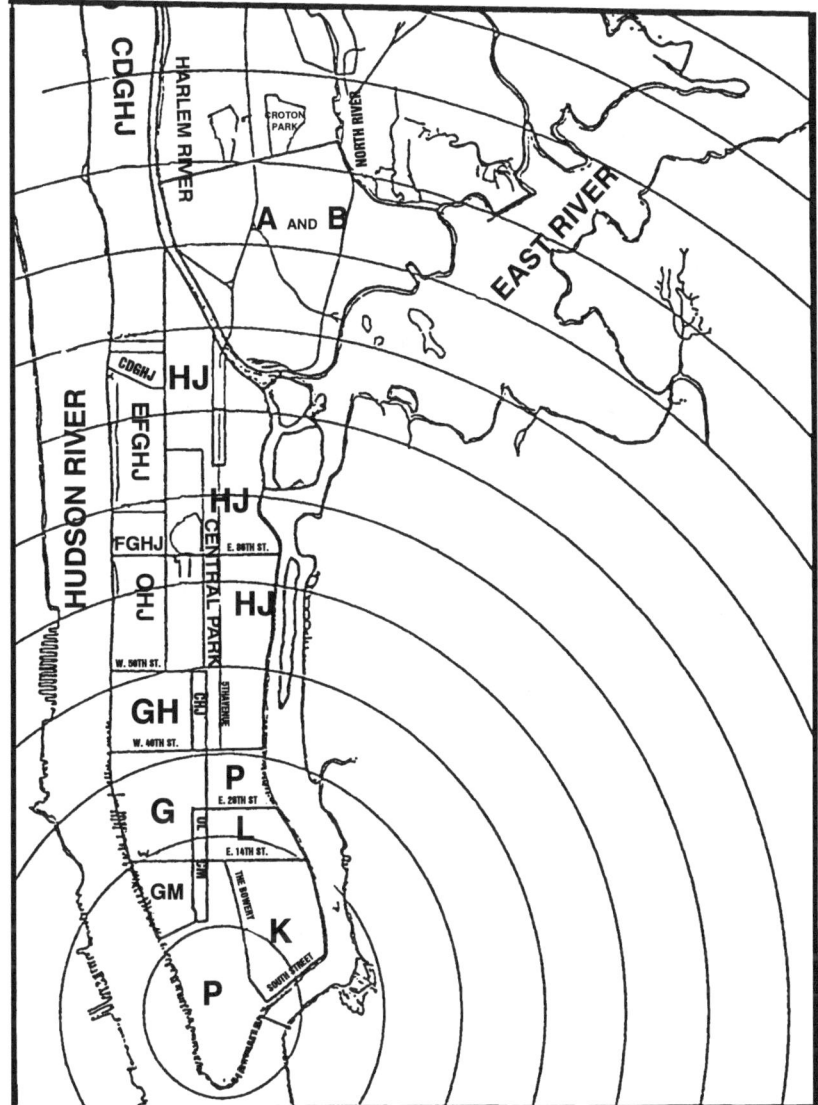

Figure 3.1.
Map showing sections of Manhattan and the Bronx protected by real estate associations.

INDEX FOR THE MAP

A   The Taxpayers' Alliance
B   The 23rd Ward Property Owners' Association
C   The Washington Heights Progressive Association
D   The Washington Heights Taxpayers' Association
E   The Riverside Drive and Morningside Heights Association
F   The West End Association
G   The West Side Taxpayers' Association
H   The 12th and 22nd Ward Real Estate Owners' Protective Association
J   The 12th and 19th Ward Taxpayers' Association
K   The 10th, 11th and 17th Ward Taxpayers' Association
L   The 18th Ward Property Owners' Association
M   The 9th Ward Improvement Association
N   The Park Avenue Property Owners' Association
O   The North Manhattan Taxpayers' Association
P   Uncovered

NOTE: The original key contained no I.
SOURCE: "Extent of Real Estate Association," *Real Estate Record and Builders Guide* (February 1901), p. 228.

II: Housing Reform and the Failure of the Building Trades Lobbies

During the last third of the nineteenth century, lawmakers passed a variety of tenement house laws and building and sanitary codes. However, as noted in Chapter 1, enforcement agencies were weak, underfunded, understaffed, and the laws were unenforced by hosts of corrupt officials in the city's Health and Building departments. With the Tenement House Commission of 1900, however, middle-class reformers began to make progress in forcing builders and landlords to alter some of their practices. As recounted by Roy Lubove in *The Progressives and the Slums*, this commission became the springboard for Lawrence Veiller, secretary of the Charity Organization Society (COS), to launch a successful career as housing reformer and staunch advocate of city planning. Ironically, this commission (along with the Building Code Revisions debate of 1899) also served as a platform for William J. Fryer, implacable critic of housing reform. In many ways, the Commission of 1900 also represented a swan song for Fryer's nineteenth-century style of real estate advocacy. In his forty-year career as municipal official and lobbyist, Fryer was a steadfast defender of New York's building and propertied interests, and over the course of the tenement reform battles that occurred between 1899 and 1901 his personal dislike for housing reformers and for Veiller specifically became well-known. While Veiller brought a heightened sense of pragmatic realism to the tenement reform movement, in many fundamental ways, Fryer's career showcased an older form of political activism, one that allowed landlords to sleep easy as institutional forces thwarted reform. However, Fryer was not simply a political obstructionist. When faced with the Tenement House Law of 1901 and the reality of reform, Fryer spent his final years establishing the United Real Estate Owners Association, New York's first permanent, city-wide real estate lobby that included tenement owners.

The passage of the Tenement House Law of 1901 owed much of its success to the widespread anger prompted by the Building Codes Revision debate of 1899. At that time, the city's building interests pushed to have the city's already weak and inefficient tenement regulations emasculated. Their vehicle was a set of proposed revisions in the building code initiated in January by the Municipal Assembly. For decades, landlords and builders had relied upon corrupt and partisan officials from the Buildings Department to ignore building regulations, and they tended to view the agency as an effective bulwark against reform. Thus, when the Assembly placed the revision process in the hands of a Buildings Department Commissioner, building organizations such the Plumbers Association foresaw major changes in the code, changes favorable to their interests.

The building lobbyists were not disappointed. The revised code not only undercut existing fire codes, but also allowed landlords to add new floors to existing tenements, and weakened provisions governing the existence of air shafts.[14] It placed responsibility for interpreting, altering, and (if they thought it appropriate) putting aside building regulations all together in the hands of the Building Commissioner, the same one who revised the code to begin with. One critic observed "that twenty-four to thirty provisions of the code were all practically nullified by the discretion given to the Buildings Commissioner to change them under certain conditions. The principal danger . . . lay in the placing of this discretionary power with one man, no matter whether he used the power so given him honestly or not."[15] The building interests supported this "end run" around all housing laws because they knew they could trust the Building Commissioner to safeguard their interests. In 1899, this Commissioner was William J. Fryer.

By birth, training, and disposition, William Fryer made the perfect advocate for real estate interests in the late nineteenth century. Born in Albany in 1842, Fryer boasted ties to one of the state's most prominent, landed families, the Livingstons. Through his mother, he had access to the highest social circles in the capital city. He studied architecture and engineering, and moved to New York in 1865 to immediately immerse himself in the building trades. He specialized in ornamental iron work, and eventually became a partner in the Etna Iron Works. His business interests gradually became intertwined with New York City politics as his firm took on large-scale, public projects. His firm, for example, manufactured most of the material used in the construction of the Third Avenue elevated railroad. He also invested in fireproof construction materials and claimed to have invented the hollow tile fireproof block, a claim bitterly disputed in years of litigation.[16]

In the 1880s, Fryer began to take a more direct role in the shaping of tenement house policy in the city. In July 1880 he went to the head of the Buildings Department, William Esterbrook, and presented a wholesale revision of the building code drafted by himself and two associates. Esterbrook agreed to lobby for the new code, and the New York State

Legislature passed it in 1885. From this point on, Fryer assumed many public roles relating to construction and real estate. He was closely allied with Thomas J. Brady, the head of the Buildings Department in the early 1890s (another implacable foe of Veiller and other housing reformers). Fryer was chairman of the Building Law Commission of 1892 which established the Buildings Department as a separate agency of city government and became a member of the Board of Examiners where he heard and decided cases of appeal in which builders challenged the rulings of Buildings Department inspectors.[17]

In many ways, Fryer was just the kind of official landlords and property owners had relied on for decades to safeguard their interests. Steeped in the interests of the building trades, Fryer could be counted on to keep the builders' and contractors' associations informed about threats to the status quo, to plot strategy, and to help them lobby against housing reform. Building trades organizations looked to him for protection, and, to the extent that his offices allowed, he provided it. He had strong ties with key municipal officials and politicians, and his long-standing alliance with the building trades routinely placed him in influential positions of policy arbitration.

Due to his record of support and his position as a Commissioner on the Board of Examiners, building trades representatives asked Fryer to spearhead an industry-sponsored revision of the building code in the fall of 1895. This Committee on the Revision of the Building Code eventually produced recommendations. However, the consolidation of greater New York in 1897 altered the political landscape such that the Revision Committee could not lobby for its plans until 1899 when many of the same individuals, including Fryer, were appointed by the Municipal Assembly to a new Commission on Building Code chaired by Fryer's colleague, Thomas J. Brady. Fryer quickly resurrected the 1895 plan, much to the pleasure of the building lobbies. *The Real Estate Record and Builders Guide* noted in its review of the Commission's work that,

[w]ith great good fortune the Building Code Commission fell heir to [the Revision Committee] reports. It required, however, a master hand to adapt the changes suggested in these reports to the existing law, but with equal good fortune to the public the Code Commission contained within itself that very kind of ability. The experience of the Board of Examiners in dealing with questions not fully covered by existing laws accrued to the Code Commission in drafting

the new ordinance. The three Commissioners of Building, bring members of the Code Commission, presented their experiences in the Department of Buildings and helped along greatly the completeness and correctness of the work.[18]

Veiller, Richard Watson Gilder, I. N. Phelps Stokes and other reformers tried to have a different commission appointed by the governor. However, industry lobbies such as the Builders League, the Society of Architectural Iron Manufacturers, and others crushed this attempt, and, under Fryer's leadership, the plan moved through the Municipal Assembly, passed the Board of Aldermen and onto the Municipal Assembly's Joint Committee on the Affairs of Boroughs.[19] Following a condensed public session in which only supporters voiced their opinion while opponents (including Veiller) were not allowed to speak, the plan was rushed passed the Board of Aldermen. At one point, Fryer claimed that the Tenement House Committee of the COS had actually endorsed the Building Commission plan, much to Veiller's consternation.[20] The plan seemed destined to become law without significant opposition, and *The Real Estate Record and Builders Guide*, an organ for the building trades and staunch ally of Fryer, trumpeted the code, stating that "broadly speaking, we believe that the new Building Code is the most complete and comprehensive ordinance thus far drafted and is a credit to our own city and a model for other cities to copy."[21]

However, the city's newspapers extensively covered the heavy-handed activities of the Building Commission, and when the plan came before the Joint Committee on Affairs of Boroughs, Veiller, Robert De Forest, and other opponents were ready for them. They had spent the proceeding days drawing up detailed, point-by-point denunciations of the planned revisions and had distributed them to reporters in advance of planned public hearings. On September 22, reformer after reformer stood to denounce the plan, the building trade lobbies, and Fryer himself, culminating in a blistering attack by a representative from the Citizen's Union who stated,

This is a deliberate attempt to tear down the building laws of this city, to destroy the fire limits, and to break up the tenement house regulations. . . . The whole attempt is a fraud. It was conceived in crime, and our passing it is criminal. It is a steal, a job, and a fraud. I charge that it is an outrage on the people to pass such a code, and I brand every man who has had anything to do with it and every man who votes for it here to-day [*sic*] as a criminal before God and his conscience.[22]

In methodical fashion, Veiller proceeded to demolish the Building Commission plan, and, in effect, called Fryer a "liar" concerning the COS endorsement of Fryer's plan, prompting a fifteen-minute shouting match between Veiller and Fryer. Fryer appears to have felt personally betrayed by Veiller, a former official of the Buildings Department. What followed was a public relations debacle of the first order for Fryer and the building lobbies as the heated exchanges and charges and countercharges received extensive coverage in the local papers, leaving the widespread impression that Fryer and the building trades lobbies were ramming through regressive, self-serving legislation (which, for the most part, they were). *The Record and Builders Guide* dismissed the reformers as a "set of cranks."[23] Rather than withdrawing the controversial plan, Fryer and his allies continued to push it through, calling on political friends such as Benjamin Croker to denounce Veiller (and even to disown his own previous endorsement of COS housing reform proposals). In October, in defiance of mounting public opposition, the Mayor signed the Building Code.[24]

Fryer's victory was short-lived. His strong-arm tactics galvanized tenement reformers from across the city, and under Veiller's leadership of the Tenement House Commission of 1900, the most significant housing legislation to date became law in 1901.[25] Building trades lobbyists had clearly overplayed their hand in 1899, and in the ensuing furor that followed, Fryer and other advocates for the building trades found themselves, for the moment, unable to defeat the legislation. Veiller and the COS Tenement House Committee staged an unprecedented counteroffensive designed to push elected officials, policymakers, and the public not only to undo the new building codes but also to impose strong, statewide building and sanitary standards combined with meaningful enforcement machinery. At a cost of more than $10,000, Veiller organized a tenement house exhibit in February 1900, effectively mixing dramatic charts documenting the incidence of tuberculosis and poor relief in certain tenement districts with photos and three-dimensional replicas of "new model" tenements as well as tenement blocks in the Lower East Side. Combined with the publicity generated by the 1899 Building Commission revisions, the exhibit had the desired effect of moving influential policymakers, specifically New York Governor Theodore Roosevelt, to rally to the COS cause.[26]

Despite significant opposition from Tammany Hall, landlords, and the

68

builders, the Tenement House Commission pushed through a series of reforms that produced several major changes. First, as Roy Lubove and others have noted, the law introduced a series of health, safety, and building regulations that significantly limited many of the worst elements of nineteenth-century tenements. The Tenement House Law of 1901 imposed strict new guidelines on builders that emphasized better lighting, sanitation, and new fire and safety standards. For example, the law limited the heights of newly constructed tenements to six stories and required that owners fireproof shafts and stairwells and provide water closets for each apartment. Also, by limiting the building's coverage of a 25 x 100 foot lot to 70 percent of the total area, the new law, in effect, eliminated dark inner courts.[27]

The law also created enforcement mechanisms that, while not perfect, were strong enough to induce widespread compliance from New York's builders and tenement owners. In the nineteenth century, officials largely ignored the enforcement of tenement house laws, due partly to the division of responsibility between the city's departments of health, fire, police, and buildings and partly to the ease with which landlords could influence officials from these various agencies. With the creation of the Tenement House Department, lawmakers centralized all of the responsibilities for enforcement. At the same time, they appointed Lawrence Veiller as the first Tenement House Department Commissioner. Rather than becoming a new repository for corrupt, political machine loyalists, under Veiller the department implemented a much more rigorous enforcement regime.[28] The Buildings Department ceased to be the bulwark for landlord interests. One builder described the difference in enforcement in 1906.

> Yes, it was a whole lot different ten years ago. In those days you weren't bothered while putting up your building and when it was finished it was finished and in went your tenants. Now you can't begin to think about tenants until the Department hands over your certificate. It's a round of inspections and re-inspections—tenants waiting to come in and loans due—but nothing doing until you get the certificate.[29]

In contrast with previous reform efforts that had successfully pushed through tenement laws, the COS and other tenement reformers remained mobilized to insure compliance once the Commission's proposals became law. The Tenement House Law did not eliminate all the administrative problems that had plagued previous legislation. In fact, as inspectors became more assertive, the Tenement House Department quickly built up a large backlog of cases. The department still suffered from a lack of inspectors and other staff. However, to an unprecedented degree, Veiller's administration saw a significant curtailment of corruption, flagrant influence-peddling, and political "cronyism."[30]

Veiller and other reformers wanted the tenement construction standards to be improved and the Tenement House Department to be relatively free from corruption. However, the Tenement House Law of 1901 also had some unintended consequences. Most notably, from the time the law took effect, it began pushing the most marginal tenement builders out of the market. As Richard Plunz and Janet Abu-Lughod have shown, due to the new building regulations, builders could no longer construct tenements one or two at a time. Of the 579 tenements constructed in Manhattan during the first 18 months of the law's operation, only 45 were built on single lots of 25 feet or less. Some 236 of the new structures were built on two combined lots, while the remaining 211 tenements were built on lots of at least 50 feet. Along with the new regulations requiring bathrooms and running water for each apartment, the law also imposed new health and safety specifications. As a result, as Plunz and Abu-Lughod concluded, "Small developers who built on a lot-by-lot basis could no longer participate in the production of high-density tenements. Large capital began to monopolize the tenement market."[31]

Finally, the law promoted a public debate among New York's real estate interests about the need for a city-wide real estate organization, a role the newly formed United Real Estate Owners Association tried to fill, making it for a time the city's preeminent voice of realty.

III: The Rise of a City-Wide Real Estate Organization

In 1900 and 1901, when the building trades saw their influence wane momentarily, real estate interests from across the city began looking elsewhere for protection and political and legal advocacy. At first, property owners adopted the same regional or neighborhood approach that had led to the formation of the Washington Heights Taxpayers Association in 1891. In 1900, for example, in response to Harlem's unstable housing market, a small group of local tenement owners organized the Protective

Association of Harlem Property Owners. Their immediate targets were other landlords who, out of desperation to rent unwanted apartments, had been offering months of "free rent" to new tenants. Rather than rallying Harlem's tenement owners to their cause, the new organization quickly became the target of ridicule and condemnation, as organizers were accused by prominent realtors of corruption and divisive manipulation. Instead of launching a new era in landlord cooperation, the association quickly collapsed, its brief history showcasing the inherent weaknesses of these and similar regional and local real estate lobbies.[32]

The passage of the Tenement House Law of 1901 sparked significant debate among New York's real estate leaders about the need for a stronger, city-wide lobby for property owners. Many established brokers felt that such an organization was impractical and that local groups were better-suited to address property owners' concerns. Others, perhaps reflecting on the Harlem association's experience, feared that leaders of a city-wide association would become embroiled in the political machine or use their office to further their own real estate careers. Many realtors also felt that the differences between small and large property owners would be in an insurmountable barrier. W. W. Niles, Vice President of the Taxpayers' Alliance, noted that "owing to the fact that that a large portion of the property owners is made up of mechanics and clerks with small salaries, considerable difficulty was encountered in raising money."[33] E. A. Cruikshank, one of the larger realtors in the city, stated frankly that, "I doubt if any organization embracing both owners and brokers would be a success. Another trouble would be that the uptown owners might not want what the owners downtown are in favor of." Some realtors like D. B. Ogden argued that real estate lobbying should remain in the hands of local, neighborhood-based groups. Others argued that a city-wide organization was necessary, but that it should follow from existing local structures. A president of a large realty trust company stated that "the best method of organization would be to use the local or district associations already in existence. . . . A central body might be formed by representatives from these that would be effective, leaving all strictly local matters to the associations as now formed."[34]

Led by Fryer and an associate, Henry Markus, established lobbyists were already moving to create a real estate association based on this concept. In 1900, even before the passage of the Tenement House Law, they established the United Real Estate Owners Association (UREO). Fryer and Markus built on existing structures to create a real estate lobby that, they hoped, would speak for all of New York's real estate interests. UREO became a confederation of local groups, in essence an association of associations. The new organization had a small staff that lobbied against taxes and housing reform in City Hall and Albany and, in general, promoted the public image of real estate in the newspapers. While most of the local associations charged annual dues of between two and five dollars, UREO required an additional forty cents a year on top of regular, local organization dues. While previous organizations were stigmatized for corruption and by officials using their positions for personal gain, UREO officials were forbidden from holding public office, and it appears that Fryer and Markus both gave up public office.[35]

Basing its membership on the member lists of these local groups, the UREO claimed an immediate membership of almost 3,750 realtors and property managers, and from its creation in 1900 to the 1930s, when other groups would surpass it in influence, the UREO was one of New York's strongest voices for real estate. The organization gradually developed a range of personal services for members, although their primary focus remained lobbying and the dissemination of information to members and the press.[36] UREO organizers formed a Tenement House Committee designed to resist any efforts by Board of Health officials to force tenement owners to make alterations to buildings already erected.[37] Fryer and Markus mobilized member organizations to challenge the constitutionality of the new tenement law. At the same time, they pressured state legislators to amend the laws and in effect nullify them. Fryer attacked the law's strict limitations on inspectors and lauded the days when city officials had discretionary authority to grant exemptions. In these efforts, UREO leaders failed. However, the organization gained significant publicity and respect from the city's real estate brokers and operators.[38]

The UREO's confederated structure gave association leaders a great deal of stature in dealing with city officials. However, UREO leaders did not exercise much control over leaders of individual member organizations. From its beginning, UREO had 150 delegates from the local organizations, and the number of delegates expanded one delegate for every 25 new members. UREO presidents could not force member organizations to follow UREO policy, and tension between UREO members and leaders became a persistent problem for the next two decades.[39]

Compounding these structural problems, between 1900 and 1913 organization leadership experienced some shocks when William Fryer died suddenly in 1907 and Henry Markus departed as UREO president. New York's realtors and brokers now had a city-wide organization, but its structure did not encourage a unified response, a uniform policy, or significant loyalty from members whose allegiance, if they had any, remained with local organizations.

Even as certain groups of realtors and developers began forming and expanding their professional associations, subtle changes in the behavior of small groups of tenement owners foreshadowed a much larger shift away from passive tenement management strategies. Between 1904 and 1906, when tenement property was in high demand across the city, ethnic, tenement curb markets began to emerge in such areas as the Lower East Side and Harlem. In these street-side markets, realtors, builders, owners, and lessees sometimes numbering as many as one hundred gathered to buy and sell lots, options, rents, and leases much like commodity brokers.[40] The behavior of these buyers and sellers stood in marked contrast with the methods of the traditional, long-term, tenement investors. At the curb markets, tenements could change hands several times over the course of a day or over several weeks. The evidence of their activity is readily discernible in ownership turnover rates. For example, in his study of turnover rates for 958 Lower East Side parcels between 1900 and 1950, Leo Grebler found that 48 percent of all sales in 1906 involved investors who had owned the property for less than a year and 64 percent had owned their properties for less than two years, more than 30 percent higher than any other year studied, and more than 50 percent higher than 1907 when the speculative bubble suddenly burst. Grebler noted that "the first decade of this century ... witnessed a hectic speculative boom the like of which was never again experienced [in the next forty years]."[41] These curb markets would appear again in 1920 when housing demand was again high.

No longer content with simply collecting the rents, these new tenement "brokers" treated their properties more like commodities or other comparable assets that were traded and circulated almost like securities. John Gilderbloom, Richard Applebaum and other housing analysts have long recognized the importance of this shift in asset management. In their overview of the central strategies of professional landlords, Gilderbloom and Applebaum state,

One reason why professional landlords charge higher rents is because they regard their units as part of a short-term investment portfolio, rather than as a long-term source of income. This, in turn, requires that rent/cost ratios be high, if the property is to command a high sales price. It also creates strong pressures to turnover property quickly. Rental units are acquired or liquidated on the basis of calculations that take into account a large range of alternative investment opportunities.... This often involves speculation — the rapid resale of units for short-term profit.[42]

The behavior of short-term operators and the periodic emergence of tenement curb markets in the first two decades of the twentieth century, to some extent, presages the dominant methods of professional tenement operators later in the century.

In critical ways, however, tenements were not stocks and bonds. High prices and accelerated turnover rates had unique consequences for renters. In 1907–1908, and again in the early 1920s, curb markets and the behavior of these tenement "brokers" indirectly contributed to significant tenant unrest.

IV. Tenant Activism and the Emergence of the Greater New York Taxpayers Association

The Tenement House Law of 1901 affected tenement operators in three important ways: it pushed undercapitalized, small-scale builders out of the market; it helped mobilize the city's real estate interests; and it forced some builders to modify their practices (an important development in the history of the city's real estate industry). However, the laws had no immediate impact on the daily experiences of the city's large tenant population. In fact, tenants played no role in the debates over tenement reform, and it did nothing (at least initially) to advance the interests of tenants vis-à-vis their landlords. Regulation of building construction never shifted to regulation of the practices of tenement managers, and the courts still remained the landlords' province. In reality, most middle-class reformers viewed revision of landlord-tenant law with deep suspicion, considering the general workings of the law too vital to the city's basic economy for idle tinkering.

And yet, as the decade progressed, the legal imbalance between landlords and tenants quickly emerged as the *central* concern of the city's working-class tenants. On the heels of their legislative setback in 1901, tenement landlords across the Lower East Side faced the most significant, organized challenge to their right to set rents. Between 1902 and 1908, sporadic episodes of tenant agitation shook the Lower East Side, episodes that showcased new tenant strategies, most notably the rent strike. This agitation had its roots in local immigrants' heightened level of political awareness and activism concerning a range of basic, bread-and-butter issues.

In the nineteenth century, landlords and other business people on the Lower East Side had experienced very little sustained opposition from working-class immigrant families. However, this passivity began to change significantly in the new century as housewives and working women began staging organized protests. As managers of the home economy, women had a heightened awareness of cost increases in staple items such as food and rent. So it began in 1902 when women on the Lower East Side organized kosher meat boycotts. At the time, when kosher meat prices jumped from a high-but-affordable twelve cents a pound to an unaffordable eighteen cents a pound, housewives organized themselves into the Ladies Anti-Beef Trust Association. Relying on local institutions such as synagogues, labor unions, and mutual aid societies, organizers brought significant pressure to bear on meat sellers until the meat wholesalers agreed to lower prices to pre-strike levels.[43]

Tenement landlords failed to appreciate the experience of the meat merchants. In early 1904, following a period of widespread demolition and significant immigration on the Lower East Side, landlords began increasing rents dramatically. As the traditional May 1 moving day drew close, many observers predicted that, in their drive for higher rents, landlords would evict thousands of tenants who could not afford the increase. In response, seventeen-year-old Bertha Liebson, dubbed the "new Joan of Arc" by local papers, organized other Jewish tenants to form the New York Rent Protective Association. Liebson and other organizers specifically targeted the weakest class of landlords, the lessees, knowing that they were in no position to hold out financially. Tenants staged rent strikes, blocked evictions, and began to form alliances with local Socialists and Jewish social activists such as Abraham Cahan, head of Jewish Charities in New York.[44]

Liebson and other organizers specifically targeted the municipal courts, long the ally of landlords when they wanted to remove unwanted tenants. The strike leaders' plan was to overwhelm the courts with eviction cases and force judges to dismiss them *en masse*. According to the *New York Tribune*, tenant activists took "advantage of every technicality, delay and dispossess obstruction that the law permits." Organizers assumed that, while the law favored the landlord, judges and the public would sympathize with tenants once they became aware of their plight.[45]

However, Liebson and the other women who started the strikes quickly lost control of the movement they helped found. Rather than advancing the specific issues of tenants (Liebson's approach), many Socialist leaders tried to exploit the movement to win new converts to Socialism. Liebson and others resisted this shift only to be completely driven out of leadership positions. By mid-April, 1904, the tenant leadership had no women at all.[46]

Liebson was not the only one to become frustrated with the Socialist activists. Setting a pattern that would persist through the 1910s and 1920s, tenants began abandoning the movement and making whatever deals they could with their landlords. Moreover, many tenants began resorting to violence, despite the movement's commitment to nonviolent protest. Attacks on landlords, small riots, and conflicts with police and city marshals were (for a brief time) a daily occurrence.[47]

As fears of violence and the growing influence of the Socialists mounted, the Mayor, the Chief of Police, and other city officials began turning against the strikers.[48] Municipal court judges viewed the rent strikes with grave apprehension, and they were determined not to capitulate based on a crowded court calendar or due to fear of violence. One judge, while deploring the avarice of many landlords, stated flatly that the "court is bound to enforce the law and if the tenant will not pay the increased rent, his only alternative is to go elsewhere."[49] As a result, some courts stepped up their processing of eviction cases, pressuring many tenants to abandon the strike strategy and sign new leases or move.[50] Even as evictions increased, the courts exercised some subtle discretion in the processing of cases, discretion that singled out tenant leaders. Individuals, such as Bertha Liebson, faced swift eviction along with many other tenant leaders while many average tenants remained in possession of their apartments.

The crisis ended in a stalemate. City and state officials pressured judges and the police to delay processing some evictions, and tenants achieved significant short-term victories. These delays hit the financially vulnerable lessees the hardest, and many of them caved in and reduced their rents. However, the fissures in the tenant leadership only widened, so that the tenant organization itself ceased to exist once the crisis passed. The rent strikes produced no change in landlord behavior nor any legal reform in landlord-tenant law. To some extent, this allowed both sides to claim some measure of victory, as many tenants remained in their apartments while many landlords felt satisfied that evictions would ultimately be processed. However, in the broader picture, the tenants' lack of support from the courts, city officials, and the larger renting public critically undermined the nascent tenant movement. Some tenants benefited but their organized political power evaporated.[51]

Tenant unrest, however, ceased only for a brief time. Renters on the Lower East Side resumed their organized assault on landlords and the courts in December 1907, and this time there would be a less ambiguous outcome. Landlords, assisted by the city's courts and the police, decisively crushed the protest, leading to the eviction of hundreds of tenants and the creation of a new association firmly committed to protecting landlords from tenement reform and tenant activists. The 1907 strikes had other outcomes as well. In their efforts to organize landlords on the Lower East Side, landlord activists openly broke with tenement lessees, purposefully excluding them from any benefit derived from organization.

Landlords (and many other observers) blamed the 1907 rent strikes on lessees who were desperate to make the most of greater demand for low-income housing. Increased demand for apartments had continued to rise in 1906 and 1907, and new groups of lessees rushed to exploit the conditions.[52] The *New York Herald* stated that the principal cause of the crisis was,

> the greed of the lessee landlords. There swept over the [Lower East Side] two years ago a speculative craze to own real estate. Men who had accumulated a few hundred dollars borrowed more and bought tenements, giving back mortgages. The prices they paid were in many cases exorbitant and their equities in the property shadowy. In order to pay off the interest and accumulate the remainder of the purchase money[,] they would lease the premise entire[ly] to the highest builder.[53]

Once again, women on the Lower East Side were in the forefront of the tenant agitation. Led by a shirtwaist factory worker, Pauline Neuman, East Side residents in the Grand Street area began to organize in December 1907, pressing owners and lessees to lower rents from 18 to 20 percent. Neuman and others organized more than 400 women and engaged the support of the region's active Socialist Party. Activists from the Socialists' Anti-rent Agitation Bureau once more focused their attack on lessees.[54] From the organizers' perspective, the success of the rent strike rested on the landlords' inability (or unwillingness) to quickly and effectively use the legal system to assert their rights. When landlords served tenants with eviction notices, strike leaders instructed renters to contest the case in court, where Socialist Party lawyers pressed to have their cases tried separately from all other dispossess cases. In theory this strategy, if widely followed, would quickly overwhelm the judicial system. Organizers were also well aware of other costs and obstacles landlords faced in getting large numbers of tenants evicted. Each processed eviction, for example, required the services of city marshals. Not only did landlords have to cover the cost of hiring the marshals, but also by law the marshals could only execute one eviction a day for any given house. According to one Socialist Party organizer, the "tenements hold from twenty to one hundred families each. We will arrange that any evicted family shall be harbored at once by some other family in the same house. This the landlord cannot prevent. Thus we would have an endless chain of evictions, by which the landlords will accomplish nothing."[55] Tenant leaders raised the specter of a massive uprising in January 1908, when rents were due. One leaflet proclaimed, "Let the landlords try to dispossess thousands.... Imagine blocks and blocks filled with furniture.... Remember the first of January is coming."[56]

Besides withholding rent, tenant activists devised other more confrontational methods of pressuring landlords. Through the Socialist Party's Anti-Rent Agitation Bureau, families organized to keep new tenants from moving into the apartments of evicted tenants. For particularly recalcitrant landlords, tenant activists used numerous forms of harassment and provocation to bring them around. While hanging American flags and red banners in windows, tenants often subjected resident landlords, lessees, and their families to verbal abuse, pelting them with debris, and, in some cases, burning the landlord in effigy.[57] Moreover, some women activists assaulted the wives of landlords, pulled their hair, and even threatened to burn down the landlords' tenements.[58]

For the first time, activists also began to systematically use municipal agencies to pressure landlords. They threatened to make complaints to the Tenement House Department and the Board of Health about code violations, a particularly potent threat for landlords lacking resources, given that these violations were very widespread and often expensive to remedy. Furthermore, once city inspectors posted violation notices, they placed a lien on the property so that it could not be transferred free and clear until the landlord made repairs. During the strike, a steady stream of Tenement House inspectors toured the East Side, attesting to the organizers' resolve to press this issue.[59]

The Socialists and other strike organizers enjoyed some initial success. In only a few short days, other groups of renters from around the city followed the example of the Lower East Side activists, and the number of strikes dramatically increased.[60] The Grand Street offices of the Socialist Party teemed with tenants. Strike leaders pressured desperate landlords to meet with arbitrators and negotiate new leases. These negotiations, according to one tenant leader, usually involved the strikers dictating to the landlord how much he would reduce his rent. Treated with contempt and often showered with abuse in a circus-like atmosphere, many landlords quickly capitulated. By the end of December, the strike leaders had secured settlements in more than 180 houses, involving a total reduction of nearly $5,400 a month.[61] These figures do not include the large number of private settlements that tenants made without the involvement of the strike committee.

Despite these successes, strike leaders and their Socialist partners greatly overestimated the strength of their movement. As they had in 1904, they had not anticipated the reaction of city officials, landlords, or even their own organizers and supporters once some gains were made. Reaction began three days into the agitation when a group of city marshals brandishing nightsticks dispersed a meeting of 3,000 strike supporters at Rutgers Park, initiating a prolonged period of skirmishes with marshals and the police. Hoping that mass arrests would prompt public outrage, strike organizers called for more civil disobedience. The police, never sympathetic to Socialist organizers and their "foreign influences" in the first place, responded by more actively supporting the city's landlords. In a confrontation with tenant activists, Police Commissioner Bingham declared, "If you don't like your rents get out. If you are not satisfied with our system of rents go back where you came from."[62] Tenant activists had also misread the sympathies of the city's municipal court judges. Judges stiffly resisted the strikers' "clog-the-courts" strategy and began to issue eviction notices by the thousands.[63]

The tenant movement itself began to show signs of disintegration as well. From the beginning, leadership had been very decentralized among the various local groups, and Socialist organizers showed inexperience or naiveté in their handling of day-to-day affairs. For example, the *New York Herald* described the relations between top Socialists and tenant organizers;

There seems to be everywhere a waste of effort on the part of those who are agitating the cause of reduction, and whenever any one who is recognized as a leader appears, he or she is promptly frowned upon by the socialists who are conducting the very loosely organized campaign. The idea of leadership is foreign to the Marxian theory or life, and for that reason the strike, as nearly as can be ascertained, is in the hands of about sixty committees and one hundred volunteer advisers.[64]

Once again, Socialist leaders also began pushing women out of key organizational roles. Even the popular Pauline Neuman was quietly advised to return to her job at the shirt factory.[65]

With the daily humiliation of landlords and regular clashes between police and activists, landlords began organizing for their own protection. In early January 1908, one hundred Lower East Side tenement owners gathered at Pythagoras Hall on East Broadway. With 2,000 tenants demonstrating outside, the landlords formed an organization to defeat the rent strikers and to protect themselves from financial ruin. Led by an attorney, Harold Phillips, landlord organizers appealed for funds to assist those landlords facing rent strikes or continuous vacancy. At first, in their zeal to present a united front of all interested parties, the organizers even agreed to admit lessees. Phillips proclaimed that "landlords must stick together.... [T]he organization should not allow one owner to be ruined by an empty house for that was what the politicians backing the rent reduction campaign were working for—to ruin several owners and thus put fear into the hearts of the whole class."[66]

Despite these calls for unity, tenement owners in the organization quickly moved to have the lessees pushed out. Two days after the first meeting, in a raucous, multilingual meeting, organizers began to lay down the basic principles and policies of this new organization. Pushing aside any prospect for inclusion, one wealthy tenement owner blamed lessees for the unrest, stating that "landlords on the east side were not responsible for the high rents, but ... the lessees were." He advocated not only for the exclusion of lessees from the new association but also for the abolition of the lessee system altogether and that landlords rent their houses directly to tenants. Ultimately, association officials barred lessees from membership.[67]

Participants also began pushing for a range of programs to protect landlords. One landlord suggested that they should "establish their own bank and their own insurance company and could defeat legislation that might throw additional financial burdens on the shoulders of the tenement house owners." He also proposed that each landlord contribute a hundred dollars to a fund to defeat the rent strikers. This brought howls of protest from small owners. The nominal chairman of the meeting, Phillips, had to balance the demands of the handful of wealthy tenement owners with those of many small owners. Finally, organizers agreed to collect ten dollars for each house held by landlord members.[68] In a matter of days, the new organization which organizers called the Greater New York Taxpayers Association (GNYTA) had attorneys on hand to assist landlords with tenant difficulties, and they had a war chest of over $20,000.[69] The new organization's membership tripled to 300, and Phillips began looking beyond the immediate crisis, stating that the fund would be used, not only for legal expenses, but would also help an owner "over a hard mortgage hill" in the future.[70]

Phillips began guiding the organization toward meeting the needs of a specific group of property owners, long-term tenement owners, in many ways the old-style passive investors of the nineteenth century. Lessees were excluded. The outcry against so-called "leasters" had been particularly severe during the rent crisis, and Phillips and others may have viewed them as a public relations liability. At the same time, he may have been simply acknowledging the divergent interests between lessees and owners. Either way, the larger landlords and owners cut the "leasters" adrift and, for most, the lessees' only choice was to settle with the rent strikers under the most favorable terms they could manage.[71] Many individual tenants exploited the desperation of the lessees to get their rents reduced. Led by officials from the new GNYTA, more substantial owners held out, waiting for tenants to come back and accept no reduction in rents. These landlords used their influence to force tenants to return or, when especially embittered, to evict the worst tenant organizers selectively.[72]

Along with lessees across the Lower East Side, the other clear losers in the rent conflict of 1907–1908 were the tenant organizers' partners, the Socialists, who had hoped to use the tenant agitation as a springboard for advancing their own political agenda. However, rather than embracing new political beliefs, strikers tended to use the Socialists, their services, and initiatives, simply to strengthen their own position in negotiation with their landlords. They often did not wait for the sanction of the organization to strike their own deals on an individual basis. In the closing days of the agitation, as lessees pressed for these individual, non-publicized settlements, the Socialist strike leaders saw their support slip away. These renegades left the Socialists to face the hostile police and court justices alone, along with a more determined, less financially desperate class of landlords. By early January, their strike fund had dwindled, and tenants complained that attorneys were not showing up to defend them in court.[73] While some tenants benefited, as in 1904, tenant activists in general met defeat in the face of sustained opposition from courts, the police, and newly organized landlords.

V. GNYTA's Basic Policies and Programs

The Greater New York Taxpayers Association had, like many similar real estate groups in the nineteenth century, mobilized in the face of a clear threat. As the threat receded, the normal course of events was for the group to have drifted apart, unable to sustain its coherence given the competition and divergent interests of its naturally distrustful membership. Initially, the association moved in that direction. For the first years of GNYTA's existence, its membership experienced little growth, and the organization's activities revolved around the lobbying of the Law and Legislative Committee. Organizers had few responsibilities, and, for many years, they operated out of the offices and homes of GNYTA officials.[74]

While Harold Phillips helped found GNYTA, two others came to assume more control over its long-range policies and programs. In the 1910s, Ignatz Reich and Isidor Berger, two prominent Lower East Side businessmen, quickly assumed central positions as President and General Manager. They exercised a decisive influence over the organization's policies for decades. Ignatz Reich was born in Austria in 1867. He emigrated to the United States in 1888 and settled in New York City, where he became a successful diamond merchant on the Lower East Side. Reich went on to form a joint real estate holding enterprise that managed tenements and other properties. He first joined GNYTA in 1916, eight years after its inception, and became chairman of the association's Finance Committee, after which he was elected President in 1921, a position he would hold until 1941. In 1927, he also became President of the Greater New York Taxpayers Mutual Insurance Association, a full-fledged insurance company designed to meet the insurance needs of GNYTA's members and other landlords. In the 1930s and beyond, the Insurance Association gradually became the raison d'être of the whole organization.[75]

As GNYTA's General Manager, Isidor Berger was more instrumental in implementing the organization's programs and overseeing its day-to-day operations. Born in 1872, he became involved in Lower East Side real estate at an early age. He was a marginally successful hardware store owner and landlord, and, with 266 other landlords and property owners, Berger helped start GNYTA in 1908. In 1914 he became Chairman of the association's important Protection and Defense Committee. In 1919, he became GNYTA's General Manager where he operated, in his own words, a landlord's "first aid" department, offering advice and solutions to a steady stream of landlords seeking relief.[76] Berger and Reich represented GNYTA at city and state public hearings, and they both routinely spoke out for the interests of landlords across the city.[77] Along with Harold Phillips, they also represented individual members in New York's municipal courts in cases involving accident liability, rent withholding, building safety, and health code violations, and almost every other kind of action that related to landlord-tenant relations. In the 1920s, New York's municipal courts frequently appointed Berger as an arbitrator of disputes between landlords and tenants. In 1927, he became General Manager of the new Insurance Association. He was a member of the Christie-Forsythe Project Property Owners Committee in 1928, a member of the Multiple-Dwellings Law Revision Committee in the early 1930s, and ran for councilman for the Borough of Manhattan in 1937. Berger remained General Manager for over forty years and eventually succeeded Reich as GNYTA's President following Reich's death, a title Berger would retain along with his others until his own death in 1954.[78] Berger and Reich molded GNYTA from a weak association with a small membership into a greatly expanded organization that offered landlords a host of services combined with one of the most active real estate lobbies in the state.

Berger and Reich helped to shape GNYTA's ideological agenda, one that focused upon the needs of a specific type of landlord, the long-term tenement investor with small holdings. Their views were logical products of their own business experience. Like many nineteenth-century owners, they both came to tenement real estate having already established themselves in other lines of work, Reich as a diamond merchant and Berger as a hardware store owner. Emphasizing their commitment to long-term owners, GNYTA officials, as a matter of policy, tried to exclude some of the more dubious speculative builders, short-term purchasers, and lessees whose strategies tended to emphasize quick profits. In 1924, one GNYTA member noted that the association "did not want them as members and is doing all in its power to impress on its members and landlords generally that they must be satisfied with a fair return on their investments."[79]

Between 1908 and 1920, GNYTA's Executive Board slowly developed programs and policies for assisting their landlord clientele and spoke directly to the goals tenement owners had enunciated at the raucous landlord meeting held at the height of the 1908 tenant agitation. To defend their members, GNYTA leaders adopted three basic strategies. First, they developed essential protective services, such as liability insurance and legal assistance for accident and rent-withholding cases. Second, GNYTA acted as a political lobby for the interests of long-term investor landlords both in the state capital and at City Hall.[80] Third, GNYTA leaders acted, in most of these matters, in cooperation with some of New York City's other real estate groups to defeat legislation, challenge existing laws in state courts, and promote strategies for the successful management of tenement property. The first two GNYTA strategies will be discussed below, while the third will be analyzed more thoroughly in later chapters.

Following a brief period of dormancy, GNYTA began to expand its protective services in 1914. At the same time, it also began to form substantive ties with other real estate organizations, laying the groundwork for more comprehensive alliances, organizational crossover of personnel, as well as other forms of professional and intellectual exchange.[81] The immediate cause of this expansion of services was the critical financial challenge to long-term purchasers represented by skyrocketing liability and fire insurance rates.[82]

Lawsuits against landlords began to affect the entire business of tenement management, especially for those tenement investors who neglected their properties. In the late nineteenth century, as noted in chapter 1, civil courts had held landlords liable only for accidents that occurred in public areas such as halls, entranceways, and sidewalks. Even in these cases, a court had not actually ruled against a landlord until 1896. Moreover, within tenement flats, landlords were not negligent at all if, for example, floors caved in or ceilings collapsed. However, beginning in the early 1910s, civil court decisions began turning against landlords. With the tougher standards established by the Tenement House Law of 1901, courts began ruling against landlords on the grounds that blatant violations of health and safety standards established by statute were, by definition, negligence. In 1914, one law journal stated the reasoning, noting that, "Upon common law principles, . . . , when the legislature had by public statute established a certain standard of conduct in order to prevent a danger that it foresaw, it has in this regard forewarned 'the ordinary prudent man' and through him the defendant in a civil action, whose conduct must always coincide with this common law criteria."[83] Under this new standard, landlords increasingly found themselves in court facing damage claims.

These problems dramatically increased in 1913. With the passage of the state's first workmen's compensation law, workers saw their ability to sue employers and property owners expanded. As Arlene Newman has argued, "the whole concept was revolutionary; it mandated that employer's absolute liability, i.e. the mere happening of an accident created the liability." The law stipulated that the employer must provide insurance or give other security for the payment of claims.[84] Further supplementing these new court decisions and legislation, both the Socialists and reformers such as Lillian Wald and other settlement house workers had, for years, been educating tenants about their rights in just these areas.

As a result, the number of liability cases dramatically increased. In 1913, tenants filed a wave of accident liability suits against landlords, particularly in the Lower East Side. In response to this upsurge, insurance companies raised their liability rates for landlords from 100 to 700 percent. Many landlords in the Lower East Side found that insurance companies would not offer them insurance at any price.[85] A GNYTA member later recalled the distress this caused for tenement owners.

[S]uits for alleged accidents said to have occurred in buildings were served on owners in ever increasing numbers. These actions for injuries, some fancied but in most cases fictitious, all demanding financial sums in settlement, were becoming an everyday event. The situation looked threatening and owners began to fear for their equities. To fight was costly, to settle would only aggravate the situation. Something had to be done![86]

With their members staring at unprecedented levels of liability litigation, GNYTA officials repeatedly sent delegations to Albany to complain to the Insurance Commissioner about insurance companies' failure to provide coverage for New York's tenement owners. The Commissioner informed the delegations that he lacked the authority to force the companies to change their policies.[87] In February, 1914, in desperation, GNYTA officials called a mass meeting of landlords to make a formal protest. Along with Stewart Browne, the Chairman of the Insurance Committee and future President of UREO, Harold Phillips attacked the insurance companies on the grounds that

the very increase in claims for accidents can be laid to the doors of the very insurance companies themselves. Railroad companies and street car companies have learned from experience that cases for damages should be carefully investigated and minutely scrutinized before any offer of compromise is made. . . . If the insurance companies adopted a similar attitude, they would find that the vast majority of cases are without merit . . .[88]

While calling for concessions from insurance companies, Phillips had already decided that GNYTA needed to offer insurance and form a protective service to deal with all issues relating to landlord liability. In response, GNYTA leaders formed the Defense Committee, offered insurance, and appointed Isidor Berger as Chairman. Initially modeled as an insurance group, the Defense Committee monitored owners', landlords', and tenants' rates and tried to safeguard landlords from "accident bandits."[89] Over time, however, the Defense Committee became the central agency for a host of other protective legal services for landlords.

The central mission of the Defense Committee was to provide liability protection which mainstream insurance companies had made too costly or had withdrawn altogether. Berger and Phillips set up their offices in the parlor of one of the founding members and began collecting premiums, paying claims, and defending actions in court. In the beginning, they placed a cap of $5,000 on any one claim. This was the highest exposure they were willing to accept. Even with this modest ceiling, between claims and litigation and other legal fees, the association owed Phillips more than $100,000 in legal fees by the time GNYTA received its license.[90] When it came to the insurance business, Phillips, Berger and other GNYTA founders were amateurs, largely ignorant of its intricate workings. As Arlene Newman has noted, GNYTA officials obtained all of their expertise through on-the-job training. They did their own underwriting, their own rating, and their own claims handling. Moreover, all of GNYTA's officers worked on a voluntary basis.[91]

Given their lack of expertise, how then did they function and succeed in providing liability protection for such a high-risk class of property? Simply stated, GNYTA officials made up for their amateurism through sheer aggressiveness and "brass knuckles" intimidation. In a survey of the basic ways the committee operated, this strategy becomes apparent. When landlords applied for GNYTA membership, the Committee required them to register all of their properties with the Defense Committee's inspection department whereupon trained inspectors visited the properties and submitted reports describing all defects and potential liability risks. The inspection department forwarded these reports to the owner who, in theory, had to make all necessary repairs. To insure compliance, follow-up inspections became part of the program. As a matter of policy, noncompliance was supposed to lead to the suspension of coverage for the owner's property. In 1920, the chairman of the Defense Committee tried to maintain inspection standards, arguing that "suppose the inspection department overlooked an important defect in the building in question. . . . should an accident occur as a result the Association is at once a loser whether the case comes to court or not."[92] Once landlords had their property registered, GNYTA's Claims Department handled any suit brought against the owner resulting from accidents. Most importantly from the members' perspective, GNYTA agreed to cover all judgments found against the landlord. With a small staff of attorneys, Isidor Berger and Harold Phillips devised various ways of heading off legal trouble or, once legal action had been initiated, of undermining a tenant's case. For example, the Defense Committee urged members to adopt preventive measures, to maintain their property and incorporate the latest safety features as they appeared on the market. They promoted items such as protective coal bin covers and iron plates for stairs to eliminate the most common cause of accidents.[93] GNYTA officials, in essence, constructed an elaborate first line of defense against the new tools the Tenement House Law of 1901 and the state's civil courts had inadvertently placed in the hands of individual tenants.

When tenants had accidents, GNYTA's more aggressive, more adversarial face comes into focus. The Defense Committee strongly urged members to notify them immediately if any accidents occurred on their property. Kahn argued that early notification "gives us the opportunity to be first on the scene, enabling us to get all the information, fresh and unadulterated and greatly aids us preparing a defense which 99 chances out of 100 spells victory."[94] Early notification allowed Defense Committee staffers the opportunity to confront tenants before they had had a chance to make a complaint or even contact their own attorneys. If the tenant did make a claim, Berger and his staff went to some lengths to undermine the veracity of the complaint, confronting the tenant both in and outside the courtroom and using their records to undermine claims concerning dangerous defects. Confrontation was an integral component of their defense strategy, and Berger, Phillips, and the Defense Committee staff developed a reputation for relentlessness. In 1919, one GNYTA member noted proudly that the Defense Committee's success was due to the "sheer aggressiveness of its attack in every case whether small or large coming within its auspices."[95]

Given the rather tenuous finances of many tenement owners, the Defense Committee offered significant benefits to its members. Its influence may explain the organization's growth from only 800 members in 1910 to well over 3,000 by 1918, the period when GNYTA created most of its services.[96] GNYTA's staff also expanded following the creation of the Defense Committee, going from one employee in 1914 to more than forty trained attorneys, clerks, inspectors, investigators, physicians, and photographers by 1924.[97] There is also evidence that Berger and his staff were effective at protecting landlords against liability claims. In 1919, for example, adjustments and judgments paid out by GNYTA amounted to $100,000 while the total amount sued for aggregated annually to more than a million dollars.[98] GNYTA's aggressive, "brass knuckles" policies would become even more pronounced when members faced particularly recalcitrant tenants.

Despite GNYTA officials' claims to the contrary, the organization's insurance programs were only "quasi-legitimate." The Defense Committee was not licensed to sell insurance, and it was staffed by amateurs who used strong-arm tactics and other questionable procedures. Newman has argued that the state of New York tacitly allowed GNYTA to operate largely because no other companies offered insurance to this class of property owner.[99]

GNYTA officials tried to maintain the association's veneer of a legitimate insurance company. One of the key purposes of the Defense Committee was to undermine the tenant's right to sue through a system of building registration that was nominally designed to raise the safety standards of buildings. Because of the inspection committee's lack of funds and staff, the registration system acted as a poor stimulant for real improvement.[100] What registration did allow, with its attendant paperwork, was to lay the evidentiary groundwork for a legal defense against accident claims.

GNYTA not only took on the courts and tenants but also other institutions that threatened the vital interests of landlords. For example, when members had difficulty meeting their financial obligations to banks, lenders, and loan operators, GNYTA leaders created a Mortgage Committee to mediate between property owners and lenders. Berger felt that this was one of the most valuable services offered by the organization, arguing that by forestalling foreclosures and even obtaining extensions or new mortgages, the Committee had "saved many a widow or helpless owner from poverty." Reich and other staffers negotiated with lenders to reduce temporarily a member's obligations until the member's fortunes improved.[101] The Committee was exceedingly active before World War I when, according to Reich, "mortgage money was not only scarce but practically extinct ... and the foreclosure notices glutted the real estate columns of our daily papers."[102]

GNYTA officials also interceded for members in their dealings with city departments, offering important services dealing with taxation and assessments. Berger, like most other New York real estate operators, felt that the tax structure unduly burdened landlords and other property owners while catering to the needs of the non taxpaying masses. Given their mistrust of government, GNYTA's Executive Board established special committees to monitor public spending and to oversee property assessments in an effort to assure members that they were not being overtaxed. Berger even urged members to submit their income and expense accounts to GNYTA so that the association's representatives could present the figures to the city's Tax Commission and argue for a reduction in assessments.[103]

In dealing with the city, GNYTA's leaders, at times, formed alliances with other real estate groups to work toward common goals. The Real Estate Board of New York and the Allied Real Estate Interests Association often formed loose ties with GNYTA.[104] GNYTA, like many real estate groups around the city, became a member of UREO, and for a number of years the two groups created joint committees to address common concerns. Through the 1910s and 1920s, information passed freely between them, and they often formed joint delegations to attend public hearings.[105] Between 1914, and the 1930s, UREO leader Stewart Browne frequently addressed GNYTA members in the association's official publication, *The Real Estate News*.[106]

How effective was GNYTA? The limited data on membership indirectly suggests a basic level of satisfaction with GNYTA's performance. While the association experienced its greatest growth during times of economic distress and tenant activism, its membership did not decline when the crises were over. In fact, the figures on membership were remarkably stable following the emergency rent crisis of the early 1920s, staying at approximately 7,000 until well into the 1950s, this despite the decline of the Lower East Side and the movement of members to other parts of the city. There are no figures on the number of cases successfully defended. However, by 1927, the Defense Committee had handled more than 30,000 accident claims, and ample evidence exists of the successful defense of individual landlords.[107]

Conclusion

GNYTA's policies and programs were, for the most part, designed to protect landlords from the financial demands created by new regulations, liability lawsuits, and shifting insurance rates, all of which revolve around the central issue of tenement maintenance. Since 1901, political and economic pressures had challenged many of the fundamental precepts of long-term tenement investors. Previously, landlords had set the rents and, for the most part, maintained their properties as they saw fit. By 1915, new state regulations and economic pressures from within the real estate industry itself began undermining these traditional approaches. GNYTA leaders, brought together in the tenant unrest of 1907–1908, quickly turned to these larger challenges. In effect, GNYTA's overarching purpose became, to a large degree, to protect those landlords who still treated tenement ownership as a passive investment.

GNYTA's emergence also had an impact on landlord-tenant relations and on the ability of tenants to exercise their rights. GNYTA's corps of attorneys and representatives offered services and fought hundreds of relatively minor court cases, which, when seen in their entirety, represented an important victory for private real estate interests in New York City. From building codes to tenant's rights laws, the meaning of these legal forms was wrestled out in these minor cases and in the individual interactions between GNYTA, landlords, tenants, and tenant organizations. Associations like GNYTA complicated law and code enforcement to the extent that tenants were deterred from asserting claims or pressing for proper enforcement, which was clearly GNYTA's intent. More broadly, so many of the services offered by GNYTA, while unsuccessful in uplifting landlords, were, for a time, successful in weakening the position of individual tenants and tenant organizations. That time came to an abrupt end in 1918 when a new type of tenant, the middle-class renter, began protesting against traditional landlord practices. These new protests will be the focus of chapter 4.

Rent Strikes and Tenent Activism

Left

The rent strikes of 1917–1918 encompassed many neighborhoods. In September, 1919, these striking tenants picketed outside their Harlem tenement where every tenant was on strike. As strike momentum built, landlords and politicians began attacking tenant leaders as socialists and foreigners. When Abraham Levew, the landlord of this building, accused the three-member committee that led the strike of running a "soviet," one of them, Ann Breitman, retorted that she would slap anyone's face who said she was not "100 percent American." SOURCE: UPI/Corbis-Bettman.

Above

Facing dramatic rent increases, many tenants living at 856 and 864 East 172nd Street went on strike in January, 1919. The landlord responded with evictions that left several families out on the street with their furniture. Here and elsewhere, mothers and their children were often the most conspicuous picketers. Here, the Chairman of the Strikers Committee, Abraham Stupnicher, feeds hungry children on the picket line. SOURCE: UPI/Corbis-Bettman.

While editors from many of New York's mainstream newspapers viewed the rent strikes with disfavor, socialist editors from such papers as the *New York Call* and the *Jewish Daily Forward* embraced the strikers' cause and, at times, lobbied hard for more intervention by government authorities. This 1918 editorial cartoon from the *New York Call*, captures the visceral anti-landlord sentiments felt by many striking tenants. SOURCE: *The New York Call*, June 24, 1918

CHAPTER 4

Rent Strikes and the Landlord's "Reign of Terror"

With their victories in 1904 and 1907, tenement landlords appeared to retain (and even enhance) their privileges. The tenant groups were crushed and the legal rights and authority of landlords remained undiminished, while tenement owners now had their own lobbying organizations more closely monitoring political affairs. The Socialists (for a while) moved on to other issues, and tenement overcrowding, degradation, and unhealthiness seemed to recede from public view. Many tenement landlords in the Lower East Side and elsewhere quickly fell back into traditional patterns of tenement management.

Even as landlords struggled to adjust to the changes brought by the Tenement House Law of 1901, unforeseen, long-term changes in the tenant population began effecting landlord tenant relations and tenement management. While New York's working class had, for generations, confronted the abuses and neglect of the city's landlords, the upper classes had little direct experience or detailed understanding of all the tactics and privileges landlords had at their disposal. In fact, as Elizabeth Collins Cromely has argued, until the 1860s and 1870s, well-off New Yorkers viewed apartment buildings as "morally dubious" dwellings and a challenge to the social order. With their obvious links to working-class tenements, multiple dwellings in general were seen as corrupt by their nature and a betrayal of traditional notions of privacy and decorum. As a result, living in rental housing in the 1860s and 1870s was overwhelmingly a choice exercised by the city's workers, not the upper classes.[1]

These attitudes began to change following the Civil War with the development of so-called "French flats" and the construction of a relatively small number of upscale apartment buildings. As the studies of Elizabeth Collins Cromley and Elizabeth Hawes have shown, middle- and upper-class New Yorkers slowly began to see the advantages of multiple dwellings. By the turn of the century, as servants became more of a luxury, apartment living, with its fewer arduous housekeeping requirements, became more attractive. Apartment dwellings also provided New Yorkers with easier access to stores, mass transit, and other centralized modern conveniences. As apartment living became more acceptable to the middle class, the construction of single-family, private homes virtually ceased. By 1910, apartment buildings had replaced single-family house construction in Manhattan, and multiple dwellings became the foundation for residential living in the city.[2]

At the same time, many working-class tenants in the Lower East Side began to accumulate enough capital to materially separate themselves from the desperately poor that had so characterized the area's tenants in the late nineteenth century. As tenants achieved modest gains in their incomes, they began to adopt the trappings of the more affluent. While many in the Lower East Side remained extremely poor, the modest increases in wealth experienced by some in the working class provided them with greater economic and political clout. In the late 1910s, these two trends, the shift of New York's middle class into multiple dwellings and the modest economic and political gains made by the working-class tenants transformed the consciousness of tenants and fostered a dramatically different environment for landlords and tenants.

On the surface, little had changed following the rent strikes of 1904 and of 1907–1908. Between 1909 and 1916, tenement owning even experienced an economic downturn as tenement construction outstripped demand. For these years, tenants (as they had for generations) exploited market conditions to obtain favorable leases. These favorable economic conditions masked the magnitude of the demographic change in the tenant population since the nineteenth century. All that was needed to mobilize the city's renters was a crisis: a city-wide reduction in essential tenant services, an unprecedented housing shortage, or widespread landlord abuses that affected the middle class. In 1918, New York's tenant population got all three.

I. Stage One: The Heat Crisis and Tenant Mobilization

World War I rationing precipitated the tenant crisis of the late 1910s. When war was declared in April of 1917, federal and state agencies in New York took measures to coordinate and build up the region's war industries. In New York City, these measures included temporary workers' housing projects designed to handle the influx of workers into local shipyards and factories.[3] To support these and other efforts, government contractors and suppliers received preference over private firms. These initiatives, combined with other factors, led to severe shortages in housing and in fuel for private home use. In New York City, private construction of tenements fell dramatically in 1917 and almost completely ceased by the end of 1918. Between 1914 and 1916, for example, the number of tenements constructed annually in New York hovered between 1200 and 1365. In 1917, this number dropped to 760 and in 1918 to 130 as state officials diverted construction to wartime needs. A corresponding drop occurred in the number of apartments, declining from 23,617 in 1915 to 14,241 in 1917 to only 2,706 in 1918. These numbers, if anything, mask the depth of the problem since they do not reflect the corresponding rate of demolition, which was accelerating.[4]

War-induced scarcity quickly caused an unprecedented, city-wide shortage of fuel. Government agencies such as the Federal Fuel Administration and the Federal Food Board established mandates in large urban centers like New York City to ration coal, gas, and other items. In January 1918, Federal Fuel Administrator Harry A. Garfield initiated a series of "Heatless Mondays" to conserve coal and to reduce private freight on the nation's railways.[5] While fuel shortages occurred in many areas, the coal shortage in New York City became especially acute when the region experienced an abnormally cold winter. The County Fuel Administrator noted in early February, 1918, that "the zero weather has . . . frozen the rivers, the kills, and the slips so that it is well neigh impossible to move coal barges." With growing alarm, state administrators noted on February 5, that the city had received only 14,000 tons of coal at a time when hospitals and charity institutions alone required more than 20,000 tons a day.[6] The situation in the Bronx was severe. According to the Deputy Fuel Administrator of the Bronx, the borough had on hand only 1,300 tons when the normal daily consumption was 5,000. Another official described the situation as a "catastrophe," with more than 400 apartments in the Bronx reported to be completely heatless, and with 300 people besieging the fuel administrator's office in the Bronx Board of Trade Building.[7]

In New York's tenement districts, cold tenants looked to their landlords to provide coal for heat. Previously, coal was exceedingly cheap and did not significantly diminish landlords' profits. For middle-class and upper-working-class tenants, building owners customarily provided coal for heat or at least for hot water if the building had the facilities. However, with the fuel shortage, landlords often ran out of coal for their furnaces or, in the face of steadily increasing prices, chose not to burn their precious supply.

The laws made few allowances for the tenants' need for heat. Courts required landlords to provide heat only when they had expressly agreed to do so in the lease agreement. Even those tenants who had agreements often had difficulty getting their landlords to honor them.[8] Many tenants chose to withhold rent to cover the cost of portable heaters or as compensation for the inconvenience and risk to health that they had to endure. In a typical example, in January 1918, the landlord of 83 Northern Avenue informed his tenants that there was no coal in the cellar to heat the tenement, and he advised them to supply themselves with their own sources of heat. One of his tenants purchased an oil stove and deducted the cost from the following month's rent. The landlord in this case, as in most others, demanded full payment and refused any responsibility for the cost of the heater. The courts supported the landlord, holding that the tenant had no right to withhold rent for any reason except if a landlord denied possession.[9]

As the coal shortage grew worse and winter temperatures dropped, the crisis cut across class lines with both working-class and middle-class tenants feeling the effects. In January, cases relating to heat and the withholding of rent overwhelmed the Bronx Seventh District Court. Indeed, the *Bronx Home News* described the situation as "unprecedented inasmuch as a large portion of the West Harlem and [Washington] Heights was without coal during the severe cold, necessitating the apartment dwellers to purchase oil and gas stoves to keep themselves from freezing."[10] Led by working-class and middle-class housewives, rent payers began forming tenant organizations in January 1918, as individual tenants in the Bronx and elsewhere began withholding rent to cover the cost of heat.[11] Middle-class tenants, like their working-class counterparts in 1907–1908, began organizing and attacking their landlords. These early groups of activists benefited from an unusual alliance between poor and more affluent tenants created by the coal shortage. Tenants in the Bronx and in Brownsville began holding "indignation meetings" and retaining legal counsel to explore options to force landlords to provide heat. When 49 tenants on Riverside Drive withheld rent for lack of heat in December 1917, observers were surprised that the strikers lived in a "high class apartment" in a fashionable part of town. In January 1918, when landlords brought dozens of tenants to court for withholding rent, the *Bronx Home News* noted again that the strikers, some driving up in limousines, were "persons of refinement and culture and whose apartments are in some of the most modern apartment dwellings within . . . the five boroughs of the greater city."[12] Legal counsel often accompanied these better off tenants into municipal court to fight eviction proceedings.[13]

The depth of the crisis and the range of tenants affected significantly altered the response of New York's municipal court judges who had to deal with the wave of eviction notices. This change benefited both middle- and working-class tenants. Early in the crisis, the judges began ruling against landlords. In a well-publicized case, Morris Joshnoff, the landlord of 419 W. 129 Street sued his tenant, Austin Wall, for nonpayment of his January rent. Wall contended that, since he had not received any heat, the landlord had, in essence, forced him to purchase a gas heater and that he had withheld part of his rent to cover the expense. Further, Wall argued that the landlord had agreed to supply heat and hot water in his written lease. The courts ruled in Wall's favor, and, in an *ad hoc* manner, Bronx municipal court judges began using various formulas for ascertaining proper deductions. Municipal Court Justice Gengung, for example, allowed one dollar per room per month, while Judge Robitzek and others allowed ten percent of the monthly rent to be deducted.[14] Later, to provide for a more uniform system of reductions, a local assemblyman introduced a bill establishing set rates of reductions.[15]

The Wall case referred strictly to situations where landlords had agreed in writing to provide heat. However, just days later, the state supreme court ruled that, even in cases where leases contained no covenants concerning heat, the landlord had to provide it if the facilities existed in the tenement. In the case, three tenants refused to pay rent even though they had no written agreement with their landlord, the Owners Syndicate Company. Since they still lived in their tenement, they could not claim constructive eviction. The courts ruled that the tenants, even if they remained in possession, could deduct the amount for damages or costs sustained from the lack of heat. As a result of these two court cases and a wave of subsequent rulings, landlords encountered barriers when they tried to evict rent striking tenants.[16] Tenant leaders noted with surprise the favorable treatment that tenants began to receive in the early months of 1918.[17]

Within the context of the heat crisis of early 1918, this shift by the courts assumed larger importance for landlord and tenant organizations. In contrast to the rent strike of 1907–1908, landlords could not evict large numbers of tenants without extreme difficulty. The courts' more pragmatic approach filled this first line of defense with obstacles. Rather than being eradicated in a wave of eviction notices enforced by city marshals, these measures allowed tenant groups slowly to expand their activities to include more direct assaults on the landlords' control over rental rates and their use of eviction proceedings.

As the heat crisis worsened in December 1917 and January 1918, working-class activists moved to the front of the tenant movement. The Bronx Tenants League emerged as a central organizing body for striking tenant activists across the city. With the support of New York's Socialist Party, the Tenants League effectively used the crisis to strengthen the contacts between disparate tenant groups across the Bronx and to sponsor more broad-based activism on issues besides the provision of heat. For example, under the leadership of a Socialist Alderman, a group of eighty Bronx tenants staged a rent strike due to the lack of heat at 1172–1174 Washington Avenue. The landlord had dispossess notices served. The justices ruled in the tenants' favor and allowed them to deduct ten percent from their rent. Following this success, the tenants agreed to join the Bronx Tenants League.[18] At the same time, Socialist Assemblyman and tenant activist Samuel Orr, introduced a bill that required landlords to keep their tenements at 68 degrees from October to April. According

98

to the bill, landlords who failed to do so would be denied the benefits of the summary proceedings law.[19] With this unprecedented level of activity, numerous other local groups began joining the Tenants' League.[20]

New tenant groups began to emerge, many with a broader agenda than simply the provision of heat. In early February, tenant activists formed the Washington Heights League. The organizers stated that their first goal was to "see that landlords furnish coal and heat as per the leases and contracts which they made with tenants, or suffer the consequences that courts impose." They also advocated a standardized lease for all apartment dwellers and charging landlords with a misdemeanor if they failed to provide heat. However, the Heights League leaders also began to articulate a larger agenda, stating that they had formed their organization for the purpose of "fighting owners and lessees of property who have no regard for the rights of the tenants of their buildings."[21] In late February, they moved beyond the issue of heat to broader issues relating to eviction proceedings and rental agreements. William Henry, the League's chairman, proposed a state amendment increasing the notice for removal from three days to ten days.[22]

These tenant organizations began to consolidate, and a clear leadership structure started to emerge. A group of experienced lawyers and activists, mostly from the Socialist Party, began to give the organization more coherence and direction. For example, from 1918 to 1922, Samuel Orr spearheaded the league's legislative agenda, organizing other Socialist legislators and presenting numerous bills in Albany. Attorney Morris Gisnet organized the league's growing staff of attorneys in defense of rent strikers around the city while Mary Mardfin, a gifted local activist, served as liaison and grass-roots organizer.[23]

While none of the proposals for legal reform immediately became law, the tenant groups of 1918–1920 (unlike their counterparts in 1907–1908) received far more favorable press coverage and obtained access to numerous city and state officials. In late January, Mayor John Hylan and many state legislators began making tours of the Bronx and attending public meetings with groups of tenants.[24] In February, a delegation of activists claiming to represent more than 10,000 tenants met with Mayor Hylan and the Board of Health to complain about unheated homes, frozen gas pipes, and a lack of hot water and to add to pressure for official action. They asked Hylan to support a proposal requiring landlords, lessees, or agents to list on monthly receipts the amounts spent on hot water and steam heat. They also wanted Hylan to endorse the establishment of "municipal steam heating plants" so that tenants would not have to rely upon the discretion of the landlord.[25] The mayor did not endorse any of these measures, and, in general, city and state officials monitored the situation but did little to alleviate the crisis.

Caught off guard by the court's favorable rulings for tenants, tenement landlords and landlord activists reacted defensively to the flurry of anti-landlord bills and the daily landlord-tenant confrontations. Initially, many landlord representatives argued that tenement owners suffered as much as tenants. GNYTA's Harold Phillips stated that most landlords were unable to purchase coal at any price, and that "in the vast majority of cases, the failure to provide heat and hot water was due to circumstances beyond the control of the landlords who had nothing to do with the condition of the weather or the various developments that combined to create a fuel shortage." Even those landlords who had coal on hand, according to one landlord representative, often had to cope with freezing pipes and other problems caused by the weather.[26] Phillips even advocated an educational campaign directed at tenants and designed to explain the coal shortage's impact on the landlord's ability to provide heat. Phillips noted that landlords should "be kind but firm" and that "the tenants would be able to see the 'great light' without unkind measures having to be resorted to."[27]

Beneath this paternalistic facade, however, landlord leaders such as Harold Phillips moved to reduce the influence of tenant organizers. He attacked the Socialists' legal counsel and other "lawyers in the Bronx" who "exploited the uneducated tenants."[28] A master at creating landlord organizations, Phillips began sponsoring locally based spinoff groups in the Bronx and elsewhere to take on the tenant groups. For example, with Morris Morgenstern, he helped organize the Federation of Bronx Property Owners, a group of more than 4,000 Bronx tenement owners. Organizers stated that "We expect to be able to supply heat, but we assume no obligation to do so."[29] In his efforts to rally landlords, Phillips stated contentiously that "We will make tenants pay up. . . . If they refuse, the owners will combine and refuse to let them stay." He stated flatly that "If 500 owners start dispossess proceedings together, it will be hard for the tenants to stay or for the courts to rule that they can stay."[30] In their frustration and unaware of the impact of tenant organization's new middle-class constituents, Phillips and many other landlord leaders completely misread the mood of the courts and of the public at large.

Denied satisfaction in the municipal courts, Phillips and others tried a different approach. Since written leases, in part, held landlords responsible for heat and hot water, they tried to simply rewrite the leases and (backed by threats) absolve themselves of any responsibility. They advised member landlords simply to adjust their leases to deny explicitly tenants' rights to heat and hot water. They brusquely issued an ultimatum to tenants stating that "Your rent pays for the rooms you occupy. Not for steam heat or hot water. Agree to this or vacate." To simplify the process, Phillips and Morgenstern attached notices to vacate with instructions to disregard the notice if the tenant chose to stay under the new conditions. Federation member Jacob Leitner, an owner of 75 apartment houses throughout the Bronx, stated that "By notifying [the tenant] to quit [the premises] . . . we believe . . . that all previous understandings will be canceled. If they stay without heat they will have no remedy in the courts, we think." Morgenstern felt that this measure would make the landlord's business safe from the ravages of an "autocratic, unreasoning tenantry."[31] The courts, however, took no notice of this legal maneuver and continued to side with tenants.

Despite many favorable rulings for tenants, in general the courts proved a poor vehicle for real reform in landlord-tenant law. The courts suffered from two limitations. First, the justices themselves differed over exactly which tenants would get reductions, thus leading to the common perception that certain justices such as Robitzek and Gengung of the Bronx favored tenants while, in seemingly similar cases, other judges did not. Without legal clarification from City Hall or Albany, judges made decisions on an *ad hoc* basis guided largely by their own disposition. Second, while landlords had difficulty evicting tenants on the issue of heat and rent withholding, this obstacle hardly exhausted the landlord's arsenal of legal options to use against tenants. For example, eight families at 1345 Washington Avenue in the Bronx complained to their landlord that they received no heat. When the landlord refused to provide it the tenants began forming an organization to protest. They did not advocate rent strikes, and all the families continued to pay rent. The landlord, however, immediately had eviction notices served to all of them on the grounds that they were "undesirable." When the tenants tried to pay the next month's rent, the landlord refused, stating that he "would not take a $1,000 a month for them." On the basis that they were indeed undesirable tenants, the courts gave the tenants the standard five days to move out after which city marshals placed their furniture out in the street.³² Despite unfavorable court rulings, landlords still retained means to evict tenants.

Between December 1917 and April 1918 the heat crisis dominated the conflict between landlords and tenants. Established local landlord groups had tried to break the rent strikes and other protests using the same strategies that had worked in 1908. They tried to pressure the courts into evicting tenants *en masse* in the hope that the tenant groups would be intimidated into silence. They also tried to marshal public support against the tenants. However, due to the depth of the crisis and its impact upon a broad cross section of New York's population, these efforts failed. As the crisis continued, many landlords resorted to more violent tactics to reassert their old privileges.

II. Stage Two: The Housing Shortage and the Setting of Rents

As warmer weather came, many landlords hoped that the agitation would subside. However, tenant activism actually increased in New York's tenement districts. The major tenant groups, the Bronx Tenants League, the Washington Heights Tenants League, and the Williamsburg Tenants League (which emerged out of the Myrtle Avenue strike—to be discussed below) consolidated into one large organization, the Greater New York Tenants League (referred to hereafter as the Tenants League), and, with the cooperation of more radical tenants groups in Brownsville, they began to broaden their attack to include the rising rents charged by landlords. Like the heat issue, rising rents cut across class lines as middle-class apartments and flats also saw significant increases in rents.

While the coercion and the evictions did not break the tenant movement, postwar housing conditions in New York seriously aggravated landlord-tenant relations. Many tenants felt tremendous pressure to fight the higher rents due to a lack of housing alternatives. The origins of the housing crisis stemmed from the war shortages. Because of the manpower demands for the expeditionary force and for war industries, labor costs in New York City, which had averaged $3.40 a day for common labor in 1913, rose to $7 a day in 1920. Building materials became scarce, and supplies of mortgage money declined.³³ In Manhattan, the number of new-law tenements erected dropped from 154 in 1916 to 5 in 1919, and the number of apartments from 5,021 to 144.³⁴ The vacancy rate dropped from 5.6 percent in 1916 to 2.18 percent in 1919 to .06 percent in 1920.[35] After conducting a survey of vacant housing, Tenement House Commissioner Frank Mann stated that the great majority of remaining vacancies, while legal, were "humanly not fit places to live,"[36] and judges even began postponing evictions because of the housing shortage.[37]

Shaken by the unfavorable court rulings, many local tenement owners began demanding more direct action from landlord associations. Militant landlords began organizing actively to resist tenant groups using whatever means they had available. In Brownsville, for example, a number of local landlords organized into several groups, including the Landlords' Protective Association and the Brownsville Landlords League, to evict Brownsville strike leaders. They also began using the police, city marshals, and hired thugs to break the rent strikes and curtail the growing influence of tenant groups in the city's ethnic neighborhoods. The conscious decision of landlords to escalate the conflict triggered months of violence, a period tenant activists called the landlords' "reign of terror" that extended well into 1919.[38]

This more violent phase of landlord-tenant conflict began in the Brownsville section of Brooklyn. Organized by the Workmen's Consumers' League, 1,000 tenants at 563 Hopkinson Avenue, 545 Stone Avenue, and a whole block at Powell Avenue near New Lots had staged periodic rent strikes between February and April of 1918. Unlike many other strikes that focused on heat, the Brownsville strikers attacked their landlord's policy of multiple rent increases in one year, going from approximately $14 to $23 a month for a four room apartment. Following these demands, the landlord precipitated a crisis by accompanying his lawyers and the police to several of his tenements and ordering the arrest of some of the strike leaders.[39] Facing similar increases, hundreds of Brownsville tenants refused to pay, and landlords were able to obtain eviction notices.

Increasingly, GNYTA representatives began assuming a more prominent role in opposing tenant groups. In late May, according to the *New York Call*, GNYTA organizers hired gangs of men to interfere with picketing women in Brownsville, seriously wounding one in an attempt to provoke a riot. In response to tenant complaints, the courts refused to issue warrants against the landlords, the organization, or the hired men. GNYTA's private detectives often harassed rent strikers, and, on occasion, got in pitched battles with picketers. In one publicized case, a GNYTA executive led a gang of detectives in an eviction that turned to violence.[40] In March 1920, the East Side Tenants League staged a rent strike in a tenement of a GNYTA member. The landlord appeared with a group of thugs and assaulted the tenant organizer and a picketer. In one of New York's Socialist newspapers, officials of the East Side Tenants League leaders claimed that GNYTA officials were "endeavoring to make a test of the strike in the hope that if it is broken the backbone of the tenants' organization on the East Side will be broken."[41]

For a time, GNYTA advertised their "protective" services to desperate landlords. In mid-1919, for example, GNYTA officials began distributing circulars to landlords that read as follows:

> Hundreds of houses
> throughout Manhattan, Bronx, and Brooklyn are on
> RENT STRIKES.
> All windows of such buildings contain signs such as:
> THIS HOUSE IS ON STRIKE.
> Glasses and Doors broken and halls defaced.
> Plumbing and other parts destroyed.
> Hundreds of houses are listed for STRIKES for October, not to pay rent.
> The Greater New York Taxpayers Association has a membership controlling over 5,000 houses, well equipped and in a position to protect you.

Register your houses under our protection against RENT STRIKES. Interested landlords went to GNYTA's headquarters on Second Avenue where the association offered them certain benefits in return for an annual membership fee of six dollars plus ten dollars for each tenement for "protection in event of strike." "Protection" included the provision of private detectives to "prevent mutilations" of houses by striking tenants.[42]

Faced with intense pressure from tenants, many landlords considered making concessions. However, GNYTA representatives began applying pressure to stiffen the resolve of wavering landlords. They threatened to go to mortgagors and pressure them to foreclose on landlords who did not resist the demands of rent strikers.[43]

Landlords still had critical allies in the municipal police. For example, in Brownsville, the police, led by Chief Isaac Frank, openly sided with landlords and began a campaign to undermine the Tenants League.

Working together, landlords and police arrested tenant leaders and tried to curtail the tenants' ability to demonstrate publicly. They arrested strike leaders on trumped up charges and allowed landlords to arrest uncooperative tenants. For example, two landlords ordered their way into an apartment where tenants displayed a strike sign, and dragged a tenant off to the police to be arrested.[44] Chief Frank refused to issue permits to demonstrate, and, increasingly, officers began ordering picketers off the streets, tearing down signs, and ordering women not to wear slogans on their clothes.[45] Through May and June, the police, landlord groups, and individual property owners worked together to suppress tenant activism.[46]

Why did GNYTA officials and others turn to violence and intimidation? In GNYTA's case, their reasons were threefold. First, association organizers had already demonstrated through their aggressive handling of accident claims a propensity for "brass knuckles" intimidation. Moreover, they viewed tenant leaders as dangerous radicals who directly challenged the fundamental interests of tenement landlords. Finally, in light of a series of unfavorable rulings, both GNYTA officials and landlords generally did not trust municipal authorities to safeguard their interests. Motivated by their deep-seeded mistrust of government, landlords and their leaders (both in GNYTA and elsewhere) embraced vigilantism as a last line of defense against what they perceived as an intolerable shift in power toward tenants.

GNYTA was only one of many landlord organizations promoting confrontation—and they certainly were not the worst. More reactionary landlord groups employed detectives and routinely used confrontational tactics and even encouraged landlords to adopt the types of "profiteering" strategies that led to rent strikes. The most notorious group that followed this pattern was the Brownsville Landlords Association (also referred to as the Landlords' League or Landlords' Association), led by a Brownsville tenement owner, A. Ellman.[47] From the beginning of the tenant agitation, the Brownsville section of Brooklyn witnessed the most politically extreme forms of tenant and landlord agitation and violence. Brownsville Tenants League leaders advocated a city-wide general strike and, according to some sources, even proposed the seizure of tenements. In response, the Landlords Association attacked the rent strikes as "a direct result of Bolshevist agitation that was nurtured in a nest of radicals who held their meetings in the Brownsville Lyceum."[48] They demanded that Brownsville landlords not "give an inch" to strikers, and they hired gangs of thugs to disrupt tenant meetings, assault picketers, and, with the assistance of the obliging Police Chief Frank, arrest tenant leaders.[49] The Landlords' Association pressed local landlords to allow it to arbitrate landlord-tenant disputes on their behalf and even punished landlords who gave in to strikers.[50] In arbitration meetings, Ellman and other Association negotiators tried to stall and equivocate, at times claiming a willingness to negotiate and then backtracking.[51] Socialists and some city officials even accused the Association of encouraging landlords to exploit the housing shortage by establishing a "Brownsville Stock Exchange" where, at the height of the housing shortage, property owners could buy and sell tenements quickly and use the turnover strategy to raise rents.[52]

To make matters worse, many landlord organizers in the Bronx and Brownsville tried to actively pressure local property owners to raise rents and to stop landlords and lessees from negotiating with tenant leaders. One investigating commission, for example, found a Bronx property owners' association that was "using every possible means to bring pressure to bear upon those landlords who have thus far refused to raise rents above the fair profit mark."[53] According to one observer, when the tenants at 1756 Park Place in Brownsville went on strike they "spoke to the landlord and tried to settle and to avoid indecency. We had nearly come to an agreement when the Landlord's Association intervened. . . . [As a result,] things are now run by the Landlord's Association."[54]

In some ways, the summer of 1919 was also the tenant's "reign of terror" on a small number of landlords. Unlike 1908, wholesale evictions only seemed to strengthen the tenant groups as tenant organizers devised new tactics to pressure landlords. Large groups of activists picketed the tenements of uncooperative landlords, and neighboring tenants staged sympathy strikes against their own landlords. The Brownsville courts ordered between thirteen and fifteen evictions a day. Frequently, as movers took furniture from one apartment to the street, strikers moved the tenant's belongings into another apartment of someone willing to take them in.[55] Tenant groups mobilized in some communities to the extent that landlords also had difficulty getting new tenants. For example, rent strikers at 928 and 934 Myrtle Avenue in Brooklyn assaulted a tenant who tried to move into the building following an eviction. The landlord, unable to attract new tenants or evict the rent strikers without difficulty, came to terms with tenant organizations.[56] Despite support from the police and some municipal court judges, landlords could not contain the agitation. One observer described the scene in Brownsville just days into the strike.

Entire blocks are being organized. On almost every block there is a procession of women wheeling baby carriages back and forth in front of a "struck" house or a row of them. Groups of women congregate on the corners "to talk it over." The court houses are filled with women with dispossess notices in their hands. Many times the number inside remain outside the court room to greet their women folk and encourage them as they come out.[57]

As tensions increased in Brownsville and in the Bronx through the summer of 1918, tenant activists became more involved in violent confrontations with individual landlords. In May, police arrested a group of Brownsville strikers who had threatened to destroy their landlord's building while in July, Harlem rent strikers severely beat their landlord, threatened his life, and made him afraid to return to his property. Tenant leaders felt that landlords deserved the hatred of their tenants but expressed concern about their own powers for "controlling the popular fury that is growing against them."[58]

Despite their tremendous growth across the city, tenant groups began experiencing setbacks. In the municipal courts, justices issued more dispossess notices. In one day in August, judges ordered more than 300 striking tenants in the Bronx to move, and in one day in September, the Bronx Municipal Court issued over 500 dispossess notices.[59] At the same time, landlord groups had appealed the Wall and Joshnoff cases concerning the provision of heat, and the Appellate Court rolled back some of the tenants' earlier gains, ruling that tenants could deduct only the cost of purchased heaters, not the fuel used in them in the months following the purchase.[60] In a related case, the Appellate Court reasserted that the landlord's only obligation was to leave tenants in peaceful possession. According to a newspaper account, "after acknowledging that a contract between a tenant and landlord implies that the tenant must be assured 'quiet enjoyment' of the premises, the court holds that the contract is broken only by eviction.... In order to have a breach of this contract, there must be an eviction."[61] Landlords were jubilant about these successes, and many felt, in light of the new decisions, that tenants would "pay their month's rent without a murmur."[62] Even tenant leaders began to waver. According to organizers, they "had been fighting a losing battle against the greed of New York landlords"[63] "The intimidation," the *New York Call* reported, "by the combination of judges, landlords, policemen, and detectives . . . broke the spirit of the tenants at the beginning of the summer."[64]

Landlord groups, however, had not defeated the Tenants League. Tenant activists continued to broaden their attack on the discretionary authority of landlords, deepening their assault on the landlords' regulatory powers to determine rents and to choose tenants as well as his remedial rights, specifically the landlords' responsibility to maintain the property. In August, for example, 53 families went on strike at 1708–1710 Webster Avenue. High rents were not the issue; rather they accused their landlord of maintaining conditions "in direct violation of the rules of the health department," and they demanded that he make the needed repairs.[65] Tenant leaders had discovered a new weapon to use against landlords.

Tenant groups also began attacking landlords who refused to lease apartments to families with children. Many New York landlords had long claimed that children caused excessive damage to apartments, driving up costs and making it difficult to retain janitors.[66] When the 1918 housing shortage created favorable market conditions, many landlords became more selective in choosing families with children. In the Bronx, some landlords refused to rent to families with children on any account.[67] One city official noted that if the "profiteering landlord has his way, the presence of children in modern apartments will become a curiosity."[68] Landlords' increasing selectivity only placed greater pressure on the limited housing available.

Even as landlords, tenants, and city marshals engaged in pitched battles across the city, local authorities did nothing. They preferred instead to let the municipal court justices defuse tensions without any legislative guidance. As New York endured its second winter of tenant agitation, city magistrates began rebelling against this neglect and demanding that legislators act against profiteering landlords. One magistrate said in early 1919 that, "when unscrupulous landlords and lessees, who have no ownership interest in the real estate, advance rents from 60 to 130 per cent, the court should have the power to provide for an adjustment of these differences. Unless some such relief is given, the helplessness of tenants and their inability to comprehend present inadequate laws will breed

Bolshevism."[69] Magistrates themselves began challenging the landlords' regulatory right to determine rents, choosing instead to exercise their own discretion on a case-by-case basis. One observer described one magistrate's approach. "In some of the cases heard where he considered that the increase was a reasonable one, he advised the tenant to pay it.... He threw out cases where he considered that landlords were taking advantage of the lack of adequate housing facilities." The magistrate stated frankly that he "was disregarding the statutes for the law of common sense justice."[70] Randolph Bergstrom, in his study of negligence cases in New York City, has argued persuasively that court judges were not simply administrators of the law but active policymakers in their own right. To an extent, the activities of municipal court during the postwar housing crisis reaffirms Bergstrom's view.[71]

Court justices were not the only city officials to stretch their authority to address the needs of tenants. To head off another winter of tenant agitation, Health Commissioner Royal Copeland pressed for an amendment to the city's sanitary code which would force landlords to maintain a temperature of 68 degrees in rented apartments between October and April. Once approved by the Board of Health, the commissioner did not require any legislation from Albany. Health officials not only changed the code but also mobilized their staff of fifty officers to enforce the new provisions.[72] With this action, the heat issue gradually receded and was replaced in 1919. The landlords' right to determine rents then took center stage.

III. Stage Three—Rent Strikes and the City Government

Landlord groups used very coercive measures to bring the Tenants League and other groups to heel, and they succeeded in accelerating the pace of evictions and putting pressure on tenants. In the Bronx in early 1919, justices often issued eviction notices for as many as 85 percent of the dispossess cases they heard. Increasingly, landlords tried to evict recalcitrant tenants and rent to new tenants at higher rates.[73] According to a legislative committee investigating housing conditions, the "attempts of some landlords to obtain more rent by taking tenants to court month after month and the granting of short stays from time to time subject families to great anxiety."[74] At the height of the crisis, according to one source, the Bronx Municipal Court was handling more than 8,000 dispossess cases a month, and some courts handled 300 to 400 cases a day on a regular basis.[75]

As many landlords sought evictions, others pursued strategies that only made the housing crisis worse for tenants. Many landlords tried to exploit the favorable market conditions by raising rents or finding ways to increase the number of renters. Landlords and lessees began converting buildings into boarding houses, or single-family houses into multi-family dwellings, while others tried to auction vacant apartments to the highest bidder.[76]

The year 1919 also saw the return of real estate curb markets. Once more, many tenement owners began quickly buying and selling tenements, some in notorious open-air markets. Tenants began protesting about the return of these so-called "leasters," landlords or lessees who bought tenements, immediately raised rents, and quickly sold the property to another buyer at a higher price based upon the new rates. One observer summed up the causes of the shortage. "There is an absolute shortage of houses which has brought about the rapid increase of rents, in part due also to the increased cost of operation of buildings, in part to the bidding of tenants for accommodations, and in some measure to an attempt of some landlords to take advantage of the necessities of those living in their houses."[77]

The effect on tenants was disastrous as tenements rapidly changed hands, each time leading to new increases.[78] Many tenants, when pressed for higher rents and seeing nowhere to move, turned to the Tenants League and other tenant groups. In a typical case, the landlord of 1394, 1398, and 1402 Clay Avenue in the Bronx notified his tenants in early 1919 that their rents would increase. The landlord agreed not to raise the rates further until October. However, he immediately sold the property in April and, according to the *New York Call*, "the new landlord, upon assuming possession of the houses, concluded to raise the rent." The tenants quickly joined the Tenants League and organized a rent strike.[79] Tenants from across the city told of similar notifications, sometimes five or six times in one year as the property changed owners with increases ranging from between $15 to $50 a month.[80] In a study of one block of tenements, the *Bronx Home News* found a tenant turnover rate of 56 percent in 1919.[81] Tenants and many city officials argued that these and similar actions pushed tenants toward radical solutions. According to state investigators, tenants threatened with higher rents and eviction "have no place to go, lose respect for the laws and the courts, who to them seem unable to protect their rights. They readily fall victim to the agitator."[82]

Public antagonism toward tenement landlords, so-called "leasters" and short-term sellers in particular mounted. Following the heat crisis and the patriotic rhetoric of World War I, journalists often portrayed New York's landlords as parasitic "profiteers" and "un-American" exploiters of people's hardships.[83] Joseph Schwab, President of the Real Estate Owners Association, strongly urged his members to avoid taking undue advantage of the housing shortage and to pay closer attention to public attitudes for fear that the government would act against them and impose "the menace of oppressive legislation."[84] Stewart Browne, President of UREO, sounded a similar cautionary note, stating that, if landlords did not "go easy" on rent increases in 1920, the state legislature would introduce bills "that will cause landlords to regret that they ever raised rents, no matter how little."[85]

Even though public anger was clearly increasing, many landlords remained adamantly opposed to any voluntary decrease in rents. Many property owners viewed the previous decade as one of economic stagnation, with landlords receiving low profits from their holdings. They had little patience for reformers and tenants who wanted them to rent for less than "the market would bear." Douglas Elliman, one of New York's more successful apartment managers, summed up their view.

I have always found the tenant ... asking for free rent or a reduction, without any thought of whether the owner was securing an adequate return for his money or not.... Tenants have had their way so long that perhaps they are a trifle spoiled. They have almost always dictated to the owner in the past, and now that owner, for the first time, is able to dictate to them, they show a very different spirit, than the owner did when the situation was reversed.[86]

Faced with landlord intransigence and the mounting threat of Socialist activism in tenement districts, city officials *finally* began to address the tenant agitation and the increasing rents. Mayor John Hylan organized the Mayor's Committee on Rent Profiteering (MCRP) in April 1919 and appointed Nathan Hirsch as its chairman. Hirsch, the Tax Commissioner, a former realtor, and a member of UREO had just completed recommendations for the Mayor's Committee on Taxation, a board organized to lessen the tax burden on New York's real estate interests. Hylan felt that Hirsch, who had a reputation as a real estate maverick, could speak effectively to both landlords and tenants. Hylan's mandate for the committee was exceedingly vague, "to investigate and take such measures as would be proper and lawful to put an end to a condition which is most deplorable in the eyes of all our cities." Hylan noted that city officials had to act to "prevent the situation from becoming really critical."[87]

These programs were not necessarily designed to address the housing crisis. They had other purposes. Hirsch, Hylan, and other officials on the MCRP clearly viewed the threat of Socialism as the "condition," and they viewed the committee's central role as the defusing of Socialist influence. Hirsch clearly stated his views about the rent crisis and how he hoped to solve it. "The spirit of unrest, by many called "Bolshevism," is gaining very rapidly and will soon, if not checked, be a great and grave source of danger to the republic . . . I have come to the conclusion that "Bolshevism" is the result of a misunderstanding which, by proper education, mediation, publicity, and conciliation, could be overcome."[88]

The policies of the MCRP focused largely on limiting the influence of tenant organizers, not landlords. While Hirsch sincerely hoped to limit the exploitative practices of tenement landlords, his attitude toward tenant radicalism was unequivocal, and he worked deliberately to undermine public support for the Greater New York Tenants League and other tenant groups. The MCRP emerged in response to organized tenant agitation, and its policies emphasized the symbolic use of power and moral suasion to siphon off public support for radical tenant groups such as the Tenants League.[89]

In their policies and programs, officials on the Mayor's Committee adopted a conservative approach that promised no long-term solutions to the rent issue but focused instead on a potpourri of short-term *ad hoc* measures. In large part, the committee became simply a coordinating agency for traditional municipal relief efforts. Hirsch became involved in fundraising, organizing and directing charities, locating and acquiring temporary housing, distributing cash gifts to particularly needy cases, and coordinating with state agencies such as the Joint Legislative Committee in the creation of bills. More importantly, the MCRP began challenging tenant leaders' efforts to arbitrate landlord-tenant disputes by establishing a competing arbitration board organized by Hirsch and staffed by Democratic Party attorneys. The arbitration board became the agency's public centerpiece. The committee took pressure off the municipal courts and created a public forum for tenants to raise concerns, vent their anger, and reduce the influence of the Socialists, the main purpose of the city's efforts.

In order to be taken seriously as an advocate for tenants, Hirsch needed some leverage to use against landlords. From its inception, however, the Mayor's Committee lacked the power to seriously challenge landlords' discretionary control over rents. Instead, Hirsch tried to create "legitimate" arbitration mechanisms to compete with and render harmless already existing Socialist agencies. In April 1919, he established a viable arbitration board to settle landlord-tenant disputes. With the assistance of a small staff of clerks on loan from other departments, four members of the committee began arbitration hearings in New York City's Municipal Building. Desperate tenants immediately overwhelmed the committee's assigned quarters with more than 500 complaints or applications for relief in the board's first two days of existence. Between April and August 1919, the arbitration board received more than 17,000 complaints, and the committee had to expand its offices to accommodate the daily crowds.[90]

Hirsch modeled the arbitration board and its services after similar arbitration committees offered by the tenant groups. Like the Tenants League, Mayor's Committee officials tried to assemble a staff of attorneys to help tenants facing eviction. As an observer from the *Sun* noted cynically, "Tammany Hall saw the possibility of making friends with oppressed rent payers and offered to aid the committee in its work."[91] With the assistance of Justice Robert Luce and the Executive Committee of the Democratic Organization of New York, Committee officials obtained the services of seventy-five lawyers from the organization's Law Department.[92] Hirsch publicly argued that the tenant organizations were "unnecessary" and that the committee could handle all grievances.[93]

With his credentials as unbiased arbitrator established, Hirsch began attacking Socialist tenant groups directly. Hirsch was especially severe with the Brownsville Tenants League. Committeemen refused to recognize the league or any other organization where "Socialist tenants were terrorizing the owners of properties and were refusing to pay any rents whatever."[94] When tenants and Socialist organizers formed the East Side Tenants League in September 1919, Hirsch, Hylan, and others quickly attacked the group's leaders for misuse of dues, conspiracy, and intimidation of nonmember tenants. The Mayor and committee officials initiated highly publicized criminal proceedings against the organizers. The trials became a forum for Hirsch and others to decry the evils of radical tenant groups and to promote the more moderate policies of the MCRP.[95] Police arrested other tenant organizers for similar charges. In November 1919, judges sentenced three members of the Harlem Tenants League to the workhouse for conspiracy. League members charged that they were victims of an "organized attempt to disrupt their efforts to obtain better conditions for tenants."[96]

The committee's arbitration sessions served as grand public theater, as hundreds of disgruntled tenants packed the committee's hearing rooms, jeering, whistling, and pelting landlords and their attorneys with debris and insults. The sessions frequently saw pushing, shoving, and mild scuffles, and on occasion the rowdiness escalated into small riots.[97] For the landlords and tenants who appeared, the committee seems to have had some success in getting landlords and tenants to agree to settlements. It is impossible, however, to determine the precise number of settled disputes. As noted, landlords frequently did not appear, and even when they did, they often did not honor the settlement in practice. According to the *Bronx Home News*, the Mayor's Committee had handled more than 12,000 disputes in the Bronx and reached settlements in 65 percent of the cases.[98]

Rather than focusing on systemic inequalities in landlord-tenant relations, Hirsch used the hearings to showcase and punish "bad" individual landlords. Besides the threat of fines and penalties, Hirsch's most potent weapon was public pressure both from the tenant galleries at the arbitration hearings and from the city's major newspapers. Local papers such as the *Bronx Home News* and the *Daily North Side News* routinely published the names of intransigent landlords along with the sad tales of dispossessed tenants. While the *New York Times*, the *New York Herald*, and *The Sun*, at times, allowed landlords to present their views, Hirsch and Goldsmith dominated published reports. Hirsch treated reporters and editors like insiders, granting frequent interviews and conducting public arbitration hearings in a circus-like atmosphere guaranteed to make good copy.

Hirsch found it difficult to keep the tenants' faith as the board's lack of real authority became apparent. Customarily, tenants brought complaints against their landlords for rent gouging, threatening ejectment, neglecting maintenance, or not providing heat, and board members responded by summoning the landlord to appear before them. From the start, many New York City property owners deeply resented the label of "profiteer" widely used in the press, and they viewed the MCRP as simply an institutionalized arm of "the mob" where they could not get a fair hearing.[99] One member of the Real Estate Board of New York noted that,

> With public officials and the atmosphere about some of the local courts encouraging the rabble to believe that every owner of habitable real estate is a wanton profiteer, it is perhaps small wonder that tenants, even some of naturally decent instincts, are gradually coming to believe that it is a highly moral thing to do to get rid of the necessity of paying rent is to resort to "direct action" and dismiss the landlord out of hand.[100]

Other landlords viewed the board with contempt, arguing that the MCRP had no legal right to ask landlords to reduce rents.[101] Even those landlords who did appear often remained intransigent, refusing to reduce rents or to moderate their demands. In the beginning, almost 40 percent of summoned landlords did not bother to appear, and, throughout the committee's existence, the absence of summoned landlords remained a problem.[102]

As more landlords snubbed the Mayor's Committee, Hirsch desperately sought the resources of a host of scattered city departments to cobble together a more meaningful enforcement mechanism. He looked to commissioners and inspectors of the Health Department, the Buildings Department, the Fire and Tenement House Departments, as well as the Police Department and the Department of Water Supply, Gas and Electricity. When dealing with intransigent landlords, Hirsch threatened to invoke the city's regulatory powers embodied in these various departments to force them to come to terms. For example, the Tax Department's Commissioner of Accounts, David Hirshfield, actively used his authority to assess property taxes on tenements to buttress the authority of the committee. According to newspaper accounts, Hirshfield turned the short-term selling strategies of so-called "leasters" against the landlords by arguing that, when property owners dramatically raised rents, there had to be a corresponding and *de facto* increase in property value, a logical conclusion based on standard selling practices at the time. Hirshfield threatened to reassess the recalcitrant landlord's property taxes based upon the higher rents and any other improvements the landlord might have made. The increased taxes usually outweighed any financial incentive landlords had to raise rents. Threatening the imposition of fines, higher taxes, and other penalties, commissioners and inspectors from other departments helped (for a while) to bolster the committee's authority.[103]

The agency, however, continued to suffer from a number of problems. First, despite the assistance of department heads and their staffs, the committee simply did not have the resources to deal adequately with the overwhelming number of tenant grievances. Only four or five of the committee members ever held hearings at any given time, and they often faced thousands of cases. For example, in September 1919, the committee's chief arbitrator held hearings in the Bronx only twice a week from 8 p.m. to 2 a.m., and he often had to ask tenants to come back another time or conduct time-consuming investigations.[104] Committee arbitrators frequently told tenants they would have to wait a week or more before an official hearing could take place. Tenants, however, often had court cases pending or their landlords had already served them with eviction notices, giving them at most five days before marshals came to remove them.[105]

The MCRP also did little to address tenants' well-grounded fear of landlord retaliation. For many tenants who complained to the agency about a landlord charging excessive rents, the accused landlord often reacted by cutting off heat, harassing the tenant, or looking for an excuse to evict the tenant. According to Hirsch, a significant number of tenants who filed complaints never appeared for their hearings, and he felt that this was often due to landlord intimidation.[106] Traditionally, landlords used intimidation to silence tenants' complaints about bad tenement conditions and, in some cases, to bully tenants into paying higher rents.[107] During the housing crisis, many tenants complained to city departments about health or safety violations. However, Hirsch noted that, "by some subterranean methods, the landlords discovered the name of the offending tenant and at once proceeded to dispossess."[108] While the committee addressed some of the needs of tenants who appeared before them, many tenants chose to stay away rather than risk swift eviction at a time of severe housing shortages.

Furthermore, the Mayor's Committee suffered from its inability to enforce arbitrated decisions. Hirsch could coerce landlords into honoring a committee summons by threatening higher taxes, fines for code violations, and other penalties. In September 1919, the Board of Aldermen even began issuing subpoenas to landlords who did not appear.[109] Hirsch found, however, that landlords often refused to agree to a settlement and frequently ignored the committee's decisions. For example, the tenants of 1165 Longfellow Avenue in the Bronx went to the agency, complaining about excessive increases in rent. The arbitrator from the MCRP, Judge Lewinson, asked the landlord, Michael Somerstein, to give the tenants a one-year written lease guaranteeing no further increases. The landlord refused. The *Bronx Home News* described the landlord's attitude of impunity and his indifference about committee sanctions.

The owner was then informed that while Lewinson did not have judicial power, he did have the authority to request the Health Department and other agencies of the Municipal Government to investigate and see that Somerstein's house complied in every detail with all laws and ordinances.... Somerstein told Lewinson he did not fear the Health Department as he kept the rooms of his apartments as well supplied with heat that the tenants were compelled to keep the windows wide open in zero weather. Then he left the building.[110]

In the first nine months of the agency's existence, landlords and tenants failed to reach a settlement in more than 35 percent of the disputes where arbitration was attempted.[111] Of those cases where settlements were reached, it remains uncertain how many landlords violated their agreements. Many observers noted, however, that landlords often ignored their agreements, knowing that the Mayor's Committee had no legal authority to force compliance. An attorney representing tenants described his experience.

In the beginning we accepted the loudly proclaimed offer of the Mayor's committee to assist the tenants and referred all matters to the Mayor's committee for investigation. I have attended many hearings of the committee, and I must say that Captain Goldsmith and myself have adjusted many disputes. This was, however, only where the landlord was willing to make a concession. In many instances the landlords refused to appear before the Mayor's committee, and when I appeared in court to answer to dispossess proceedings begun by the landlord and requested adjournment of the cases so as to enable the Mayor's committee to investigate, the landlords refused on the ground that the Mayor's committee had no power to do anything. This statement was confirmed by the courts, and the judges invariably held that the adjustments must be made either by the court or by agreement between the landlord and the tenants.[112]

Representatives from the Tenants League and other groups labeled the committee's arbitration hearings a "farce."[113]

Conclusion

At the end of 1919, New York's landlords and tenants remained deadlocked in an economic and political battle over the fundamentals of urban rental housing. Bolstered by a larger renting public sympathetic to their plight, tenant organizers attacked landlords across many fronts. They also overtaxed the city's municipal court system and prompted judges to impose their own reforms on landlord-tenant laws. As a result, they created an array of new precedents and shook the business of tenement management to its core.

The city's landlords opposed tenant activists in many ways. However, the club-wielding tactics of GNYTA and the Landlords League only created fearful public scenes of street violence often directed against women and children. Moreover, the significant involvement of New York's middle-class tenants (as well as simply the huge number of tenants involved) crippled the state's usual methods for dealing with rent strikes, methods that had almost always worked in the landlord's favor. Pilloried in the press as "war profiteers" and exploiters of the poor, landlords desperately sought some way to reinvent themselves in the eyes of the public. In 1919 and 1920, as the Red Scare became a national phenomenon, they found it. However, the fear generated by the Red Scare had unforeseen consequences for the city's tenement owners. This will be the focus of chapter 5.

CHAPTER 5

Shades of Activism During the Red Scare

Landlord advocacy groups emerged in New York City in the first decade of the twentieth century, and by 1920 many landlord leaders were well known in City Hall and in Albany. However, just as tenement management embraced a wide cross section of actors from different social and economic groups, so landlord groups served widely different types of tenement owners. Each organization relied on its own distinct programs and policies reflecting their own ideologies, members, and personnel. While landlords often used the common language of real estate and approached tenement operation from broadly similar philosophical perspectives, more fundamental economic, ethnic, and political differences greatly diminished their political unity and effectiveness.

These differences would become apparent as the Red Scare expanded, and landlords from across the city became intransigent in their opposition to "reds" and Socialist "radicals." Despite their common opposition, many of the major real estate lobbies in the city failed to overcome their deep-seeded mistrust of each other. If anything, they became even more divided. Fractured along the lines of class, ethnicity, and political world view, landlord leaders routinely forged brief alliances with other associations only to see them dissolve in acrimony.

As landlord advocates became mired in internecine discord, tenant organizers continued to build on their successes of 1918 and 1919. However, following the ineffective performance of the MCRP and the so-called "reign of terror" of 1919, tenants faced a more formidable opponent—a new, more activist state government.

I: Tenant Organizers and the Red Scare

The anti-radical policies of Hirsch's Committee echoed broader national trends as fear of immigrants and foreign ideas quickly spread across the country. Between 1918 and 1920, the United States experienced the so-called Red Scare, which strongly influenced public attitudes and the state's response to the tenant agitation in New York. The drive to suppress radicalism and to promote "100% Americanism" grew out of both long-term economic tensions and immediate events linked with the Russian Revolution and the end of World War I. Inflation increased sharply during the 1910s, severely affecting public employees, white-collar workers, laborers, and people on fixed incomes and leading to widespread discontent. By late 1919, the cost of living for an average family was almost double what it had been in 1914.[1] At the same time, many workers had high expectations following a period of modest gains for American unions during the war. For the sake of wartime mobilization, President Wilson had made a number of concessions to organized labor and had helped certain moderate unions, notably Samuel Gompers's American Federation of Labor. As the cost of food, building materials, and other commodities increased, organized workers tried to consolidate the gains they had achieved during the war. Union leaders tried to hold onto these concessions at the same time that corporate leaders wanted to return to "normalcy" and roll back labor-management relations to the practices common a decade or more before.

Economic tensions combined with the recent gains of organized labor capped a period of significant growth in membership of many radical groups in the United States. Just as New York City's tenant groups attracted large followings in 1919, on a national scale the American

Socialist Party's membership expanded from 80,000 in 1917 to 110,000 by 1919.[2] Many of these gains were from recent immigrants, particularly those from Eastern Europe who were influenced by the Bolshevik Revolution. In the Socialist Party of America, for example, members who spoke a foreign language constituted 35 percent of the total membership in 1917. By 1919, this figure had increased to 53 percent.[3] Initially, many Americans viewed the Russian Revolution favorably, often drawing parallels with America's own revolutionary past and hoping for the advent of a more democratic government. Once the Bolsheviks seized power in November 1917, and openly advocated the abolition of religion and the destruction of capitalism, public opinion sharply turned against the revolutionaries.[4] Many American radicals remained fascinated with Lenin's new government, however, and some of the most militant pressed American workers to follow the Russian example. Anticommunism began to increase in early 1919 following bloody battles between the Industrial Workers of the World (IWW) and the American Legion in Centralia, Washington. Public hostility also increased with the bombing of the home of U.S. Attorney General, A. Mitchell Palmer, followed by a series of attempted bombings of homes of other prominent citizens.

As antagonistic fervor increased during the war, state and federal officials began attacking political agitation, and many government agencies broadened their activities. Federal authorities had used the Espionage Act of 1917 and the Sedition Act of 1918 to quell political dissent, leaving the IWW and other targeted groups in disarray. During the war, the U.S. Congress passed the Immigration Act of 1918 that imposed new barriers to European immigration. The Bureau of Immigration supplemented this law with bolder policies on deporting aliens engaged in unpatriotic or radical activities. Various federal and state agencies in league with private groups also assisted the Department of Justice in persecuting political agitators. With the assistance of the American Protective League, the American Defense Society, and other patriotic organizations, Attorney General Palmer and a youthful J. Edgar Hoover staged a series of raids on political organizations and labor groups across the country, leading to more than 6,000 arrests.[5]

With the end of World War I, much of this legislation lost its legal rationale, leaving state officials to find other means of suppressing political agitators. Many states had already passed criminal syndicalism laws, and state and federal authorities began targeting Socialists and unionists of almost any kind. In March 1919, the state legislature formed a Joint Committee to Investigate Seditious Activities and appointed Clayton R. Lusk as chairman. Between June 1919 and February 1920, the committee staged a series of raids in New York City and across the state, arresting thousands of suspected agitators and seizing large quantities of radical literature. New York's Attorney General Charles D. Newton resurrected a "criminal anarchy" statute passed in 1902 following the assassination of President William McKinley. The law defined "criminal anarchy" as the doctrine that the government should be overthrown by "any unlawful means." It prohibited not only actions but also simply the advocacy of such a doctrine. Under this law, a number of anarchists and communists received lengthy prison terms.[6] New York City's District Attorney staged raids against the Tenants League in early 1920, seizing the League's records and temporarily weakening the group's organizing efforts.[7] The legislature also passed laws in 1919 forbidding the waving of red flags from striking buildings, and city ordinances banned the use of foreign languages in street meetings.[8] In New York, the Red Scare reached its crest when the New York State Legislature expelled five Socialist members in January 1920; two of them were Tenants League leaders Samuel Orr and Charles Solomon.[9]

II. Landlord Attacks on Socialism

Landlord leaders had been exploiting anti-radical sentiment from the earliest days of the heat crisis. In February 1918, Morris Morgenstern of the Bronx Federation of Property Owners and Harold Phillips of GNYTA had tried to shift public attention away from landlord activities by blaming the tenant protests on professional agitators, and they pressed legislators to arrest or punish the so-called ringleaders.[10] While such efforts were largely ineffective in early 1918, by October 1919, GNYTA leaders had stepped up their publicity campaign against the Tenants League, at a time when press reports were revealing that tenant leaders were channeling membership dues into the Socialist Party's general fund and that the East Side League and other groups were demanding "security fees" along with dues which members forfeited if tenants did not support rent strikes.[11]

Many landlords used the Red Scare to adopt a patriotic veneer and deflect tenant criticism. One GNYTA executive even turned tenement ownership into a badge of honor, stating that, "it is against the spreading evil of Socialism that the realty owner as the leading exponent of our American form of Government must concert all his efforts. . . . Thus, . . . the real estate owner is the one who is continually fighting for the rights of mankind and our present system of society."[12] Reflecting a common perspective of many landlord leaders, a commentator in the *Real Estate Record and Builders' Guide* lauded the state legislature's efforts to combat Bolshevism, and praised the Federal authorities for their "various plans to hold lawless elements in check."[13]

City officials, in many ways, promoted anti-radical passions and even encouraged landlords to pursue their own initiatives against tenant activists. In April 1919, for example, the Board of Aldermen passed a resolution designed to punish landlords, agents, or owners of buildings in which speakers made "anti-government utterances."[14] While the Aldermen designed the measure to hurt owners of public halls, property owners in general viewed these and other measures as clear inducements to deal with tenant organizers as they saw fit.

Landlords began establishing their own self-help services and arbitration agencies. Berger and Phillips, for example, created special programs for GNYTA's tenement landlord members in addition to their normal array of privileges, including legal aid and arbitration services embodied in a Rent Adjustment Committee chaired by Isidor Berger. Berger clearly wanted this committee to serve as a *landlord's* alternative to court-administered arbitration, the MCRP, and the even more hostile arbitration services offered by tenant groups. Berger argued that, "Reputable business men (not politicians) should be requested to form Conciliatory Boards, in different sections of the City, to settle disputes between tenants and landlords. These men using common sense could more than all the laws combined, appease the warring elements and consequently very few cases would reach the courts."[15] After its inception, a GNYTA executive noted, "Let us hope that in the course of time our offices shall become the universally recognized clearing house and authority on all such matters not only so recognized by the parties immediately affected but by the courts confronted with similar cases."[16] Committee arbitrators demanded that members submit figures of rentals and expenditures, and they calculated what they considered to be a fair rental. As a preventive measure, Berger and other GNYTA executives pleaded with members to bring their books to the association before raising rents or pursuing actions in court.[17] Rent

Adjustment Committee members often went before municipal court judges and the MCRP with the cost estimates to defend member landlords.[18] Berger claimed that the committee successfully arbitrated 75 percent of the landlord-tenant disputes they heard, and GNYTA officials prided themselves that the committee did not always rule in favor of the landlord and that many "received an unfavorable decision."[19] Isidor Berger cultivated a lasting reputation as an arbitrator.[20]

Despite their deep mistrust of municipal authorities, GNYTA leaders began forging closer ties with city agencies and officials. One GNYTA President described the period of the mid-1910s as one of "phlegmatic inactivity" for the organization.[21] The rent strikes and the housing crisis pushed GNYTA leaders toward greater public activism. Berger, Phillips, and other GNYTA representatives appeared regularly at MCRP hearings representing member landlords, and they often helped draw up settlements. Unlike organizers of the Brownsville Landlords' League, Berger and Phillips also began sponsoring research and formulating data to support their proposals at public hearings and in meetings with officials. In mid-1919, for example, GNYTA officials conducted a noted survey of vacancies in the Lower East Side. While the survey's methodology was flawed, Phillips was able to use the data to good effect to attack the whole notion of a "housing shortage" so strongly proclaimed by tenant leaders and reformers.[22]

Even as landlords established their own services, they began to assume a larger role in the administration of the MCRP. Committee leaders increasingly appointed GNYTA attorneys, particularly Isidor Berger, as actual arbitrators. This shift may reflect the more politically conservative views of committee leaders following Arthur Hilly's appointment in January 1920. Hilly moved more forcefully against tenant activists, and Albert Sokolski, a real estate operator affiliated with the Real Estate Board of New York and the United Real Estate Owners Association, and also a member of GNYTA's board of directors, became a member of Hilly's new Mayor's Committee board.[23] Berger became GNYTA's most prominent arbitrator, and his reputation lasted for decades, long after the housing crisis had diminished.[24] Much of this activity dramatized GNYTA's movement toward direct engagement with city officials and agencies, and demonstrated the landlord leaders' growing awareness of their need for greater influence on political processes and policymaking.

In this move toward less political marginality, GNYTA officials even became involved in electoral politics. GNYTA leaders began advising members how to vote and attacking candidates they viewed as most hostile to real estate interests. For example, Harold Phillips, the chairman of GNYTA's election committee, issued a list of "safe" candidates in 1919 and warned members to vote for legislators and judges "not tainted with false doctrines of social and economic regeneration that threaten the very foundation of our civilized life."[25] At one point, the Socialists caught GNYTA executives passing money to a candidate for the state assembly, Louis Zeltner, otherwise known as "Wireless Louie," and critics accused GNYTA and other real estate groups of paying off public officials and channeling money into the coffers of their candidates.[26] A GNYTA executive dismissed these accusations and criticized the "means and methods resorted to by the radicals to blacken our reputation and misrepresent our aims."[27] In many ways, this foray into local politics showcased two competing tensions within the organization, one toward professionalization and political legitimacy, the other toward "hardball" confrontation and heavy-handed or illegal forms of activism.

III: The Tensions of Associational Alliances: GNYTA, UREO, and REBNY

In this effort to elevate GNYTA's political influence, Association leaders began forging ties with other real estate groups, the most prominent being with Stewart Browne's United Real Estate Owners Association (UREO). With its confederated structure, the UREO depended greatly upon local organizations with their diverse memberships and often independent leaders. Like GNYTA, the UREO also catered to the needs of tenement landlords along with a host of other real estate interests. UREO's membership, however, tended to be more prominent and more diverse, containing lenders, builders, brokers, and agents.[28] UREO was led by one of New York's most prominent (and mercurial) real estate lobbyists, Stewart Browne. Born in Argyllshire, Scotland in 1854, Browne moved to Canada when he was 20, and began representing various insurance and banking companies. As representative for these firms, he traveled regularly to Latin America and Europe and eventually established in New York City his own banking and brokerage firm, Stewart Browne and Company. Around 1890, he took an interest in state politics and began appearing before legislative committees both in Albany and in

Washington. He became involved in real estate around 1900, and soon after became the president of the UREO, where he cultivated a highly confrontational style, particularly with New York's mayors, often leading to his ejection from board meetings and public hearings.[29]

Despite his confrontational public persona, Browne frequently equivocated and shifted his public positions on real estate matters, often to the bewilderment of UREO members and other real estate leaders. For example, when New York City's Board of Estimate debated the city's first zoning laws in 1914, Browne and REBNY lobbyists bitterly disagreed as Browne argued that "arbitrary districting" would worsen conditions for New York's speculative real estate firms. In contrast, REBNY representatives favored zoning because it allowed builders greater control over large-scale development. The Board of Estimate passed the zoning proposal, and, despite his earlier vocal opposition, Browne ultimately voted for the measure. In part, as we shall examine, this divergence of opinion between real estate leaders reflected differences between REBNY and UREO memberships. However, it was also very characteristic of Browne. His tendency to take both sides of an issue emerged repeatedly during the housing crisis and in debates over other real estate issues.[30] Browne demonstrated similar behavior in debates over municipal housing in the early 1920s. REBNY lobbyists were openly contemptuous of Browne as he opposed the municipal housing but then stated that he knew of no other solutions to New York's housing troubles.[31]

GNYTA and UREO representatives lobbied together in the early 1910s, and they appear to have shared similar agendas on a range of different issues relating to tenement ownership.[32] By early 1920, the two organizations began appointing each other's members to top executive posts. For example, Harold Phillips became one of UREO's vice presidents in November 1919, while UREO's treasurer also sat on GNYTA's board of directors.[33] Organizers expanded this strategy in 1921, when GNYTA's president appointed delegates to sit on virtually all of UREO's standing committees.[34] In dealing with the housing crisis and potential legislation, the most important UREO committee was the Law, Legislation, and Taxation Committee, which monitored legislative activities in Albany. In 1921, of the fifteen standing members, at least six were GNYTA executives, including Berger, Phillips, and former GNYTA president Elias Diamond. A subcommittee of five members (of which Berger was probably one) monitored events in the legislature on a daily basis. The majority determined whether GNYTA opposed the legislation, and when in doubt, (which seems to have been often), the committee submitted the bill to members with expertise on the subject matter.³⁵

With UREO and GNYTA's alliance, their leaders briefly became central spokesmen for the city's tenement landlords. However, other real estate groups had significantly greater policymaking clout than any landlord association. For lawmakers, the most respectable voice of New York City property was the Real Estate Board of New York (REBNY). Founded by twenty-seven realtors, brokers, and auctioneers as the Real Estate Board of Brokers in 1896 (it was renamed the Real Estate Board of New York in 1913), following the collapse of the New York Real Estate Exchange in 1895, its organizers focused on facilitating the regular and organized selling of real estate in all its forms. Among the earliest members were some of New York's most prominent real estate operators, including J. Clarence Davies, Edward Ashforth, Walter Stabler, and Horace S. Ely. Some of REBNY's programs reflected this concern with selling. One, a system of cooperative buying, allowed sellers to offer property before REBNY members in exclusive weekly meetings, a program that developed into a multiple listing plan by the 1930s. REBNY's first executives stated that "the Board ... furnishes a clearing house for property placed by owners for sale and rent in the hands of members of the Board." REBNY executives also began developing a forum for the buying and selling of real estate mortgages and securities, eventually leading to the formation of the New York Real Estate Securities Exchange in 1929.³⁶

REBNY executives also focused on broader issues relating to professionalization and education. Early REBNY presidents developed a real estate curriculum and a series of lectures in connection with the YMCA and later Columbia University, a program that stressed the fundamentals of buying and selling real estate and securities.³⁷ In 1908, REBNY President Joseph P. Day organized a publicity campaign not only to persuade the public that real estate was a safe investment but also to push the newspapers to give as much coverage as possible to real estate news. In the process, REBNY developed a close association with real estate editors of all the major papers.³⁸ In these activities and elsewhere, REBNY organizers continually emphasized the importance of higher professional standards and ethics for realtors, agents, and brokers, often emphasizing the role of professional building managers.³⁹

Their unequivocal stance on the professionalization of real estate operators often put REBNY at odds with UREO, GNYTA, and other, less influential groups that drew members from heterogeneous groups of nonprofessional property owners, particularly over such proposals as the licensing of tenement lessees and annual fees and permits for tenement owners. The potential for conflict became clear in early 1921 when REBNY's membership voted almost unanimously to support a bill that required the licensing and regulation of real estate brokers and agents to protect the public from fraudulent realty operators. The bill required that realtors maintain a place of business, produce references to prove competency and trustworthiness, and pay licensing fees. Stewart Browne bitterly denounced the bill as an invasion of the personal rights and liberties of property-owners and claimed that it would prevent small-scale owners from hiring anyone to represent them in the sale or lease of their property. With the support of REBNY, the Brooklyn Real Estate Board, and the New York State Association of Real Estate Boards, the legislature passed the bill and Governor Miller signed it into law in April 1921.[40] Similar ideological conflicts between REBNY and GNYTA emerged over the licensing of lessees and tenement owners.[41]

UREO, GNYTA, and REBNY lobbyists often sabotaged each other. During the height of the housing crisis, UREO members began challenging basic association policies and placing significant pressure on the organization's confederated structure. Initially, Stewart Browne led this insurgency. From late 1919 through the mid-1920s, Browne questioned the severity of the housing shortage, at times portraying it as a device manufactured by politicians, a perspective commonly held in landlord circles.[42] Many real estate leaders, including REBNY's Edward Doyle, argued that, since the shortage was perhaps not so severe, the legislature should not act against property owners to limit their profits. Browne, however, felt that New York's landlords had more to fear from the public perception of rent profiteering (real or imagined) and that unless landlords agreed to control their profit levels, the state would intervene in the face of rioting tenants. He made his case most pointedly at a UREO meeting at the Hotel Astor in March 1920, where he stated that,

> unless real estate owners do something that will protect their tenants as well as themselves the legislature will pass bills that will make owners look sick for years to come. . . . Any real estate owner who is not satisfied with 20 per cent net is going to get it in the neck. He will have the courts fixing rentals.[43]

The meeting was a public relations disaster, and when some UREO leaders later spoke at a legislative hearing, they were openly split on how to proceed, and Browne felt compelled to backtrack on his earlier statements.[44] Unable to assert their own political agenda, landlord leaders from UREO, GNYTA, and REBNY, like tenement landlords generally, became intransigent as no end of the crisis appeared in sight.

IV: The Reconstruction Commission and the Lockwood Committee

As various real estate groups clashed over how to deal with the rent crisis and the tenant movement, public pressure continued to mount for a government-sponsored solution. By early 1920, the housing crisis had clearly overwhelmed the MCRP. The huge caseload, combined with a lack of resources and powers of enforcement, seriously impaired the committee's ability to address tenants' grievances. Bureaucratic infighting and Mayor Hylan's inability to guarantee the committee a regular source of revenue exacerbated this situation. The committee's chairman, Arthur Hilly, placed much greater emphasis on undercutting radical tenant groups than lowering rents, promoting construction, or punishing landlords. Tenant activists viewed Hilly with suspicion, and average renters often experienced long delays before being heard. While the Mayor's Committee remained very active, tenants from across New York City (and from other urban areas such as Rochester and Buffalo) began demanding relief from the excessive demands of landlords and the inadequate supply of houses.

As the influence of the MCRP declined, state authorities began to take a more active interest in the housing crisis. Unlike Hirsch and Hylan, with their narrow, short-term vision of *ad hoc* reform, many state officials, informed by Governor Al Smith's broader reform agenda, strongly reflected the Progressives' willingness to advocate more systemic, government-sponsored solutions. Several state agencies had been investigating the housing crisis since early 1919. The Reconstruction Commission, led by progressive lawyer Abram Elkus, and the Joint Legislative Committee on Housing, led by Brooklyn State Senator Charles Lockwood and attorney Samuel Untermeyer, became the central foci of many tenants' hopes for reform. Governor Smith established the Reconstruction Commission in January 1919, to develop plans to meet the state's postwar needs. Specifically, Smith wanted the Elkus Commission to review the war-emergency laws to determine which to keep and which to repeal, as well as the laws pertaining to public health, taxation, labor supply, public works, and housing conditions. Smith appointed Belle Moskowitz and Robert Moses to handle the unwieldy administrative duties. Because of Republican opposition in the State Assembly, the Commission received no funding, and Elkus had to rely solely on private donations. While the New York legislature ignored many of the its proposals, the Commission's findings helped to define Smith's legislative agenda for his years as Governor of New York.[45] Abram Elkus headed the committee assigned to investigate housing conditions, and many of New York's more celebrated, progressive housing analysts and social scientists became members of the committee, including Clarence Stein and Felix Adler.[46]

From its inception, members of the Reconstruction Commission, like their counterparts in the Mayor's Committee, resisted rent regulation or reworking landlord-tenant laws as a solution to the postwar crisis. The committee noted in its final report that, "considerable caution might wisely be displayed in the passage of legislation aimed at the regulation of rents or the disciplining of landlords as such. For, to the extent that such legislation does not prove futile, it is very apt to prove undesirable, and calculated to aggravate the already unhappy state of the average tenant."[47] Instead, Elkus and others emphasized the long-term nature of the crisis, arguing that tenants' problems were different only in degree, not in kind, and that tenants had suffered the same problems for decades. They went on to argue that changing landlord-tenant laws or imposing some form of rent control unduly penalized decent landlords and, at the same time, discouraged the construction of tenements. Instead, commission members proposed greater involvement by the state in encouraging lending for the purpose of building low-income housing. In keeping with their commission's Progressive pedigree, they also advocated the construction of government-owned housing and the formation of local housing boards.[48]

Fearing accusations of "socialism," committee members were slow to push openly for state funding of public housing. Initially, they explored the more traditional route of private philanthropy. Elkus announced in May 1919 the formation of the "Housing Reconstruction Corporation," a semi-philanthropic agency designed to raise funds for constructing low-income housing at moderate interest rates.⁴⁹ Reconstruction Commission members designed other proposals to alleviate the housing shortage. Commission members began to consider tax exemptions on mortgages for new construction in New York City, a proposal strongly favored by REBNY.⁵⁰ State officials felt that these exemptions would make mortgages competitive with securities, spur construction of new, low-income housing, and help garner support from real estate groups for the Commission's larger package of reforms. However, many smaller real estate groups, particularly GNYTA, did not embrace this proposal and, in fact, leaders often spoke against tax exemptions.

With their emphasis on long-held goals of New York's Progressive housing movement, the Reconstruction Commission did little to address legal and economic inequalities in the landlord-tenant relationship, and their proposals offered little immediate help to tenants, leading Nathan Hirsch to dismiss the Commission's limited-dividend corporation as "a drop in the bucket."⁵¹ In his enthusiasm for appointing housing professionals and noted progressives, Smith, unfortunately, had left most of New York's more powerful legislators out of the process. The Governor wanted the legislature to act quickly, but lawmakers let the proposals become bogged down in committee. Eventually, the Commission's proposals laid the groundwork for the creation of the state's Board of Housing in 1926 and its development of public housing in the 1930s.⁵² These actions were far removed from the postwar housing crisis, and the legislature blocked Smith's efforts to provide immediate relief. When Smith called a special session to adopt municipal housing in 1922, the legislature continued to ignore his proposals and instead enacted tax exemptions for builders, a proposal supported by REBNY and other conservative real estate groups that represented New York's more successful builders and developers.⁵³

When New York state legislators created the Joint Legislative Committee on Housing (the Lockwood Committee) in April 1919, they established their own forum for addressing the housing crisis. Individual legislators had been presenting housing and landlord-tenant reform bills since the heat crisis of 1917–1918 but these measures rarely became law. Between April 1919 and March 1920, the Lockwood Committee conducted hearings, interviews, and commissioned lengthy studies into various aspects of the housing crisis. Initially, they were quite optimistic about resolving the housing crisis. Lockwood noted that "it appeared that except in one or two instances local authorities expressed the opinion that they had the housing situation well in hand and desired no new legislation."[54]

By March 1920, tenants and working-class organizations from across the city had become impatient with the MCRP, the Reconstruction Commission, and the Lockwood Committee over the general lack of concrete action. Conditions in the cities had seriously deteriorated. In New York City, officials from the Central Federated Union, representing more than 350,000 members, began meeting with the United Hebrew Trades (with more than 200,000 members), the Brooklyn Central Labor Union (with 100,000 members), and the city's numerous tenant groups, including the radical Brownsville Tenants League. It is unclear which organization first floated the idea of a massive May 1 demonstration, but, by late March, tenant organizers such as Leo Gitlin and Federated Union leader Edward Hannah spoke openly of a general rent strike to force elected officials to alleviate the situation. On March 30, a mass meeting of 648 delegates of tenant groups, unions, and workers' societies formed an organization claiming to represent more than 800,000 members for the purpose of staging a general revolt against high rents.[55] In fear of an "eminent uprising," some landlords began calling for federal troops.[56]

Mayor Hylan tried to defuse the crisis by calling together many realtors, lenders, and civic leaders for a conference on housing to develop proposals to stimulate construction. Hylan had completely lost confidence in the MCRP since Hirsch's resignation, and he hoped to build a coalition around some of the more conservative proposals, such as a cap on labor costs and tax exemptions for builders.[57] Real estate groups and tenant organizers were too polarized for any consensus to be reached. Hylan immediately came under fire from tenant groups for equivocating and a lack of action, and Socialist Alderman Benjamin Vladeck even attacked Hylan as "a tool in the hands of the Realty Board."[58] At the same time, landlord leaders such as GNYTA's Elias Diamond blasted the Mayor for not taking property owners into his confidence.[59] The Mayor vacillated until eventually real estate representatives became convinced that he had no intention of supporting their proposals. Led by REBNY officials, they walked out, and public attention shifted back to the state legislature.[60]

The Lockwood Committee cobbled together a set of initiatives to placate the city's tenants. However, even these measures smacked of stalling and inaction. The committee leaders had devised a two-pronged response to the housing crisis.[61] The agency's legal counsel Samuel Untermeyer staged a lengthy investigation of building costs, construction firm combinations, and corruption that led to a small number of prosecutions against sand and gravel dealers at the end of 1920.[62] However, in spite of ample evidence acquired over three years, the committee, lacking in resources, made few prosecutions. Many of those accused continued to operate. Despite months of interviews, public hearings and twelve volumes of recorded testimony, Untermeyer did nothing to change significantly the dynamics of the housing crisis.[63]

Prompted by Lockwood and Untermeyer, the committee finally developed a set of legal initiatives that really spoke to the central concerns of tenants. From the beginning, Lockwood had focused more on the problems of rent profiteering and landlord-tenant relations. Unlike the Progressives on the Reconstruction Commission, Lockwood was less interested in encouraging construction. While their preliminary report referred to many actions designed to encourage construction, including tax exemptions and federal loans, Lockwood's final report and list of proposed legislation referred almost exclusively to tenants' "suffering and distress," and how profiteering landlords were driving tenants to revolt, stating that "they readily fall victim to the agitator."[64] Committee members looked for ways to punish landlords and limit their ability to exploit tenants, and, in April 1920, their efforts led to the passage of the Emergency Rent Laws.

V: The Rent Laws

Some contemporaries dismissed the Lockwood committee as nothing more than a political showboat. This criticism was, to an extent, justified. Lockwood, Untermeyer, and many other legislators on the committee engaged in public landlord-baiting on numerous occasions. Many of their decisions can be attributed to political expediency and good public relations rather than carefully considered public policy. One REBNY critic noted derisively that "unfortunately, some of the legislators had their heads turned and with their ears to the ground, misinterpreted the noise they heard to mean the approving voice of the voters."[65]

Some scholars have viewed the Lockwood Committee and the emergency laws of April and September 1920 as of little consequence beyond the immediate postwar shortages.⁶⁶ However, these assessments fail to acknowledge the important shift in authority from landlords to the courts brought by these laws, their long-range impact on landlord-tenant relations, as well as broader shifts in public opinion concerning New York's tenant population. For the first time in the city's long history of housing reform, the legislation took aim at dispossess proceedings, landlords' access to city marshals, and the tenant's general vulnerability to landlord harassment and intimidation.

Following weeks of political haggling, public demonstrations in Albany, and intense activism among many of New York's tenant groups, the legislature passed the first series of Emergency Rent Laws in April 1920. Through 1919 and early 1920, city and state officials passed individual ordinances affecting dispossess proceedings and landlords' ability to gain swift evictions of unwanted tenants. The April laws, combined with these individual changes in the law, significantly diminished the discretionary authority of New York landlords and much of this lost authority shifted to the municipal courts. The laws attacked landlords' discretionary authority in three ways. First, they eliminated the worst abuses of oral leases by repealing the Ottinger law. The new law restored the old provisions protecting tenants who made oral leases. However, Lockwood and others stated that these protections were only a stopgap and that *written leases* were the only real protection available to tenants. These measures altered leases by placing unprecedented emphasis on tenants obtaining written leases instead of relying on more traditional oral leases. While some landlords, particularly those who rented high-class apartments, viewed this development as a positive step toward rationalizing the buyer-seller relationship between landlords and tenants, for many tenement landlords this long-term change represented a significant loss of control over their property, particularly in light of the April laws' new limitations on dispossess proceedings.⁶⁷

The laws also strengthened city ordinances that required landlords to provide services that were "necessary to the proper or customary use of a building." If landlords refused to provide these services, city officials could now charge them with a misdemeanor. Committee members explicitly designed this law to put an end to traditional forms of landlord harassment and intimidation that had involved withholding these services to punish recalcitrant tenants or force them to move.⁶⁸ Most importantly, the laws limited landlords' ability to evict tenants. They

134

blocked landlords' easy access to dispossess proceedings and made it easier for tenants to file counterclaims. Traditionally, judges assessed the merits of counterclaims but they had no authority to provide relief for tenants. The emergency laws allowed municipal court judges to assess counterclaims and force landlords to provide relief.[69] The laws also created new standards for determining if a tenant was "objectionable." Previously, the courts considered the landlord to be the sole judge of the tenant's objectionable character. In practical terms, this relationship operated as a conditional limitation on a lease's term. Under the new law, the courts shifted the burden of proof to the landlord, stating that landlord had to prove to the court that tenants were, by some objective standard "objectionable."[70]

Evictions were not only harder to get under the new laws, they also required more time to process. Previously, the courts gave tenants three to five days to move out. The shortness of this time worked great hardship on tenants, and, in practice, made it very difficult for rent payers to challenge landlords in court, especially given the difficulties in filing a counterclaim (as noted above). Tenants often saw their belongings removed by city marshals before they could even get a court hearing, a problem only deepened by the crowded court calendars created by the tenant unrest.[71] The laws also gave judges the power to grant stays of execution of a warrant in summary proceedings for up to thirty days. The purpose of this law was to give justices more authority to arbitrate landlord-tenant disputes and to give tenants more time to file counterclaims.[72]

These, in sum, were the permanent changes determined by the April laws. In many ways, these revisions of landlord-tenant relations were hardly revolutionary. Many commentators dismissed the permanent laws as of "comparatively minor importance,"[73] and noted that they faced few legal challenges. Taken individually, there was perhaps some validity to this assessment. Taken together, however, and especially when combined with municipal laws passed around the same time and with the emergency laws that came later in September 1920, the impact of legislative revision should not be underrated. The new laws initiated a slow, permanent erosion of landlord authority; they introduced the state as a far more significant player than had been the case; and they stemmed largely from a profound shift in perspective by New York's cross-class tenant population, one that viewed nineteenth-century styles of landlord abuse as a threat to all renters, not just the working class.

The Emergency Rent Laws also contained numerous temporary provisions which, to the city's landlords, were even more menacing: they attacked not only the landlords' access to legal machinery to discipline and evict tenants, but also their power to determine rent. While the permanent laws attacked landlords' traditional possessory rights, the temporary measures weakened their regulatory rights, specifically as they related to the setting of rents. Under the new laws, in cases where landlords wanted to recover rent, the tenant could claim that the landlord's monthly rates were "unjust, unreasonable, or oppressive." Lawmakers argued that the housing crisis had created a situation where normal laws of supply and demand could not function and thus "the freedom of contract had been impaired."[74] In defining contractual terms, the legislation assumed that increases of 25 percent or more were "unjust," and it required that landlords justify these increases. As in cases of tenant "undesirability," the laws shifted the burden of proof to the landlord to demonstrate that large increases in rent were indeed reasonable.[75] When judges decided that rents were "unjust," the laws further mandated that the courts determine "a fair return." In cases involving less than 25 percent increases, the burden of proof shifted back to the tenant to show that the increases were unjust.[76]

The temporary laws also imposed new limitations on landlords' access to evictions. To ameliorate the housing crisis and the congestion in New York's courts, the law permitted the courts, at the judges' discretion, to stay the execution of eviction warrants for up to one year. For these stays to be granted, tenants had only to demonstrate that they could not find suitable housing at the same rent. To a large extent, these measures robbed the landlord of his most powerful weapon against tenants: swift, court-ordered eviction.[77]

Due to intense lobbying by New York's real estate groups, the temporary provisions embodied in the first series of Emergency Rent Laws contained many limitations. The laws only applied for a set time period (initially until November 1922), and only in a select group of cities. They regulated only two forms of summary proceeding, and covered only certain types of multifamily dwellings. Nevertheless, real estate groups blasted the temporary measures, and the legislation became the center of a lobbying firestorm for the next nine years.

Most landlord leaders expressed outrage at the punitive nature of the laws and at the loss of discretionary authority. Stewart Browne, expressing a belief widely held by landlords, noted how he felt the new legislation would shift landlord-tenant obligations.

> The tenant has the right of remaining as long as he pleases and can vacate when he pleases without notice, and, when in possession, his apartment is his castle to fill it and do with it as he pleases and he has the right to pay rent in amount and when he pleases, and he hasn't a single obligation in the world, except the contingency to pay rent in amount as and when he pleases.[78]

Many New Yorkers both in and outside the real estate community began attacking the legislation on the grounds that it actually discouraged builders from investing in tenements. Progressive housing luminaries such as Lawrence Veiller and Clarence Stein expressed serious doubts about the impact of the new laws and pushed anew for the proposals embodied in the Reconstruction Commission's report, such as the construction of municipal housing and the creation of a state housing board.[79] Officials from the Advisory Council of Real Estate Interests and from REBNY stated that the new laws would simply prolong the housing crisis.[80] REBNY lobbyist Edward P. Doyle claimed that tenement owners felt the laws' negative impact almost immediately, as purchasers backed out of negotiations because they did not think, under the laws' new provisions, they could take possession.[81] REBNY officials also blasted the legislation because it failed to distinguish between honest landlords and so-called "profiteers."[82] Berger derisively stated, "the exaggerated methods employed in this emergency are identical to and as productive as curing a case of hic-coughs by beheading the patient."[83]

The effect of the April laws on New York's tenants was threefold. First, city, state, and federal authorities stepped up their campaign against radical tenant groups, especially as the Brownsville Tenants League and others prepared for a general strike on May 1, the traditional Socialist Labor Day, and one of the busiest moving days for tenants. Second, tenants from across the city began testing what the new laws meant for them in their struggles with landlords, a process that lasted through the summer of 1920. Finally, in August, tenant groups stepped up their activism, as weaknesses in the laws became apparent.

As the postwar red scare reached its height in mid-1920, city officials and many average New Yorkers directed their fear of radicalism against all tenant groups. In 1919, even though he tried to pull support away from tenant leaders, Nathan Hirsch had emphasized the importance of conciliation and mediation in arbitrating landlord-tenant disputes. By early 1920, however, the Chairman of the MCRP, Arthur Hilly, began emphasizing a much harder line toward tenant organizers. A series of disputes ensued between Hilly and the Central Federated Union led by newly appointed Mayor's Committee member Edward Hannah. Hilly argued that the Lockwood legislation would alleviate the crisis while Union officials and other tenant leaders felt that they would provide no relief.[84] The Central Federated Union continued to advise tenants to withhold rent while Hilly and other city officials discouraged rent strikes.[85] When the Tenants Defense Union began calling for a massive rent strike in May, Hilly referring to the strike as a "planned display of red-flagged disorder," claimed that "any attempt to organize resistance to the landlords would defeat the very purpose of the legislation and of orderly government."[86]

As the strike dates drew closer, officials from the MCRP, in essence, declared war on the rent strikers. Committee attorneys urged the courts to promptly issue eviction warrants against any tenants who joined the strike.[87] City officials contributed to growing public hysteria as Commissioner of Accounts Hirshfield warned of vandalism against landlords, and Hilly warned of a "Red revolution," claiming that he had reliable evidence that tenants were planning to seize houses in Brownsville and elsewhere.[88] Hilly and other city officials began pressing for greater police presence in Brownsville, the Bronx, and other areas most threatened by the general strike. The municipal police began mobilizing in force in late April, and federal agents under the direction of U.S. Attorney General A. Mitchell Palmer began to appear in larger numbers. All along, Justice Department officials had been active in suppressing the tenant groups most associated with the Socialist Party. Police had arrested many tenant leaders, and they kept tenant leaders under heavy surveillance. Agents from New York City's District Attorney had seized the Tenants League's records earlier in the year, seriously weakening efforts to mobilize tenants.[89] At the same time, landlords had many tenant picketers arrested.[90] Socialist leaders claimed that they were victims of an "inquisition."[91] In justifying the level of federal involvement in the crisis, U.S. Attorney General Palmer concluded that "the tiniest little 'revolution' that might be started in this city, long the center of Soviet activities, should be crushed with such telling decisiveness that not even momentary success would be allowed to give a false picture of American sentiment."[92]

These pressures precipitated a minor crisis within the ranks of tenant groups, as the leadership split over whether to proceed with the general strike or to cancel it. Widespread strike activity appears to have decreased following the passage of the April laws, and observers claimed that many tenants were forsaking tenant groups in favor of taking their chances in court.[93] To demonstrate their continued strength, union and tenant leaders still spoke of mobilizing for a general strike. Leo Gitlin of the Brownsville Tenants League, in particular, remained adamant in pushing for a general strike up to the May 1 deadline. As the deadline approached, however, more moderate leaders, such as Hannah, began distancing themselves from a general strike, especially after Hilly announced plans to suppress any strikes, demonstrations, or vandalism.[94] Tenant and union organizers, such as Morris Feinstone of the United Tenants' League of Greater New York, even began arguing that the threatened strike was, in reality, a Hilly creation designed to whip up public fear and to undermine support for tenant groups.[95]

There may have been some foundation to this charge. With the aid of a youthful J. Edgar Hoover, Attorney General Palmer used local authorities from around the country to incite public fears of a May Day uprising.[96] New York's district attorney convened a grand jury investigation into who initiated rumors of a rent revolt, and Arthur Hilly was subpoenaed.[97] The grand jury found no evidence that a rent revolt was imminent and, when May 1 came, none occurred, further suggesting that the general strike hysteria was a product of New York red-baiters and a handful of vocal tenant leaders.[98]

For landlords and tenants alike, problems with the April laws quickly emerged. From the perspective of tenement owners and builders, the laws did nothing to encourage construction. Aaron Robinson, President of the City and Suburban Homes Company, and a number of other moderate reformers and city officials, argued that the April laws could only provide temporary relief and that the legislature had to do more to encourage tenement building.[99] Correspondingly, tenants confronted landlords who viewed the new laws as an invitation to institute 25 percent increases in rent across the board for all tenancies. Municipal court justices seem to have encouraged this strategy by generally ruling in the landlords' favor where increases of 25 percent or less were involved. At the expiration of leases, landlords began instituting holdover proceedings without offering to renew leases. Facing increases of less than 25 percent and an uncertain fate in municipal court, many tenants found no relief in the April laws. Also, even though justices could grant stays of up to one year, they had to give landlords eviction notices for that future date at once. Many tenement owners held these notices over the heads of tenants, knowing that, once these stays expired, they could evict the tenants almost immediately.[100] In these and similar cases, the laws actually provided landlords with new tools with which to intimidate tenants.[101] City officials began to fear another "moving day" on October 1, 1920 that would include thousands of evictions, crowded courts, and the potential for violence.[102] By late August, Hilly and others pressed the legislature to abolish holdover proceedings, to bar evictions, and to fix values and rents.[103]

The legislature permanently altered dispossess proceedings in the following ways. First, the appeals process became even more favorable for tenants. The laws made it possible for courts to grant stays in dispossess proceedings to holdover tenants who retained possession after the expiration of their lease. The laws also lengthened the time tenants could respond to dispossess proceedings from five to ten days. Finally, the laws granted municipal court judges the power to vacate dispossess warrants to allow tenants time to appeal. Previously, the only way of preventing the execution of dispossess warrants was through an application for an injunction from the State Supreme Court.[104] The September measures also changed certain aspects of the temporary April laws which, as a result, abolished most holdover proceedings and barred evictions.[105]

Conclusion

With the passage of the rent laws, nineteenth-century styles of tenement management were dead. The laws not only severely curtailed landlords' access to dispossess proceedings, but also significantly limited their freedom to raise rents. Moreover, for the next nine years, they established new operating rules and procedures, and, for a time, they became embedded in the renting process. As a result of the rent laws, tenants no longer viewed dispossess proceedings as immutable. In fact, all of the procedures and standards governing landlords and tenants now stood exposed and open to revision—perhaps not in 1920 or even any time soon—but eventually.

Landlord leaders were far from finished, however. Between 1920 and 1929, the Emergency Rent Laws became the focal point for prolonged, bitter political battles that lasted most of the 1920s. GNYTA, REBNY, UREO and other groups attacked the legislation and began to devise strategies for landlords trying to cope with the new realities of tenement ownership. Initially, these landlord groups challenged the constitutionality of the laws, even as they advised landlord members of loopholes. However, between 1921 and 1925, lawmakers spent each legislative session blocking these loopholes, leading New York's tenement owners to search for more permanent ways to nullify the laws. GNYTA, UREO, and REBNY were most eager to help the landlords find them. These efforts will be the focus of chapter 6.

CHAPTER 6

Landlords in the Tenants' Court

By mid-April 1920, municipal court judges from across the city were dismissing eviction proceedings by the thousands. Judges found that the landlords' legal papers were not in order, that tenants could not find new accommodations, or that the tenement owners were demanding more than 25 percent increases in rent. In turn, they granted stays of eviction of between four to six months, even up to a year in some cases, and cut landlords' rentals. In the second district court, where many cases from the East Side were pending, one justice disposed of more than 300 cases without once ruling in the landlord's favor.[1] Certain judges routinely granted year-long stays of eviction, the maximum allowed by the law. Others, such as Justice William E. Morris, often appeared at large gatherings of tenant organizations.[2]

As Hilly, Hirsch, and other officials had hoped, with the passage of the emergency rent laws, individual tenants began turning away from organized tenant groups such as the Greater New York Tenants League. Instead, they began acting in their own interest. Renters began asserting an unprecedented degree of independence in bargaining for lower rents, demanding repairs and heat, and wringing other concessions from irate landlords. The rent laws provided the necessary cover for them to exercise this assertiveness. Tenants increasingly found ways to counter eviction proceedings and often chose to take their cases to trial. Between 1919 and 1921, the number of summary proceedings going to trial jumped by 94,443, a 400 percent increase.[3] The landlords shouldered the costs of the litigation, as well as the time and humiliation. Following the passage of the rent laws (and subsequent amendments each legislative session), many observers noted that landlords greatly diminished their demands, choosing to settle out of court rather than institute dispossess proceedings they would probably lose.[4]

Even aside from the rent cases, small-scale tenement investors were buffeted by other larger changes in the tenement operating business. New sources of investment capital were gradually supplanting the unlicensed lenders of the nineteenth century. Insurance and title companies began investing heavily in the tenement property while state regulators began clamping down on immigrant banks and other, more indigenous sources of credit.

I: Landlord Groups Challenge the Rent Laws

The municipal courts were not the only forum where landlords were losing their influence. They also saw their autonomy diminish in the offices of city agencies as well as in civil courts. New city ordinances cut landlords off from their traditional means of physically evicting tenants, the city marshals. Before the rent laws, Mayor's Committee chairman Hilly began meeting with the city marshals and pressing city and state law makers to limit landlords' access and control over them. Before the housing crisis, city marshals were basically the hirelings of landlords. Marshals assisted landlords in drawing up eviction papers, and they often represented landlords in court. If the tenant still remained after the waiting period, courts authorized the landlord and the marshal to physically remove the tenant. The landlord paid the marshal a set fee for each eviction. Under this system, by any measure, the marshals worked for the landlord, not the city.

Moreover, the widespread tenant unrest created a financial bonanza for city marshals who often found themselves evicting dozens, at times hundreds, of tenants a day. Brooke Avenue, where the Bronx municipal court was located and where many marshals had their offices, was referred to as "Marshal Row."[5] Judges began seeing self-proclaimed "marshals," who were not even members of the city's regular complement of 67, requesting and processing evictions. At the height of the crisis, according to the *New York Times*, some of these illegal marshals were making as much as $2,000 a month. Even some official marshals, the *Times* reported, maintained three or four offices and avoided legal requirements that threatened to limit their incomes.[6]

Many city officials, even Hilly, saw this relationship not only as inappropriate and an inducement to corruption, but also as specifically prohibited by the Greater New York Charter. Quietly, municipal authorities began inserting themselves back into the process. Through intimidation and cajolery, Hilly persuaded the city marshals not to process any eviction notices that did not have written approval from The MCRP.[7] Many marshals resented this interference, and Committee officials had to threaten them with the loss of their licenses to assure greater compliance. In this fashion, the agency became part of the eviction process, at least for a while, and Hilly made obtaining an eviction more problematic. In addition, critics began pressuring the courts to bar marshals from appearing on behalf of landlords in dispossess cases.[8] The courts also began increasing costs for processing legal actions. In early 1921, some landlords complained about 100 to 200 percent increases in the costs of dispossessing a tenant.[9]

Despite widespread fears of tenant activism, many landlord leaders and individual tenement owners had not forsaken the goal of outmaneuvering the rent laws' restrictions. The period from 1920 to 1922 saw numerous efforts to circumvent the laws, sometimes by measures ingenious but often silly. Landlords often used various forms of fraud or legal chicanery to circumvent the laws. For example, the Mayor's Committee reported cases of landlords trying to classify their tenements as "offices" or "hotels" to avoid the laws' provisions. Landlords also tried to falsify tenant receipts and to pressure or mislead tenants into signing receipts with inflated rental values. Landlords would then use these documents in court to mask the true level of increase that landlords were demanding.[10] One of the more persistent methods of circumvention involved landlords falsifying their list of expenses so as to strengthen their requests for greatly increased rents.[11] Landlords also tried to stretch the laws' provisions regarding "objectionable" tenants, as well as provisions that allowed landlords to take possession of tenements for their own use. Landlords tried to have tenants classified as "objectionable" for everything from slamming or leaving doors open, to blocking stairwells or stoops, to putting garbage in the hallways, to using the premises for illegal activities (ranging from running a speakeasy to operating an ice cream saloon).[12]

Local landlord leaders often tried to exploit the frustration of tenement owners by claiming that they knew ways around the rent laws and that they could somehow reassert landlords' traditional proprietary rights. REBNY officials, for example, began counseling New York landlords to pressure tenants into becoming month-to-month tenants and to press renters to sign documents that, in essence, would waive the tenants' rights under the new rent laws. Other landlord leaders told members to mark the October 1920 moving day with a wave of eviction notices, particularly aimed at month-to-month tenants who were more vulnerable to such pressures. Such tactics, however, usually prompted quick legal action from municipal court judges and legislators.[13]

Various landlord leaders tried to coordinate these and other activities to create mass demonstrations in support of the city's landlords. Bernard Deutsch of the Bronx Federation of Property Owners tried to create just such a city-wide movement in early 1921. Such initiatives, however, usually failed to lead anywhere due to the widespread mistrust of outsiders, including members of similar associations, that was characteristic of many landlord groups. Finally, becoming aware of the need to avoid adverse publicity, leaders of the Bronx Federation were very concerned about letting outsiders hear their deliberations.[14] Such fears were not without foundation, as one landlord group discovered in mid-1920 when its leaders advocated that tenants and the courts be inundated with a wave of eviction notices on the October 1 moving day. They tried to marshal the city's other landlord leaders to their cause including UREO's Stewart Browne. The mercurial Browne, however, viewed the scheme as counterproductive and promptly exposed it in the press and in public hearings.[15]

Most of the testing, probing and circumvention strategies developed by landlord leaders and individual tenement owners did little to improve the situation for the city's landlords. Within tenant communities, judges, legislators, city officials and tenant leaders moved quickly to block such strategies. The press also publicized landlord-initiated incidents surrounding these maneuvers so that the credibility of landlords suffered. During the 1920s, the city's largest landlord groups gradually moved away from these short-term, "quick-fix" deceptions and legal maneuvers.

Instead, they organized a series of legal initiatives and higher-court challenges designed to emasculate the rent laws, scale them back to the point of insignificance, or have them overturned as unconstitutional. Of all New York's real estate groups, the Real Estate Board of New York was best suited to initiate legal challenges and lobby the state legislature for repeal or modification of the rent laws. REBNY officials had the prestige, the political contacts, and the legal and professional savvy to persuade lawmakers. A large cross section of the city's landlord groups lined up behind its efforts, including GNYTA, the West Side Taxpayers Association, the Federation of Bronx Real Estate Owners, and an assortment of hotel, building, and apartment owners' associations.[16] After the legislature passed the April laws, REBNY's legal staff, led by lobbyist Edward P. Doyle and legal counsel Alexander MacNulty, began organizing court challenges and legal initiatives to undermine the laws. Unlike local landlord leaders such as Bernard Deutsch of the Bronx Federation of Property Owners and Isidor Berger of GNYTA, REBNY leaders showed little concern over individual members' problems created by the new legislation. Doyle, MacNulty, and REBNY President Charles G. Edwards worked with members of the state legislature who shared their dislike of the rent laws or with members open to persuasion to amend the laws or pass new ones.[17] MacNulty and Doyle also began mobilizing other landlord leaders to have the laws declared unconstitutional. This process proved long and cumbersome. Between 1920 and 1925, as important pro-tenant provisions were added to the rent laws, REBNY leaders challenged them all.

Between 1920 and 1925, REBNY had very little success in overturning the rent laws or even amending them to the advantage of New York's landlords. Their successes were limited to a series of defensive victories that spanned most of the 1920s and involved holding back more radical rent relief measures. Tenant groups, officials, and legislators from New York's poorer neighborhoods flooded the legislature and city hall with ordinances and laws designed to saddle landlords with greater legal costs, to place greater constraints on their ability to raise rents, to force them to repair their tenements, and to impose serious penalties for violations of the rent laws, the Tenement House law, and other fire and safety codes.[18] In concert with other real estate groups, REBNY leaders successfully countered hundreds of these proposals through a relentless campaign of focused publicity combined with private and public lobbying.[19] Their clearest victories came over the efforts by tenant supporters to disconnect rent relief from the housing "emergency," a temporary status that spelled eventual uncertainty and possible defeat for more long-term reform. REBNY officials and their supporters in the legislature never let the debate broaden to allow repair bills, heat bills, and permanent rent controls much chance of passage. In this respect, REBNY's role in the postwar housing crisis was significant.[20]

II: Tenants, Tenant Organizations, and the Rent Laws

As tenants exploited the rent laws, they also looked for (and received) more concerted action from the municipal agencies. Tenants began filing complaints in unprecedented numbers with the Tenement House Department, the Department of Health, and other municipal authorities charged with monitoring conditions and standards in tenement districts. Tenants did this, of course, in part to better the conditions of their apartments which, according to Tenement House director Frank Mann and others, had deteriorated in recent years. Looking back on the 1910s, Mann noted that owners "had no incentive to do anything that would attract tenants. The demand for apartments was far greater than the supply. Hence, the owners of tenements did nothing for the comfort of their old tenants. . . . Tenants soon found that all appeals involving an expenditure of money fell on deaf ears when made to the owner or his agent."[21]

With the rent laws in place and following three years of tenant activism, tenants exercised greater initiative in challenging landlord neglect. Even in cases where the rent laws did not specifically apply, tenants felt greater freedom to resort to these agencies to pressure landlords. Reflecting back on a study of more than 32,000 homes conducted in 1919–1920, an inspector for the Department of Health described the "unprecedented fear of landlords, on the part of tenants, so that the conditions, in many instances, could not be obtained by questioning of tenants."[22] Such reporting dramatically increased after the passage of the rent laws.[23] In cases where landlords completely ignored the department's warnings, the landlords were summoned to the magistrates courts. With the housing crisis, city officials began coordinating planned inspections from the Fire Prevention Bureau and the Building and Tenement House Departments. The magistrates' courts also abolished the Board of Review, which had customarily allowed landlords a leisurely grace period to make necessary repairs. Instead, the courts began bringing in landlords promptly and issuing fines. Some property owners even ended up in jail.[24]

Tenants had other motives for placing complaints. Calling in municipal authorities strengthened their position when negotiating with landlords. Since the number of substandard tenements was great, the threat alone was often enough to make landlords moderate their demands. A degree of malice may also have influenced some tenants' decisions. Landlord leaders and the city's press reported numerous instances of tenants deliberately damaging wallpaper, pipes, and other fixtures and then reporting their landlords to the municipal authorities. Acknowledging the tradition of landlord neglect, the *Real Estate News* described the new insecurities for landlords, noting that

> Heretofore it mattered little to an owner if the tenant made himself obnoxious by causing a tenement house violation to exist. The owner could easily remove the tenant from the premises. [Under the rent laws] some of the malicious ones are creating all kinds of conditions. . . . It has become a common practice for tenants aggrieved at the landlord for raising rents to file complaints with the various city departments having to do with property.[25]

Stewart Browne claimed that tenants engaged in numerous forms of harassment and vandalism including

> allowing water to overflow, destroying plumbing, cutting holes in the tiled floor bathrooms, poking holes in ceilings, breaking plaster on the walls, breaking interior windows, ripping off wallpaper and then going to the Tenement House Department and Health Department and making complaints so that violations may be placed on the landlord's property and he be compelled weekly, at his own expense, to rectify the vandalism purposely caused by tenants.[26]

Some tenants also left windows open in the winter, whereupon they reported their landlords for violating city ordinances requiring a temperature of at least 68 degrees in their buildings.[27]

Landlords' complaints may have been little more than attempts to rationalize neglect of their properties. Conviction rates for tenement house violations in magistrates' courts in Manhattan did, in fact, increase substantially during this period from 23.1 percent in 1918 to 68.3 percent in 1921.[28] However, the situation did reach a point where Tenement House director Frank Mann felt compelled to issue public warnings to tenants concerning vandalism of their apartments. With the support of GNYTA, REBNY, and other real estate groups, he pushed to have ordinances passed that increased the penalties against such tenants.[29] When the rent laws and supporting municipal ordinances expired in 1929, GNYTA's official organ, the *Real Estate News*, charged that the rent laws had been of no use to tenants "other than giving them a weapon of harassing landlords."[30]

III: The "New Tenant Organizations"

Until the passage of the rent laws, both middle-class and working-class tenants organizers had pushed for reform. However, once the housing crisis began to subside, middle-class tenant groups began supplanting the Socialist and working-class tenant organizations of the late 1910s. Tenants increasingly turned away from tenant organizations such as the Greater New York Tenants League and the East Side Tenants League. While these organizations remained active through the 1920s, they faced fundamental challenges as new groups appeared. Organizations such as the Fair Play Rent Association, the Citizens' Protective Housing League, and the Tremont and Melrose Tenants Association had few, if any, links to the Socialist Party. In fact, these new groups often broke formally with tenant organizations that had been most active in the pre-rent laws era. This was due in part to the Socialist Party's decline and growing ineffectiveness. Between 1920 and 1925, the Socialist Party became fractured over basic strategy. Its left wing split off to form the Communist Party which, in turn, established services and organs that competed directly with the more centrist Socialists. By 1922, the Communist Party was strong enough to establish its own daily, *The Freiheit*, that competed with *The Forward*. By 1929, even in formerly militant sections of the city such as Brownsville, the Socialist Party was, according to Historian Alter Landesman, "a shadow of its former self."[31]

Middle-class leaders dominated the new tenant groups, and they were more willing to work with city and state officials. In the late 1910s, tenant activists such as Charles Solomon of GNYTL, Abraham Beckerman of the East Side Tenants League, and Leo Gitlin of the Brownsville Tenants League regularly lashed out at city and state officials as "tools" of real estate interests and political opportunists. They viewed with skepticism official efforts to co-opt their movements and draw tenant leaders into a more inclusive, consensual relationship with elected officials. In contrast, In the early 1920s, members of the Fair Play Rent Association, the Tremont Tenants' League, and other tenants came mostly from the middle class.[32] Moreover, these new tenant leaders celebrated their close association with city and state legislators, and they allowed policymakers to exercise much more influence over their deliberations. Many tenant activists embraced their roles as "nonpartisan" and "law-abiding" tenant advocates. Katherine Meyer, an activist associated with the Bronx Council of Tenants Leagues and Columbia University, studied tenant groups in the Bronx in the latter half of the 1920s and her views are quite instructive. In assessing the success of tenant groups in 1929, she stated that these organizations "formed during the crisis were of great aid to the state and can continue to be if their members are not made to feel inferior. They can serve as effective media of co-operation."[33] These nonconfrontational middle-class tenant leaders became easy prey for politicians accustomed to catering to middle-class tastes and concerns. Meyer describes the general treatment accorded tenant representatives in their increasingly deferential dealings with city and state officials. He states, "Many of the legislators come to know some of the leaders of these associations because of their repeated appearances and ask if their organization had any requests to make. This was highly flattering to these organizations even though legislators gave little lasting thought to their poorly framed proposals."[34] These groups showed much more reluctance to resort to more radical strategies, such as seizing tenements, deliberately overloading the courts, organizing mass demonstrations, and confronting police, that had been standard among some tenant groups in the 1910s.

Tenant leaders in the 1920s also appear to have abandoned the high idealism and sense of mission that had so defined the earlier tenant movement. They put aside higher visions of tenement flats as a public resource, or demands that landlords accept collective bargaining principles from tenant leaders. To a degree, this change may stem from the more general decline of the Socialist Party in New York City and the ravages some tenant groups sustained during the Palmer raids, experiences from which the Greater New York Tenants League, for example, never seemed to fully recover. Many older leaders invested their hopes in cooperative housing while others, such as GNYTL's Samuel Orr, focused his energies on the creation of municipal housing.[35]

The more moderate political orientation of these new organizations was reflected in the programs they routinely sponsored in the early to mid 1920s. While they, like their predecessors, continued to donate funds to individual members when they faced eviction, the organizations also donated money to groups such as the Salvation Army, homes for the terminally ill, Catholic churches, veterans associations, as well as for specific causes such as Christmas funds. Their legal aid and educational programs harkened back to programs fostered by mainstream housing and relief groups, such as the Charity Organization Society and even the Settlement House Movement. The leader of the Fair Play Rent Association, for example, began conducting regular inspections of tenements to advise tenants about cleanliness and good housekeeping. By 1926, tenant groups such as the South Bronx Tenants League had to cut back on these donations due to dwindling funds and a shrinking membership.[36]

Through the 1920s, one issue remained constant. Both new groups and old tenant organizations made the rent laws, to a large extent, the centerpiece of their existence. Their meetings became dominated by tenants' queries concerning various aspects of the rent laws and how tenants should respond to individual problems. Meyer noted in 1929 that most tenant groups in New York City adopted similar strategies, and that their "primary purpose . . . is to explain the rights of members and to protect these against infringement."[37] Leaders of groups such as the Tremont and Melrose Place Tenants Association fostered ties with city officials, and focused their organizational efforts most forcefully when the rent laws came up for renewal each year.[38] Moreover, in some ways, tenants began using tenant groups in the same way that they used the courts and the municipal departments: as a resource to enhance individual bargaining power in dealing with landlords. With limited personal investment in or commitment to their organizations by tenants, and lacking any unifying series of principles or effective programs to foster greater group loyalty, New York's tenant groups, to varying degrees, drifted to the margins.

IV: Landlords at Risk

GNYTA and other real estate groups tried to assist landlords in adjusting to the new environment. They devised new programs to help landlords deal with the practical problems created by the rent laws, specifically tenants' growing independence and their increasing reliance upon litigation and complaints to city departments. As noted in chapter 3, GNYTA officials had originally designed the Defense Committee to deal with landlord liability insurance rates in 1914. With the new problems created by the rent laws, this committee seemed ideally suited to expand its services. Led by GNYTA General Manager Isidor Berger, the Defense Committee continued to monitor owners', landlords' and tenants' rates and tried to safeguard landlords from "accident bandits."[39] However, the Defense Committee also became the central agency for a host of other protective legal services for landlords. The Inspection Department was supplemented in 1919 by a repairs department that assisted landlords in locating competent hired help at reduced rates.[40] Also, when landlords made more substantive repairs or renovations, the department provided advice, methods for saving money, a list of reputable contractors, and even a consulting architect. All of these measures supplemented GNYTA's central service, landlord liability insurance.[41]

By the 1920s, tenement landlords required liability insurance more than ever. Tenants had filed negligence cases in the past and, between 1870 and 1910, their numbers had steadily increased.[42] In the early 1920s, landlord liability insurance rates rose, the number of cases increased, and landlords expressed unprecedented concern over accident litigation and keeping down landlord liability rates.[43] As early as 1918, the Superintendent of the State Insurance Department noted that "the Lower East Side of Manhattan is the worst section [for insurers] to handle, and companies were unwilling to handle any large volume of business in this section."[44] According to one estimate, liability insurance rates jumped from between $15 and $25 per house before World War I, to $150 to $200 for an average small tenement in 1925. At the same time, the cost of fire insurance more than doubled.[45]

As noted in chapter 3, civil courts were already holding landlords liable for public areas in and around the tenement and, to some degree, for blatant violations of tenement house law. However, beginning in 1922, new decisions dramatically raised the stakes. That year, Appeals Court

Judge Benjamin Cardozo heard the case of *Altz v. Lieberson*. The plaintiff was a tenant in a New York City tenement house and, in 1917, a dilapidated ceiling in the apartment collapsed and injured him. The landlord, the defendant, had been previously notified of the faulty ceiling, but, following traditional patterns of tenement management, he did nothing. The tenant sued the landlord for damages in New York City's lower court. In every previous case, following precedents established in the nineteenth century, landlords had nothing to fear from such cases. However, in *Altz v. Lieberson* the landlord lost and was forced to appeal the case. As Arlene Newman has argued, the central issue of the case was whether the landlord had committed a breach of duty when he did not repair the ceiling. Previously under common law, as noted in chapters 1 and 2, the courts had found that landlords had no duty to make repairs within leased premises. However, Cardozo *overturned the common law* and ruled for the tenant and dramatically expanded the landlords' responsibility to tenants. In his decision, Cardozo concluded that "At common law there was no duty resting on the landlord of an apartment house to repair the rooms demised. His duty of repair was limited to those parts of the building which the occupants enjoyed in common. The Tenement House Law has changed the measure of his burden. . . . Every tenement house and all parts thereof shall be kept in good repair."[46] Thereafter, landlords were liable for failing to maintain their premises.

As much as the rent laws, this shift in landlord liability shook tenement managers across the city. Tenants did not wait long before they began filing law suits, and, by 1924, one Bronx Supreme Court Justice stated flatly that, "ever since the famous Cardozo decision was handed down, the courts of the city have been overwhelmed by the most unprecedented wave of litigation in the history of court practice." GNYTA officials appealed to their members about the urgency to coerce the legislature to modify the Cardozo decision or else tenement owners and insurance companies would expend millions to cover the claims.[47]

State law makers did quite the reverse. They actually went on to write the law into the statutes with the passage of the Multiple-Dwellings Law in 1929. The new law, combined with the numerous court cases that followed, greatly expanded landlords' vulnerability to tenant law suits. Even as the Cardozo decision clearly established that landlords were responsible for residential tenants in their buildings, further litigation in 1931 and later extended landlords' responsibility to include business tenants as well as guests. In 1934 and 1939, the courts found landlords liable for work done by independent contractors. By the mid-1940s, the dramatic expansion of landlord liability from late-nineteenth-century levels caused one insurance company official to note,

> The common law liability of the landlords to tenants and third parties has been so modified and enlarged by statute and judicial decision that there is now little resemblance to the duty with which a modern property owner is chargeable and that of a nineteenth century land holder. Of course, the changes and modifications which have been made are all praiseworthy and each one marks a milestone in a constantly improving social pattern. Formerly, and under the original scheme of things, many persons whose rights were outrageously violated, were left uncompensated for their grievances against landlords who kept their overhead low by refusing to make the improvements which decency and common sense demanded, but which were not required by the law.[48]

Through the 1920s, the responsibilities of GNYTA's Insurance Committee steadily expanded and, along with the Defense Committee, it developed greater autonomy.[49]

The biggest change for GNYTA was its abandonment of a "brass knuckles" approach to landlord-tenant relations. At some point in the mid-1920s, Reich and Berger decided that GNYTA had to shed its "quasi-legitimate" status, particularly in regard to its insurance services. While the Association had been offering insurance since 1914, it was not licensed by the state, and, as noted in chapter 3, GNYTA's inspection procedures provided more the veneer of safety and enforcement rather than the substance. In 1927, State Insurance Department officials began investigating GNYTA's operations as an unlicensed insurance provider. Some sources suggest that large numbers of complaints about the Association's business methods had prompted state officials to act. Moreover, as Arlene Newman has noted, attorneys and other court officials had expressed substantial hostility toward GNYTA due to their tactics, and mainstream insurance companies that provided landlord liability insurance viewed GNYTA's competitive price structure with suspicion. Finally, as Newman concludes, anti-Semitism against GNYTA's Jewish officials and Jewish membership almost certainly played a role.[50]

Even as the state clamped down on GNYTA's insurance activities, it allowed them to reorganize the Association from a cooperative venture to a business venture. Berger and Reich decided to elevate the Insurance Committee into a full-fledged, fully licensed insurance company. On August 10, 1927, the State of New York licensed the Defense Committee as an authorized mutual insurance company. In 1928, the Association began opening branch offices in other parts of the city and, by 1939, it had more than 15,000 policyholders.[51] Still closely tied with GNYTA, some real estate leaders described the insurance association as the "foremost landlord liability insurance company in New York," and a leading force in combating the accident claims of tenants.[52] However, this move came at a price. The officers went from receiving nominal fees for services to paid officers whose activities were subject to regulation. For the first time, their books were subject to audit. The state also regulated GNYTA's rates, set minimum resource requirements, and, as Newman has noted, the legislation gave the State Insurance Department "virtual dictatorial power over the financial affairs of insurance companies."[53]

As the civil courts became more open to tenant law suits, tenants also began to demand better amenities in lower-grade apartments, including tiled sinks, toilets, and bath tubs. Others simply moved to better sections of the city. Many tenants were ready to pay higher rents to obtain better features.[54] Tenants looked for better accommodations due to a general rise in standards of living that many workers experienced in the Lower East Side in the 1920s. The income of men's clothing workers, for example, tripled between 1914 and 1925, while the number of work hours per week actually declined. These trends, according to Leo Grebler, encouraged many tenants to look for better housing and improved amenities.[55]

Just as GNYTA officials themselves had to put their own house in order, they, in turn, urged landlords to assert more control over their property. For those landlords who did not live in their buildings, for example, the Defense Committee strongly urged them to assert more control over their janitors, agents, lessees, and others whose responsibility it was, in theory, to maintain the property. Reformers and city officials had long decried the incompetence of janitors and housekeepers. The Tenement House Department noted in 1903 that,

> the majority of janitors, unfortunately, are not in any way fitted to perform the functions that they are expected to perform. They are generally ignorant people, often women with large families of children to care for, and who are sometimes physically unable to do the work which they are expected to do. Most of

the bad conditions which exist in the tenement houses, the department finds, are in the public parts of the house and not in the private apartments of the tenants.[56]

Berger urged landlords to supervise their properties by monitoring their janitors and lessees more closely, even advocating, at times, the use of professional property managers.[57]

V: New Tools for a New Environment

Landlord leaders had not given up on reestablishing their old prerogatives. Many of these efforts were ineffective (and, at times, farcical). However, other initiatives clearly pointed toward the future of working-class tenancies in the city. As the rent laws took hold in the early to mid-1920s, landlord leaders tried a number of strategies to reestablish the discretionary prerogatives these laws had helped to demolish. REBNY's court challenges clearly established that the temporary provisions of the rent laws would eventually be put aside. GNYTA's leaders offered services that provided landlords with a certain degree of protection against accident claims, municipal housing violations, vandalism, and holdovers. These strategies, however, were largely defensive in nature. Many landlords wanted simpler, more permanent, and more comprehensive ways to reassert control over their properties and their tenants. Stewart Browne and UREO's organizers had been working on numerous strategies for evading the rent laws, most of which proved cumbersome, short-lived, and often ridiculous. However, in the process, Browne did publicize two methods that, under certain conditions, offered landlords substantial new protections. These methods would long outlive the rent laws and go on to become central elements of property management in New York City and elsewhere. The methods were a request for security deposits, and the "iron-clad" lease (or written leases that minutely define the responsibilities of landlords and tenants).

Security deposits and iron-clad leases have become so commonplace by the 1990s that many Americans who rent today cannot envision a time when they were not in use. And yet, in 1920, security deposits were virtually unheard of for working-class tenancies: on the rare occasions when individual landlords introduced them, tenants and the public at large criticized them as un-American and even immoral. Security deposits and iron-clad leases conflicted with two time-honored traditions among New York's tenants and landlords alike, traditions that allowed both parties considerable latitude and discretion. The first tradition involved tenants' reliance upon oral leases. The great majority of New York's tenants in this period relied on oral leases with their landlords. Some New Yorkers placed the percentage of tenant families with oral leases as high as 80 and even 90 percent. In the nineteenth century, written leases were impractical due to high levels of immigration, illiteracy, and turnover. In the tenement districts of New York, traditional moving days fell on May 1 and October 1 of each year, and the city's streets were jammed with moving vans, carts and crowds of people relocating.[58]

The oral lease gave both tenants and landlords a certain degree of freedom. By their nature, the leases were quite short, and thus they could not address all the needs and contingencies of both parties. This tended to enhance the discretionary authority of landlords, as issues such as the provision of heat, repairs, and basic aspects of habitability were left to the landlord to adjudicate as he and his purse saw fit. As noted earlier, tenants were in no position before 1920 to challenge their landlords legally for fear of reprisals, and the courts and municipal departments did not encourage them. In reflecting upon the operations of the Tenement House Department, for example, Frank Mann said that strict enforcement of the Tenement House law and the city's health and building codes was neither possible (due to lack of resources) nor necessarily desirable. As a consequence, tenant groups, on occasion, accused him of ignoring their complaints.[59]

Before the coal shortage and housing crisis of the late 1910s, the difficulties in enforcing oral leases did not always work to the landlord's advantage. Since the finances of many landlords and lessees were precarious, tenants usually had to pay their monthly rents for the landlord to make ends meet. Thus, tenants who felt ill-used could, as a last resort, break their own part of the oral lease and steal away before the agreement was due to expire. This option gave tenants a tremendous sense of freedom, and tenants routinely ignored their agreements and, without notice, moved on to other quarters. For example, Julius Grunfeld and his family immigrated to New York around the turn of the century. Their first residence, located in Ninth Street and Avenue C, had foul privies in the basement which they found intolerable. They stayed at the first flat for a month, and then moved to 76th Street. Again they disliked the bathing and toilet facilities, so they moved to 92nd Street. There, the Grunfelds found that the courtyard gave off foul smells, so they moved once more to 81st Street near the East River. The family moved *four times* in one year. The agreements they made with their landlords were not an issue. As Julius Grunfeld's daughter later recalled, "There were no leases in those days. At least, not where we lived."[60]

Tenement managers called families like the Grunfelds "rent-beats," and they were a bane to most landlords. Given the uniformity of the leasing calendar imposed by the traditional moving days it was not always easy to find new tenants and make up for the lost rent. Landlords were especially vulnerable when housing was plentiful and tenants were free to pick and choose, as was the case in the early 1910s. At such times, tenants expected landlords to provide two and even three months free rent before they would to come to terms. Some tenants made a practice of skipping out after the period of free rent expired, simply to move onto another building and another landlord who was willing to make such concessions.[61] Tenants with families or established workplaces could not easily exploit this weakness.

The landlord's authority was, to an extent, further enhanced by a second tradition that defined landlord-tenant relations before 1920: monthly leases. Here again, according to contemporaries, a clear majority of tenants chose to renew their leases every month rather than agree to more long-term arrangements. This practice suited tenants with seasonal work or other types of employment who experienced frequent layoffs or idle time. Customarily, landlords considered the lease automatically renewed when tenants paid the next month's rent. However, if the landlord wanted to get rid of a tenant, all he had to do was not accept payment and have the tenant evicted. Monthly leases, whether written or oral, were brief, with particular emphasis placed on the amount of rent and mutually understood indicators of the tenant's desire to renew the lease at the end of the month. A typical example from 1900 is shown below.

Agreement made May 1st, 1900 between John Doe as Landlord and Richard Roe as Tenant, as follows:

Doe rents unto Roe, and the latter hires and takes from Doe, the first floor of house No. 1 Broadway Borough of Manhattan, New York, for the term of one month from May 1st 1900, at the monthly rent of twenty-five dollars, payable in advance. This tenancy expires at the end of said month. It is expressly understood that if the said John Doe accepts rent after the end of said month, such acceptance shall operate as a renewal of the tenancy for another month, and so on for each month for which he accepts rent. But in case the said John Doe refuses to accept further rent, the tenancy is to terminate with the month for which rent was last accepted.

John Doe

Richard Roe[62]

Oral, monthly leases were acceptable for both landlords and tenants because they established and assumed that a degree of equilibrium existed between the two parties, founded on the basic principles that tenants needed a place to live and that landlords wanted to keep their properties filled with tenants paying rent. The heat crisis of the late 1910s and the postwar housing shortage destroyed this equilibrium, as municipal court justices reluctantly adopted the practice of protecting only those tenants who had written leases and evicting tenants with oral agreements.[63] An assemblyman introduced a bill that would have provided stronger protections for tenants with oral leases in early 1920.[64] Other legislators, members of the MCRP, and initially even some tenant activists took a counter approach, favoring reforms that forced all tenants and landlords to adopt year-long, written leases. They did this, in part, to curb the quick turnover strategies of some of the worst speculators.[65] The rent laws were an attempt to protect desperate tenants from a marketplace where demand outstripped supply to an unprecedented degree.

Issues such as the oral lease led to a rupture in the relationship between GNYTA and UREO officials. Long before the passage of the emergency laws, Browne began publicly moving away from the position of GNYTA leaders Isidor Berger, Elias Diamond, and Harold Phillips. As early as September 1919, for example, GNYTA leaders had declared that increases in rent "must be made to meet the increased cost of material for construction and maintenance." In response, Browne described himself as a "semi-paternal socialist" and declared that tenants could not afford any increases.[66] Following passage of the emergency laws, GNYTA leaders condemned Browne's softness, and the organization publicly broke with him and UREO in 1922. Reflecting on this break in 1923, Browne summed up the differences he saw between himself and members of GNYTA.

[GNYTA's members] are composed of the owners of the cheapest tenement houses in the city; they noisily and bitterly opposed every rent law bill and building tax exempt bill from 1920 to date.... Affiliation [between UREO and GNYTA] was discontinued because they objected to my pro-rent law and pro-tenant views and claimed I had no sympathy with the owners of cheap tenements.[67]

Browne endorsed the rent laws because their existence drew rentpayer support away from the most radical tenant groups. Also, from the beginning, he felt confident that landlords could quietly manipulate the legal process to their advantage and mitigate the harshest aspects of the rent legislation. In mid-1921, for example, Browne began circulating a booklet to New York's landlords that gave explicit directions on how legally to raise rents and deter tenant activists. For example, the booklet told landlords, "Never give a tenant big or little possession until after he has signed the lease and paid three successive monthly installments of rent.... Make the first month's installment of rent payable three days before possession, the second month's rent two days before possession and the third month's one day before possession."[68] This complicated system of installments, in theory, disqualified tenants from appealing to the courts on the grounds that the rents were "unreasonable," because the courts had already ruled that a tenant who paid rent for three successive months was barred from any appeal to the rent laws. When reporters confronted Browne with the booklet, he claimed that it simply instructed landlords on how to comply with the law. The Committee's legal counsel responded by distributing its own booklet to tenants, which either denied the legality of most of Browne's strategies or informed tenants about how to counter them.[69]

In July, 1923, Browne and UREO staffers began circulating a new form of lease to member landlords, the so-called "iron-clad lease." This lease tried to nullify not only most of the harsher elements of the emergency rent laws, but also central features of the tenement house law and numerous building, safety, and heat ordinances enacted in New York City. The new lease's provisions, if legal, would have largely reestablished the landlord's discretionary authority, and greatly limited the tenants' newly won independence and ability to pressure landlords. The lease undercut the tenant's access to the civil and criminal courts and the city departments; it even tried to turn these institutions into landlord support mechanisms by either classifying certain responsibilities as "extras" that were specifically not paid for through the rent, or by explicitly shifting the responsibility to the tenant. A *New York Times* article described some of the lease's protective features.

Third clause—Provides for tenant complying with the regulations, and violations of the Labor, Tenement House, Health, Building and other departments and failure to comply authorize landlord as tenant's agent to do so and provides for dispossess for non-payment of cost of so-doing and for all fines payable by landlord. Tenant does all repairs &c. . . .

Seventh clause—Contracts landlord out of penal code to supply heat and hot water. . . .

Eighth clause—Contracts landlord out of public liability inside building and makes tenant responsible for all damages to landlord's property caused by tenant, his family, or employees.[70]

Browne was not the first to use leases in this fashion. Through the course of the heat crisis and the housing shortage, individual landlords had tried to exempt themselves from various laws or ordinances or had tried to hold tenants to a more specific account than oral leases had allowed.[71] Indeed, standard leases had for decades made certain demands on tenants in regard to maintenance. A standard written lease from 1899, for example, simply required the tenant to "comply with all the requirements of the board of health, municipal authorities and police and fire departments of the city of [New York]." The standard lease described no penalties for tenants if they ignored the requirements. The so-called "Astor form" of lease demanded more of tenants, requiring them to make some repairs and "to not call upon the [the landlord] for any disbursement or outlay during the hereby granted term; and at the end . . . of the term shall deliver up the premises in good order and condition, damage by the elements excepted." Here again, however, the lease described no penalties. As a matter of practice, landlords had no means of collecting when such penalties occurred. Like the iron-clad lease, standard leases for flats did demand that tenants "make and do all repairs required to walls, ceilings, paper, glass and glass globes, plumbing works, ranges, pipes and fixtures belonging thereto, whenever damage or injury to the same shall have resulted from misuse or neglect." Despite such provisions, however, landlords rarely required month-to-month tenants in the city's tenement districts to use written leases. When they did, the leases were short, concise, and largely unconcerned with holding tenants to any standard of accountability regarding repairs, maintenance or safety.[72]

By recommending a written lease for working-class tenants, Browne realized that he was challenging these long-held customs in New York City. He felt, however, that landlords should make these demands given the housing conditions of 1923, and he argued that landlords had simply been short-sighted in the past for not pressing the case. He stated that,

> The lease has been made necessary ... and the whole trouble has come about because 90 per cent of the tenants are month to month tenants. They have no agreement with the landlord other than the price of their rent. They can sublet the premises the landlord rents to them and the landlord is powerless to stop it. ... The housing landlord with month to month tenants has lived in a "fool's paradise" for 100 years and hasn't known it and does not know it yet. When told to get a month to month tenant to sign a month to month lease, his reply is "What's the use? The tenant isn't any good." Suppose he isn't? Most tenants aren't whether month to month or yearly. Why not get them before they take possession to sign a lease under which the tenant agrees to do everything and the landlord agrees to do nothing but collect the rent, and if in possession, serve a tenancy notice containing similar provisions. Any landlord who doesn't is a "gol-darn fool."[73]

As a legal instrument, the iron-clad lease itself was flawed. Tenants could not sign away their rights. Public officials and leaders from REBNY and GNYTA quickly condemned the lease as unworkable in its specifics.[74] Former Mayor's Committee chairman (and UREO member) Nathan Hirsch resigned from the UREO, publicly stating to Browne that, "a lease such as you insist that the landlords use is, in my judgment, a step backward and reminds me of the laws existing hundreds of years ago when the Lord of the Manor in England had certain legal rights the nature of which newspapers today would hesitate to discuss. . . . I can only see harm in waving a red flag before thousands of already harassed and infuriated tenants."[75] At first, Browne argued that UREO's legal counsel would take any challenges to the lease's legality to the Court of Appeals. However, following a week of withering public condemnation, Browne retreated somewhat and claimed that he was putting aside the original version of the lease and would eliminate its most onerous elements in UREO's future leases.[76]

Two issues are noteworthy regarding the UREO lease. First, the iron-clad lease controversy sent a chill through New York's tenant community and tenant supporters, and their reaction is instructive. They attacked the legal flaws in the document, as well as the document's implicit threat to tenant freedoms that landlords had always built into oral, month to month leases. Critics attacked the document and the basic strategy as un-American, "communistic," and verging on treason since it was likely to cause riots and general unrest. Leaders from the Greater New York Federation of Tenants Leagues, egged on by the Lockwood Committee's Samuel Untermyer, actually went to the extent of pressuring state officials to have Browne, who had never applied for U.S. citizenship, deported back to Great Britain.[77]

Furthermore, while many activists put aside UREO's iron-clad lease, the basic strategy was not lost on New York's landlord leaders, particularly the real estate professionals who were looking for ways to rationalize and standardize rental agreements. In modified form, UREO, GNYTA, and other groups began promulgating standardized, written leases for all tenants, leases that not only explicitly defined landlords' responsibility but also set out specific penalties for tenants. In broad outline, landlords began pressuring tenants with oral agreements to sign written leases shortly after the legislature passed the rent laws.[78] By the beginning of 1924, the Commission of Housing and Regional Planning noted with dismay the tenants' loss of bargaining power in the "tendency of new leases toward explicit release of the landlord from responsibility and obligations heretofore resting on him by force of custom or law, in the gradual reduction of services afforded by landlords and owners of rental property and their refusal to make necessary repairs."[79] By 1925, despite their initial opposition to Browne's specific lease, REBNY officials began stressing in their YMCA real estate lectures the importance of holding month-to-month tenants to an explicit written lease.[80]

What made the "iron-clad's" provisions any different from previous leases for flats, which had required tenants to pay the costs for repairs? Not much by themselves, however, the basic strategy of explicitly defining responsibilities and penalties happened to coincide with the emergence of a new mechanism of enforcement for landlords, the security deposit. Like written leases which had been customary for middle- and upper-class tenants, the security deposit was not customary for working-class tenancies. When individual landlords tried to use them, tenants routinely claimed that they were illegal since they assessed penalties before any crime or damage had occurred. For example, during the early stages of tenant activism in 1918, a group of Belmont Avenue tenants in the Bronx staged a successful rent strike against a landlord who had demanded one month's rent as a security deposit.[81] Once the legislature passed the rent laws, the press reported more cases where landlords demanded security deposits. A *Bronx Home News* reporter described the novelty of the security deposit for Eagle Avenue tenants in July, 1920.

> An example of the terrorizing methods being used by landlords in forcing tenants to sign leases at advanced rentals and at the same time extracting from them permanent deposits equal to a month's rent to be held as "security" was brought to the attention of the Home News a few days ago.... Standing out prominently among the provisions of the leases was the demand that the tenants give the landlord one month's rent to be kept by him until the tenancy expired. The money was to be forfeited by the tenants should they violate any of the other provisions of the leases. According to tenants, there were so many stringent rules to be lived up to that there was little likelihood of them getting their money back.[82]

The practice quickly spread in the Bronx. The *Bronx Home News* noted by the end of September that,

> greedy landlords have inaugurated a new practice to victimize persons who are seeking apartments and one which is believed to be illegal. They are demanding that new tenants, in addition to signing leases for two years, deposit with them cash amounts ranging from $100 to $200, giving as the reason for the latter that they wish to protect themselves against the tenant vacating before his lease expires.[83]

Poor tenants viewed security deposits as threats to many of their customary freedoms and their ability to pressure landlords. The Eagle Avenue tenants described above, for example, feared that, with so many provisions, "their liberty would be encroached upon."[84]

While the development of the iron-clad lease, and the increased use of the security deposit for working-class tenancies were new, their overall historical importance remains uncertain. Did New York landlords really embrace these methods at this time or were they simply a momentary experiment tried out by a select few? Older traditions persisted through the 1930s, including landlords granting up to three months free rent to prospective tenants.[85] Oral leases remained in use, and the "rent beat" continued to plague landlords through the 1930s and 1940s, clearly indicating that many property owners still did not ask for security deposits.⁸⁶ The importance of this flurry of interest in security deposits in the 1920s lies in the trend it indicated toward the rationalization and streamlining of property management. In an analysis of tenement management in 1932, a time when landlords rented at an extreme disadvantage in the Lower East Side, GNYTA President Ignatz Reich had come to a similar conclusion. By that time, he took it for granted that landlords would get written leases. He summed up the larger transformation in property management this way.

> The old time type of landlords who saw nothing in a lease but duty to collect his monthly stipend and who frequently so conducted himself as to come to be regarded by the tenant as a natural enemy, must now make way for the landlord who puts his renting on a business basis and gives the same attention to it that they would give to running a bank or drygoods store. The new way means turning an uncertain line of endeavor into a permanent and profitable business.⁸⁷

Indeed, in the late nineteenth century, small-scale investors could treat their properties as passive investments, ventures that did not require specialized knowledge or a significant commitment of time or capital. By the late 1920s, the market was clearly moving away from this style of management. Instead, informal agreements, age-old landlord-tenant laws, and limited civil liability were, as Reich suggests, giving way to a more rationalized and capital-intensive business that demanded legal expertise, day-to-day oversight, and, ultimately, more money. However, this change not only represented more than a change in behavior. In the 1910s and 1920s, the need for more rational procedures and increased levels of capital ushered in a host of new, large-scale real estate investors.

Conclusion

In the 1920s, tenement landlords had to adjust to a host of new realities. Government regulation limited landlords' ability to raise rents and denied them easy access to eviction proceedings. Moreover, landlords risked their fortunes if they allowed their tenements to deteriorate to unsafe levels. Pressure from insurance companies and state agencies also significantly undermined landlord autonomy.

Some landlord leaders bitterly denounced these changes—but they also took some solace from the reasonable belief that they had weathered the worst. Through the 1920s, not only had GNYTA, UREO, and REBNY leaders helped kill the most radical proposals floated during the height of the housing crisis, but also their lobbying had weakened the laws and even brought the gradual repeal of some of them. Furthermore, by the late 1920s, the tenant agitation that had seemingly caused so much of the trouble was slowly disappearing. Lacking the hardships of the housing crisis and the confrontational leadership of Tenant's League organizers, tenants began assuming a less adversarial stance vis-à-vis the city's tenement landlords.

This lull, however, was brief. Just as an unprecedented crisis had radicalized a broad cross-section of the city's tenants, so another unparalleled crisis would again mobilize New York's renters. The crisis was the Great Depression, and its effects on the city's landlords and tenants will be the focus of chapter 7.

CHAPTER 7

The Depression and the Decline of Amateur Tenement Operators

During the Depression, market conditions, state intervention, and the emergence of established, citywide, tenant confederations spelled an end to the landlord's traditional level of discretionary authority. Moreover, the diminishing authority of the landlord further eroded the economic profitability of the properties of long-term operators and undercapitalized, small-scale landlords. Following the rent laws and the Depression, professional realtors, property managers, and large-scale lenders came to control the majority of tenement property in the Lower East Side. While small-scale landlords would remain a vital group of tenement owners, the business of renting in New York City was becoming too complicated for amateurs. In 1929, as the expiration date for the temporary provisions of the emergency rent laws approached, the *Real Estate News* noted that, "June 1st will see the end of the reign of the rent laws and complete control of tenement property will again revert to the owners. However, the legal relationship between landlord and tenant will not completely re-adjust itself to the status as it existed prior to the initial rent law enactment [in 1920] and it will take a more or less indefinite interval before the readjustment to that extent will take place."[1] In many ways, the "indefinite interval" continues to this day, as landlord-tenant relations have never returned to their pre-rent laws status.

In 1926, the New York State legislature began the process of "decontrol."[2] Lawmakers began repealing the temporary provisions of the emergency rent laws and allowing landlords greater freedom to increase rents and evict tenants. While many landlords were relieved to see a return to some semblance of prewar practices and procedures, more reflective property owners noted that their situation had changed permanently. Landlords could not fully recapture the discretionary authority that the postwar housing crisis had whittled away.[3] Despite the repeal of the emergency laws, tenant activists and legislators from New York's poorer districts pressed forward in other areas. As the Depression buffeted the city's renters, tenants from almost all classes and social backgrounds began forming tenant confederations with unprecedented influence in New York's housing policy circles.

I: The Decline of the Housing Crisis

By the late 1920s there were clear indications that the postwar housing shortage was over, at least in the Lower East Side and other white ethnic communities. The tax moratorium on multi-family houses, one of the byproducts of the housing crisis, caused a surge in tenement and apartment construction. At the same time, new lending practices appeared which made it easier for landlords to obtain mortgages with limited capital. In the early 1920s, banks, insurance companies, and, to a decreasing extent, individual investors were the principal sources of mortgage money for tenement buyers. In the late 1920s, however, new sources emerged. Title companies, which previously confined their activities to examining and guaranteeing real estate titles, gradually drifted into mortgage lending. Buyers swarmed to purchase the six and seven percent mortgage certificates for highly speculative building plots, acreage, and subdivisions. One of GNYTA's vice-president noted in 1927 that, "we have the pleasing spectacle of large lending institutions advertising their moneys for investment, indicating no doubt, a super-abundance of available mortgage funds."[4] While much of this real estate activity occurred in newer areas of the city such as Queens, the easy access to mortgages fostered a frenzied atmosphere among small-scale real estate investors across the city.[5]

Tax breaks and easy credit fostered construction and eased the housing shortage. The number of vacancies in Manhattan increased from 1,510 in 1921 to 102,158 by late 1928, while the number of tenements under construction leaped from 309 to 3,580 during the same time period.[6] Through the late 1920s, tenant activists and sympathetic legislators had argued that, despite new construction, rents were still too high for tenements and beyond the means of average workers.[7] However, even in this area, by 1929 the number of apartments available at ten dollars a month per room, close to the average prewar rental figure, accounted for more than fifty percent of the total vacancies.[8]

At the same time, there were clear indications that many middle-class and upper-working-class white, ethnic New Yorkers wanted newer, better accommodations than those available in the Lower East Side or the Bronx. Many chose to migrate to other areas of Manhattan or to the outer boroughs.[9] In a study conducted of former Lower East Side residents, Leo Grebler found that the condition of the tenements, the lack of amenities, and neglect ranked highest as the reasons why people migrated to other sections of New York. As New York's mass-transit system expanded in the 1920s, Queens and newer sections of Brooklyn became more popular, and developers and contractors built apartments and suburban homes to meet the growing demand for better accommodations. While the outer boroughs experienced impressive growth, many second-generation New Yorkers sought better housing in other parts of Manhattan, including new, middle-class ethnic neighborhoods on the Upper West Side along Central Park West, Riverside Drive, and West End Avenue. Jews began moving there in large numbers before World War I, but the big surge came during the 1920s. Moreover, as African Americans increasingly moved into Harlem, thousands of Jewish families relocated to the Bronx, Brooklyn, or the West Side.[10] New York realtors described 1928's moving day as the most extensive since 1920, with widespread migration out of old-law tenement districts such as Yorkville to Queens and other areas with new housing stock. Extensive migration caused older communities to contract, leaving more vacancies and lower rents. The Lower East Side experienced a particularly severe decrease in occupancy.[11] In 1929, according to the State Board of Housing, in the district bounded by the East River, the Brooklyn Bridge, Centre Street, the Bowery, and East Fourth Street, there were 13,000 vacancies out of approximately 79,000 apartments.[12]

Within these older communities, many workers could afford better quarters than neglected tenements. Through the 1920s, average wages steadily increased, and many tenants demanded more amenities associated with middle-class living, including steam heat, elevator service, and appliances. The decade also saw a number of experiments with cooperative workers' housing projects that were often linked with labor organizations, such as the Amalgamated Clothing Workers and the International Ladies Garment Workers Union. The significantly better housing accommodations that the Amalgamated Clothiers' housing projects and other limited-dividend corporations offered to workers in both the Lower East Side and in the Bronx promoted this trend. While the Limited Dividend Act of 1926 assisted many of these projects, others developed without any government assistance. The Workers' Cooperative Colony and the Yiddish Cooperative Heimgesellschaft built projects with strong ideological ties to larger Socialist political movements.[13]

Tenants exploited the new options and abandoned the old-law tenements in droves. The State Board of Housing noted in 1928 that most of the vacancies occurred in the worst tenement areas and in old-law tenements. In the Lower East Side, the report stated, "this section represents the worst tenement conditions in the city. Most of the residences are old cold-water flats of the poorest possible type."[14] In 1929, a Tenement House Report declared that,

As a result of the construction of a large number of new, light and sanitary apartments in buildings in various parts of the city, there has been a migration from the sections where the old law tenements predominate. This has been particularly noticeable in the lower east side of the Borough of Manhattan. This area until recent years was teeming with humanity and was the most congested section of the city, but with the migrations from this area, year by year, to other localities the vacant apartments are increasing. In many cases entire buildings have been abandoned for living purposes.[15]

As tenants migrated and vacancies increased, old-law tenement landlords who provided no amenities felt greater pressure to change their management strategies. GNYTA President Ignatz Reich observed in early 1929 that,

Owners of [old-law tenements] have all cause to feel uneasy about the future. With the constant dilution of the number of apartments by new ones erected, with the drastic rent cutting resulting both from lowered rent scales and repeated concessions, the owner of the old-law tenement, which lacks all up-to-date improvements, is facing a situation that daily is becoming worse. . . . [These owners] have failed to bring their commodities up to the standards required by the purchasing public, with the result that the latter is ignoring them for the more replete and modern apartments of recent construction.[16]

Real estate lobbyists and many legislators began pressing for the repeal of the temporary provisions of emergency rent laws. Using the favorable statistics from white, ethnic communities as evidence, many reformers and city officials proclaimed that the housing crisis was over. Such prominent legislators as the Chairman of the Assembly Judiciary Committee, Edmund Jenks, opposed the extension of the rent laws and actively courted real estate interests, including GNYTA and REBNY.[17]

In 1926, the legislature began a gradual three-stage process of decontrol. First, it repealed provisions of the temporary laws that applied to smaller cities in the state, such as Rochester and Buffalo. Second, it gradually reinstated landlords' access to dispossess proceedings (although access was not precisely in the same form as earlier). And third, it narrowed the laws' applicability to tenements that fell within a certain range of rents. For example, the legislature repealed controls on rents of more than twenty dollars per room per month. In November 1928, it lifted controls on rents of more than fifteen dollars per room per month and then lifted all controls in June 1929.[18] By 1928, rent controls covered only 37.7 percent of tenancies; even among those, only tenancies initiated before 1924 were significantly affected.[19]

A number of noted housing reformers, including Edith Elmer Wood, hailed the repeal of the emergency laws. They had long criticized the rent laws as an unnatural perversion of market economics and a dead end for housing reform. Instead, Wood, Clarence Stein, and others stressed the importance of limited dividend housing corporations, cooperative housing, and public housing. Most housing reformers rejected fundamental restructuring of the landlord-tenant relationship. While some advocated small, temporary alterations in dispossess proceedings, their priorities were clearly elsewhere.[20]

Even as Berger and Reich rejoiced over the demise of the rent laws, demographic movement and tenant demand for better accommodations hampered the return to older styles of tenement management. Neglected tenements were less profitable, and lawmakers' continued interest in new landlord-tenant regulations destabilized the entire market in old tenements.

Berger, Reich, and other realtors and builders tried to encourage landlords to renovate dilapidated old-law tenements. They argued that, with a little wallpaper and some superficial "fix-it-up," these old structures could be made attractive, profitable and legal once more.[21] However, even GNYTA's optimistic estimates could not hid the incredible investment, particularly in terms of plumbing, electrification, and new safety features, that would have been necessary. Landlords faced high liability rates and lawsuits if they allowed the structures to decline further.

Certain long-term trends also began to undercut the profitability of tenements for small-scale landlords. Rising taxes and the expanded cost of maintenance and repairs impinged upon traditional tenement management strategies. For example, landlords in "Little Italy," New York's fourteenth ward, saw property values decline, taxes on assessed values double, and the rates of foreclosure more than double. Some owners demolished their aging tenements, hoping to attract commercial developers, and others hoped that the city would condemn and buy their empty buildings.[22] In the late 1920s and early 1930s, average wages increased, driving up the cost of basic repairs and maintenance—this at a time when many tenants were looking for better accommodations. Many of these costs did not go down once the economy deteriorated. For example, in his study of New York real estate firms, Leo Grebler found that repairs and maintenance costs for walk-up apartments rose dramatically through the early 1930s.[23]

New laws combined with vigorous law enforcement made better tenement maintenance increasingly essential. The centerpiece of this new legislation was the Multiple Dwellings Law of 1929. The law included new requirements for fire protection and prevention in old law tenements, imposed new restrictions on the use of second interior rooms, and required private toilets for each apartment. The law was to take effect January 1, 1934, but, due to the Depression, the dates for compliance with some provisions was pushed back two years. In 1936, when the law took full effect, the number of violations for noncomplying properties grew precipitously, and many landlords received warnings that own-

174

ers would be held "criminally negligent" in the event of fires and fatalities. As a result, as Leo Grebler notes, "most owners either complied with the fire-retarding provisions of the law or proceeded to close buildings." Ironically, by the end of the 1930s, run-down old-law tenements were often as dangerous financially and legally to the landlord as they were physically hazardous to the tenant.

Indeed, many landlords were already choosing to simply board up their properties and abandon them. For example, on the Lower East Side, the number of dwelling units in closed buildings rose from 624 in 1929 to 4,936 in 1938, an increase of about 700 percent. Leo Grebler noted that "the overwhelming proportion of closings were caused by actual or anticipated vacate orders for violations of law, and that even in the rest of the cases the threat of criminal liability was a more forceful motive than voluntary boarding-up." In his review of Lower East Side real estate, Grebler concluded that "almost 6 percent of the total housing inventory on the Lower East Side was withdrawn from use by the closing of buildings, but the withdrawal was apparently caused by public action rather than by market forces."[24]

II: The Impact of the Depression on Old Tenement Districts

In the 1920s, many banks, title companies, and other mortgage lenders had speculated freely. Lenders had encouraged tenement buyers to take out large mortgages, often on property that was already over-appraised. Moreover, representatives from REBNY and other real estate experts had encouraged an atmosphere of endless optimism concerning real estate investment, leading many small-scale operators to grossly overestimate even their short-term profits.[25] The Depression hit small- and large-scale investors severely. As the value of many investments plummeted in the wake of the stock market crash and as more property owners defaulted, many mortgage lenders began calling in their loans to protect their investments.[26] REBNY President Anton Trunk accurately described the lenders' position in 1932, stating that "Altogether the lending institutions confronted a situation totally unprecedented. They saw values fall like a bird shot down in its flight. They saw the supposed margin of safety between market value and encumbrances shrink to the vanishing point. They had their own investors to protect."[27]

Landlord leaders from across the city, with their profound faith in the soundness of real estate as an investment, were slow to recognize the enormity of the economic crisis. Initially, some of New York's most prominent real estate leaders actually hailed the Depression, arguing that it would drive more money away from stocks and into real estate securities and the funding of mortgages.[28] An example of this misplaced faith was REBNY's belated attempt to attract investors into real estate securities through a real estate securities exchange. J. Clarence Davies, one of New York's largest tenement realtors, spearheaded REBNY's campaign. REBNY designed the exchange to exploit the enthusiasm for securities endemic in the 1920s but the market was already in steep decline by the time the exchange opened in January 1930.[29]

As the Depression tore through real estate investments in the city, large-scale lenders began, by default, taking control of large numbers of tenements. Many landlords, especially those in the Lower East Side where vacancies were dramatically increasing, faced foreclosure and even bankruptcy. GNYTA's Isidor Berger felt that these landlords, most of them small-scale businessmen and nonprofessionals, were "victims of the unwholesome practices and the frenzied and unbridled orgy of mortgage indiscretions of 1926–1929."[30] In New York, between 1926 and 1933, foreclosures dramatically increased. During the Depression, lending institutions took control of property in the Lower East Side at an unprecedented rate, increasing from less than one percent in 1920, to eight percent in 1930.[31] Lender repossession was particularly common in cases involving old-law tenements. The lenders found it difficult to recover their investments given the depreciation in the values of old-law tenement mortgages, often amounting to less than fifty cents on the dollar.[32] Due to the enormity of the crisis and their own lack of "hands-on" tenement management experience, lenders were notorious for allowing property to lose value quickly during the process of asset liquidation. Often landlords felt compelled to monitor the day-to-day affairs of tenement management in hopes that they might recover a fraction of their investments. In cases where lenders took control, landlords often found themselves still responsible for maintenance and collections. As lenders took control of more tenement property, rents and property values continued to decrease.[33]

Both by default and, in some cases, as a matter of explicit policy, lenders began assuming control of large numbers of tenements. At many points during the early 1930s, Berger and other landlord organizers attacked large lending institutions for what seemed like a calculated effort to drive out the more marginal landlords and small-scale investors.[34] As the Depression dragged on through the 1930s, many lenders found it difficult to find buyers for tenement property, especially in older districts. Thus, many turned to professional property managers and real estate agents to collect rents, make repairs, and otherwise attempt to maintain the property's value.[35]

As part of a long-term trend, the Depression also drove many individual landlords in the Lower East Side out of real estate entirely. Professional realtors and property managers replaced most of them. For example, in Leo Grebler's study of a sample of Lower East Side properties, single individual ownership went from 72.8 percent in 1900 to 45.3 in 1930 to 31.6 in 1940, where it leveled off. At the same time, properties owned by realty corporations went from 0.4 percent in 1900 to 25.2 in 1930 to 33.3 in 1940. In terms of the assessed value of the parcels, individual owners controlled 60.9 percent of the sample value in 1900, 35.0 percent in 1930, and 21.6 percent in 1940. In contrast, realty corporations controlled 2.1 percent of the sample value in 1900, 25.2 percent in 1930, and 33.3 percent in 1940. While some of the transfer from family to corporate ownership was only nominal as individuals simply incorporated their businesses, the shift, as Grebler has noted, represented a significant change in organizational structure that was driven by the increased need for financial resources and professional expertise during the Depression. Grebler also suggests that fear of foreclosure and focused efforts to limit landlord liability drove individuals to transfer their properties to realty corporations.[36] Some observers noted this dramatic shift as early as 1932, when George Edgecombe stated in the *Real Estate Magazine*,

> The Metropolis has witnessed many industrial depressions and financial panics but it is extremely doubtful whether it ever faced a crisis when over-production, inflation and business stagnation conspired with such alarming proportions to create competition in the renting of all classifications of improved property.... Out of it has already evolved a trend toward a more scientific method of planning and a return to management, operation and renting that bids fair to outclass anything of its kind ever been known. In other words, scientific management, operation and renting, such as has been developed so surprisingly by the leading agency firms since 1910, unmistakably will see an era of greater and more profitable possibilities beyond the dark abyss of the present depression.[37]

GNYTA's leaders fought to limit the free fall in rentals and with its help landlords put off foreclosure proceedings. As part of their effort to encourage the rejuvenation of old tenement districts, GNYTA's leadership actively engaged in promoting development projects in the Lower East Side. Berger and Reich hoped that new subway lines, bridges, and grand commercial and residential projects would revitalize the neighborhood and salvage the investments of local property owners. The most notable example of this strategy was the organization's involvement in the ill-fated Chrystie-Forsyth Project in the early 1930s. Mayor Jimmy Walker and housing reformer August Hechscher originally proposed a bold new housing project on a strip of seven blocks between Chrystie and Forsyth Streets, one block east of the Bowery. The city was to acquire the property and sell the parcels at cost to private interests. GNYTA leaders promoted the city administration's plan and, with Mayor Walker's approval, Berger and other GNYTA officials contacted the landlords and realtors whose property was affected and facilitated the property transfer to the city.[38] This project, unfortunately, became bogged down in corruption and bureaucratic wrangling. Rather than becoming a modern housing development, Parks Commissioner Robert Moses and the new Mayor Fiorello LaGuardia converted most of the plot into Sara Delano Roosevelt Park in 1934.[39]

The distress brought by the Depression further eroded relations between the large real estate groups in the city, as organizations like REBNY began stressing professionalization and rationalization of business practices per se as a solution to property owners' economic woes. REBNY officials began pressing for legal barriers to the so-called "concession evil" and pushed for standardized leases.[40] REBNY leaders increasingly vilified "shoestring" operators, often claiming that their practices were a discredit to the entire business. As a result, they began looking for methods to limit their ability to do business. One building manager noted in 1932 that, "building managers at this time are training the white light of science on their problems in order to reduce the element of pure speculation which has attended considerable real estate development and building investment in the past."[41] Rather than fully embracing these changes, GNYTA leaders, for the most part, continued to rely on old approaches to address the new crisis in foreclosures and collections. There was very little innovation, consolidation, or reorientation of organizational goals and methods to reinvigorate landlord activism in light of deteriorating economic conditions during the Depression.

III. The Return of Tenant Agitation

To complicate matters further for New York's financially strapped landlords, tenants in Harlem, the Lower East Side, and elsewhere began organizing rent strikes and public demonstrations. As the Depression worsened, unemployment in New York City skyrocketed over 30 percent. By 1932, of 29,000 manufacturing firms in the city, more than 10,000 had closed. Approximately 1.6 million city residents received some form of public relief.[42] These conditions left many low-income families unable to pay any rent. Not surprisingly, many landlords immediately instituted dispossess proceedings against nonpaying tenants. Following usual landlord pre-Depression practice, many of these actions were simply bargaining maneuvers to pressure tenants to pay or, at least, to negotiate. Reports from city departments revealed that landlords did not dispossess tenants until they were between two and five months in arrears; in fact, landlords dropped the vast majority of dispossess proceedings.[43] Many tenants offered their labor in exchange for rent, while some landlords lowered their rents to what the tenants could afford. Tenants also went to their local political clubs, synagogues, and churches to get donations for a month's rent, or to get local leaders to appeal to landlords for leniency. Facing eviction notices, many thousands of tenants also simply moved into smaller apartments or became lodgers. In more extreme instances, they joined the growing army of the homeless.[44]

Many tenants, however, had no place to go and refused to move into the streets. Faced with intransigent landlords, these tenants began to organize rent strikes and large demonstrations to pressure property owners and city officials to offer some relief.[45] The agitation began from disparate (yet still connected) sources in Harlem and in the Lower East Side often associated with the Harlem Tenants League and New York's Communist Party. Even though the Harlem Tenants League had declined by 1933, a number of individual groups remained active throughout the Depression in fighting racial discrimination and segregation. In 1934, these groups united into the Consolidated Tenants League. The League focused on the legal defense of tenants in dispossess cases and on lobbying for new legislation. By the late 1930s, the organization claimed 8,000 dues-paying members, a permanent group of attorneys, and a professional staff.[46]

Agitation quickly spread to the Lower East Side, Brownsville, the South

Bronx and Hell's Kitchen. New York's Communist Party, initially small and focused largely among Eastern European Jews in the Lower East Side and other self-contained neighborhoods, gradually expanded its membership, particularly in Harlem's black community. As other Socialist leaders and more centrist tenant groups explored traditional solutions to the evictions, Communist leaders exploited their experience with collective struggle and expressed greater willingness to act outside the law to make their demands public.[47]

Communist leaders developed two strategies for pressuring landlords: eviction resistance and rent strikes. Eviction resistance proved particularly effective because it involved only a small number of actual participants and did not require the political sympathy of the victim. In cases where courts ordered a tenant's eviction and marshals placed the tenant's furniture in the street, activists simply moved the belongings back into the apartment and appealed to neighbors not to allow marshals or police to repeat the process again. Many non-Communist groups that opposed evictions adopted this strategy. In 1932, the *New York Times* estimated that eviction resistance had succeeded in restoring 77,000 evicted families to their apartments.[48] Since landlords had to pay for each eviction and marshals and police were already overextended, these tactics often led to negotiated settlements and significant delays in tenant displacement.[49]

Besides rent strikes and eviction resistance, tenant activists pressured City Hall and the State legislature to develop protective measures for tenants facing eviction. To a small degree, they were successful. For example, Mayor Jimmy Walker declared that the Mayor's Committee on Unemployment had to approve all evictions before he would authorize marshals to act. This measure strongly resembled similar measures created by Chairman Hilly for the MCRP on Rent Profiteering in the early 1920s.[50]

GNYTA officials had clearly turned away from their confrontational policies of the early 1920s. There is no evidence that GNYTA leaders embraced violent tactics in their attempts to undermine Communist tenant agitation in the early 1930s. However, the organization remained at the forefront in legally challenging the Communists' eviction resistance. These challenges, though, usually took the form of actions on behalf of individual, member landlords. While GNYTA leaders occasionally engaged in broad court actions to challenge legislation (as in the case of the municipal rent laws), specific episodes of eviction resistance, rent withholding, and foreclosure dominated GNYTA's day-to-day affairs. For example, in November 1931, the landlord of the building at 529 East 135th Street, a GNYTA member, brought dispossess proceedings against a tenant for nonpayment of rent. In January 1932, a marshal evicted the tenant. As the eviction took place, a crowd of about 150 gathered. Once the marshal departed, two tenant organizers reentered the apartment and, with the crowd's assistance, restored the tenant's belongings. The police arrested the two leaders. In this case, as with many others, GNYTA attorneys handled both the dispossess proceedings against the tenant and the prosecutions against the tenant leaders. Ultimately, the courts evicted the tenants and sentenced the two leaders to thirty days in the workhouse. However, given the tensions of the times, the landlords' victory was short-lived. When the tenant was again evicted, a crowd gathered to move him back in. The police arrived and in the ensuing melee, a fire broke out which gutted the apartment, destroying both the landlord's and the tenant's property.

GNYTA's legal measures did not stem the tide of rising tenant activism. For New York's landlords, tried and accepted methods employed in the early 1920s lost their effectiveness in the widespread suffering of the 1930s. Many older landlord groups, like GNYTA, simply pursued policies and strategies that differed little from the programs of other real estate groups. They believed, for the most part, that tenement landlords would weather this crisis, and that landlord-tenant relations would eventually return to a rather idealized and mythic past when property owners had broad controls over their tenements.

These strategies did not work, however, because of two fundamental changes in New York's political context. First, New York's local and state elected officials initiated a wide range of new housing proposals, including the development of public housing, which dramatically transformed the debate over low-income housing, high rents, and landlord-tenant relations. Second, even as landlord groups fell back on traditional policies, tenant groups demonstrated a level of sophistication they had lacked in the 1920s. Their sophistication was primarily an outgrowth of experience gained during the 1920s, especially the new tensions between tenant activists and traditional, policy-oriented housing reformers. As described in chapter 6, centrist, largely middle-class tenant groups had developed by the late 1920s. These groups tried to establish relationships with New York's traditional housing leaders in City Hall and in the state legislature. Groups like the Tremont and Melrose Tenants League grew accustomed to deferring to leaders like Clarence Stein of the State Housing Board, Langdon Post of the Tenement House Department, and August Hechscher, who had spearheaded numerous campaigns on behalf of poor tenants.[51] Until the Depression, Tenants' dependence on the good will and political fortitude of established housing reformers limited their ability to challenge fundamental elements of the landlord-tenant relationship. Centrist (and even many Socialist) tenant leaders cherished their limited political contacts and could not bring themselves to break those ties.

The Knickerbocker Village rent strike of 1934 fundamentally changed this relationship. The Fred F. French real estate interests had organized this large, limited-dividend project under the Reconstruction Finance Corporation, and housing officials hailed it as a model of public-private cooperation for the purpose of "uplifting" whole urban neighborhoods. French's company built it in the heart of the Lower East Side between Cherry, Catherine, Monroe, and Market Streets. Knickerbocker Village contained 1,593 small apartments with modern amenities, including self-service elevators, playgrounds, and parks. Previous experiments with limited-dividend developments such as the Dunbar Apartments in Harlem, as well as the Thomas Garden Apartments, and the Academy Housing Project, both in the Bronx, generated significant enthusiasm for limited-dividend, large-scale housing projects.[52] Constructed in blighted neighborhoods, these projects seemed to circumvent the numerous obstacles to change that had dogged reformers since the time of Jacob Riis.

Limited-dividend housing advocates failed to note the rising tenant militancy in similar model housing projects. In the city and in the suburbs, the Depression forced many model tenement managers to make service cuts and bring dispossess proceedings against tenants. However, tenants, in turn, mobilized and forced managers to make concessions. The City and Suburban Homes Corporation had to make concessions and engage in "rent bargaining" for the first time. At the Homewood Cottages, another group of model tenements in Brooklyn, managers granted leases in exchange for rent payers' agreement not to call for repairs. In the Scholem Aleichem cooperative in the Bronx, Jewish radicals staged a rent strike that caught national attention.[53]

Ironically, tenant selection, one of the key elements of Knickerbocker Village's programs, proved their undoing. The Village's managers, like previous philanthropic ventures, hand-picked the tenants from the surrounding community, and articulate, middle-class and upper-working class Jewish white-collar and professional workers dominated the tenantry. While initially enthusiastic about the new project, when the tenants moved in, the freight elevators did not work, the parquet floors were unfinished, and Village managers treated tenants' concerns with contempt. A group of tenants organized the Knickerbocker Village Tenants Association (KVTA). The KVTA's protest committee developed into a landlord's nightmare; it included seventeen journalists and forty-five lawyers. The committee quickly gathered promises from 300 families to withhold their rent. Once more, as in the heat crisis of 1918, middle-class tenants became centrally involved in the tenant movement.

The Fred French real estate group offered some concessions but for the next two years it tried to drive out the tenant leaders. The KVTA, led by outspoken editor Heinz Norden, appealed to the State Board of Housing, the government body responsible for overseeing limited-dividend projects. Tenant leaders argued that such semi-public projects had a "social responsibility beyond that of the private landlord." They even appealed to the Reconstruction Finance Corporation. In taking these actions, tenant activists not only had greater access to a more sympathetic media than did the 1920s agitators who faced the Red Scare, they also ignored traditional, paternalistic, housing reformers and appealed directly to state and eventually federal authorities. As Joel Schwartz has argued, reform-minded managers and traditional housing officials continued to view model tenements as way stations to better private housing for worthy tenants. Most traditional reformers failed to see that, as projects became bigger and contained more amenities, they offered tenants new avenues for political activism.[54]

Rather than trying to create one massive, dues-paying, city-wide tenants league (as the Socialists had tried in the early 1920s), the KVTA leadership eventually established a confederated alliance between tenants groups, labor organizations, social welfare groups, and left-wing grassroots organizations like the Communist Party. In 1936, KVTA called together the Consolidated Tenants League, the Lower East Side Public Housing Conference (a group of settlement house workers, mothers' clubs and several organizations not explicitly devoted to tenant needs formed in 1935), and other neighborhood groups from the Lower East Side and Chelsea to form the City-Wide Tenants Council (CWTC), a unified collective bargaining organization that soon represented more than 25,000 tenants.[55]

The CWTC developed new mobilization strategies to augment traditional protest strategies. Organizers focused on fund-raising, public relations, educational programs, and legal and legislative strategies. The Tenants' Council also deemphasized its reliance upon membership dues and relied more upon autonomous, self-governing, community-based tenant groups and left-wing organizations. It did not simply wait for interested tenants to come to its door, but actively promoted the development of tenant groups in slum districts. The CWTC distinguished itself from earlier efforts to mobilize tenants by establishing close ties with the Works Progress Administration's Workers Alliance, the Lawyers Guild (which organized a volunteer staff of more than 100 lawyers to defend tenants), and many prominent figures in New York's social work community. Council activists also made contacts with well-known housing liberals such as Nathan Strauss, thus establishing themselves as important policy players in New York housing circles. Heinz Norden and other activists, for example, were appointed to the Citizen's Housing Council. During the 1930s, the CWTC also formed ties with the Housing Section of the Welfare Council, the Housing Committee of the United Neighborhood Homes, and the Charity Organization Society. By the late 1930s, even officials from the paternalistic New York City Housing Authority felt it necessary to deal with the CWTC and other tenant groups.[56]

Initially, many landlord leaders saw this growing tenant involvement in municipal housing policy as of little consequence and even as a form of poetic justice for housing "do-gooders." Model tenements had existed for decades; whatever new elements the limited dividend and public housing projects might contain posed little apparent threat to private tenement owners. In fact, the increased level of housing condemnation actually provided an economic opportunity for landlords who were desperate to unload unprofitable properties. To the extent that limited-dividend projects depended upon tax-exempt bonds, REBNY officials had long viewed them as a waste of public expenditures.[57] Others observed that the experience of limited dividend managers provided clear testimony that philanthropists should leave low-income housing to private, professional interests. Further involvement by the government, they argued, led inevitably to higher taxes and further undercutting of the private tenement market.[58]

However, GNYTA's leaders and other landlord organizers soon had to confront the real threat from these new tenant confederations. As their influence grew, these tenant groups did not limit their actions, programs, and lobbying activities to government housing, and they quickly focused on the low-end, tenement housing market. Once tenant activists became policy players backed by large numbers of voting tenants, landlord groups in New York's older tenement districts found that their old strategies for disrupting rent strikes, influencing policy, and assisting landlords lost a great deal of its effectiveness. While GNYTA and other groups remained important because of the services they offered individual landlords, their organizational structure remained somewhat static, their memberships no longer increased, and they failed to attract the new, big players in tenement ownership—the realtors and property managers who gravitated toward larger, more elite associations like REBNY.

Why were such landlord groups as GNYTA and UREO so ineffective in blocking this resurgent tenant movement? Stated simply, old-style tenement landlords, GNYTA's members, were being wiped out financially. GNYTA's leaders, along with most other landlord activists, were trying to keep their members from losing their properties. For many landlords, their attempts to pressure desperate tenants into paying rents (the same pressure that drove the tenants into the arms of the CWTC) represented a last-ditch attempt to hold onto their assets. In the city's poorest tenement districts, tenement landlords were facing financial ruin at an unprecedented rate. In the sample of 218 tenement properties discussed in chapter 2, banks and other lenders were taking these properties at a devastating pace. By 1937, lenders had foreclosed on almost twenty percent of these properties. Moreover, between 1929 and 1937, in only two cases did the lender subsequently sell the property to another purchaser by 1937. In most cases the lenders simply held onto the properties, sometimes for seven or eight years. The small-scale landlords, those most effected by these actions, were the core of GNYTA's membership, and their financial loses not only preoccupied GNYTA leaders but ultimately translated into a permanent loss of political influence for the Association.

Due to the Depression's debilitating impact on New York real estate more generally, UREO and REBNY also saw their influence wane during the 1930s. UREO almost collapsed as a viable lobby during the 1930s as, apparently, its member organizations began abandoning the UREO confederation. Moreover, Stewart Browne, the Association's President for more than twenty years, died in 1938. REBNY was able to weather the Depression but, like GNYTA, many of its members were distracted by their own financial woes, a fact showcased by the suicide in 1933 of a former REBNY President.[59]

IV: Tenant Politics and the Emergence of Permanent Rent Controls

Middle-class power now came to bear on landlord-tenant reform. Over the course of the Depression, new tenant confederations like the CWTC developed an array of effective strategies and organizational structures that remained intact (with minor modifications) for several decades thereafter. They employed expert legal representation for tenants and individual buildings, often backed by picketing and rent withholding. New tenant groups also became aggressive advocates for tenant interests and formed strong ties with liberal and left-wing organizations, as well as entrenched middle-class groups in the city's many ethnic communities. In 1937, for example, the Tenant's Council built upon its ties with unemployed organizations, trade unions, and settlement house workers by adding ten tenant groups from across the city. Tenant activists also became astute and respected commentators on New York's housing issues. They conducted several well-researched studies that gave them an intellectual edge over many real estate groups. The CWTC, for example, developed ties with the left-wing Federation of Architects, Engineers, Chemists, and Technicians to conduct housing research in the late 1930s. In combination, these various tactics allowed tenants to introduce legislation that reflected the "tenant's interest."[60] The strength of this approach is visible in the continued vitality of tenant organizations in New York to the present day. Even as racial and ethnic constituencies have changed, the basic strategies and alliances have remained largely the same.

The increased political strength of New York's tenant groups during the Depression was evident in a succession of breakthroughs that began in the late 1930s with the Minkoff Bill, and carried into the war period with the enactment of federal rent control in 1943. In this time period, Council organizers and their allies pushed through an impressive array of legal measures beneficial to tenants. Tenant leaders helped enact the Minkoff Bill of 1939, which prohibited rent increases in old-law tenements where landlords had not complied with the Multiple Dwellings Law. They also pressured the Emergency Relief Bureau to alter its policies in order to protect tenants displaced during the upgrading of tenements. Finally, in concert with organized labor, tenant groups pressured the Office of Price Administration to impose wartime rent controls in New York City.[61]

In dealing with city housing authorities, the CWTC also began influencing the placement and tenant-selection process for New York City housing projects. Once developers completed these projects, the Tenants' Council organized tenant associations in many of the larger complexes, including the Williamsburg, Queensbridge, and Vladeck Houses. In addition, the activities of the CWTC and other tenants groups forced many managers of public housing (and many housing reformers in general) to adopt a more professional approach and to diminish traditional paternalism. The campaigns of tenant groups also contributed significantly to the expansion of public housing in the postwar years.[62]

Several established real estate groups remained vital actors in creating New York's housing policies, none more so than REBNY. For many years, REBNY officials had maintained policies that paralleled those of the Tenants' Council. Not only did they lobby in Albany and at City Hall, but they also sponsored "spin-off" real estate groups and mobilized specific groups in various communities such as realtors, builders, or retailers. Through the 1930s and early 1940s, real estate leaders still exercised a critical influence over housing policy and the city budget in New York City. Former REBNY President Peter Grimm, for example, became Chairman of the Citizen's Budget Commission in 1929 and a real estate adviser to the Municipal Housing Authority in 1933. Along with other REBNY officials, Grimm also went on to become a policymaker in Washington.[63] With the numerous state and city positions held by REBNY officials, real estate interests remained entrenched in the processes of housing policymaking and implementation. Landlord groups still retained many of the strengths that had sustained them through previous eras of tenant agitation. Real Estate organizations were usually self-contained and self-supporting. Members usually came from a distinct social and political group with ethnic and class loyalties that only changed, if at all, over a long period of time. At the same time, their organizational structures allowed for a degree of long-term continuity in leadership and basic policy that tenant groups could not match. Tenant organizers, as Mark Naison has pointed out, relied on coalitions with other interest groups and with housing policymakers that often proved fragile.[64] While the basic strategies charted by the CWTC were quite successful, tenant organizations themselves experienced a good deal of flux in their membership, leadership, and ethnic and class constituencies over time.

New organizations also emerged to address the new situations faced by New York's tenement owners, especially those in expanding areas of the city like Queens. For example, the Metropolitan Fair Rent Committee (MFRC) was created in 1943 in direct response to the imposition of wartime rent controls. The MFRC was a joint venture by the city's real estate boards which they established to help owners with substantial holdings in pre-1947 apartment buildings.[65] While MFRC's officers initially came from REBNY, the organization eventually established an independent identity.[66] As tenement districts declined and as tenant influence grew during the Depression era, and as federal and state involvement in housing greatly expanded during the postwar era, old-fashioned tenement landlords and their associations became politically marginalized.

Conclusion

For New York's most marginal landlords—the part-timers, the passive investors, and those who relied the most upon neglect and undercapitalization to succeed—strong political organizations failed to counter resurgent tenant activism in the 1930s and early 1940s. In 1900, housing and landlord-tenant regulations barely affected these operators. By 1943, however, the dramatic extension of landlord-tenant restrictions, housing reforms, tenant activism, and the emergence of public housing and rent control hit the marginal landlords the hardest.

In reviewing tenant and landlord activism during the Depression, two issues are especially noteworthy. First, the Depression caused widespread suffering for both property owners and rent payers. And yet, the 1930s were clearly a catalytic period for tenant organizations, whereas most of the landlord groups established in the preceding decades declined. Moreover, their responses to the crisis failed to elicit much response from individual tenement landlords. The political and social context had changed for tenants in two significant ways. Once more, large numbers of influential, middle-class rent payers briefly experienced standard landlord practices in housing projects like Knickerbocker Village. Organizers effectively exploited the property managers' actions to push for reform.

More importantly, the broad, public suffering of New Yorkers caused by the Depression, combined with increased government involvement driven by the New Deal, transformed public willingness not only to experiment with public housing but also to allow tenants unprecedented influence in the development of housing and landlord-tenant policy. In contrast, many landlord leaders failed to adjust to this larger political shift. They still relied primarily on strategies that they had developed in the 1910s and earlier, most of which were informed by traditional concepts of government nonintervention in the private housing market. While these organizations remained important political lobbies, it would take the imposition of federal rent control in 1943 to jolt New York's landlords into proactive innovations in lobbying and mobilization, and to create new real estate groups and revitalize established associations such as REBNY.

The Depression, to some extent, sealed the fate of small-scale landlords and lessees. Legal changes, housing reforms, and higher costs for maintenance and insurance decimated this traditional class of businessmen. Between the 1890s and the 1920s, these landlords still managed to make a profit through neglect, overcrowding, and undercapitalization. With the growing intervention of the state and the increasing activism of tenants, these strategies began to break down.  Even after the repeal of the emergency rent laws, the late 1920s and early 1930s saw market changes in tenement ownership that placed small-scale landlords and lessees in an increasingly untenable situation. The permanent provisions of the rent laws, combined with changes in city ordinances, rising liability rates, fee schedules, and controls on marshals, greatly increased the cost of doing business for tenement landlords. Despite the more favorable rental market of the late 1920s, small-scale landlords had the most difficulty in shouldering these new costs. Smaller owners and especially lessees found it much harder to make profits using the traditional methods of passive investors—undercapitalization, overcrowding, and neglect. In areas like the Lower East Side, the small, ethnic entrepreneurs and even former tenants with small amounts of capital began to give way to lawyers, larger business people, contractors, and lenders. Landlords, realtors, and owners with a long-term professional outlook began replacing the small-scale, overextended part-time landlords and lessees. This important shift reflected the growing exclusion from rental property ownership of tenement landlords and lessees with exceedingly limited means and who were trying, through high-risk strategies, to pull themselves up and out of working-class ethnic communities (both economically and culturally). In the decades following the Depression, professional property managers would come to dominate tenement management in New York.

The growing dominance of professional property managers and real estate firms created troubling ambiguities for promoters who viewed real estate as the way out of the working class. For decades, tenement ownership had provided one of the few avenues out of the slums for ambitious ethnic immigrants, especially Jewish entrepreneurs from the Lower East Side. However, for lessees and small-scale landlords, this advancement came at a high cost in social standing. At times, they endured political and ethnic isolation and estrangement from neighbors. The emergence of professional property managers greatly limited ethnic access to this old avenue of economic advancement (although not entirely). In many ways, the history of tenement owning in New York City in the early twentieth century showcases cruel paradoxes such as these for ethnic property owners. Not only were relatively poor ethnic entrepreneurs pushed out of the market, but also evidence suggests that a large number of the new professionals who did the pushing were, in fact, drawn from the ranks of the amateurs of the previous generation. Having obtained higher economic status, many of these tenement owners, it seems, now turned to burn the bridge behind them.

CONCLUSION

The Tenant City

By most accounts, New York City's experiment with rent control began in 1943 when the Roosevelt Administration imposed rent regulations as a wartime emergency measure. Following the war, when most other cities put these controls aside, New York gradually institutionalized rent control's regulating structures and, for the next fifty years, passed the responsibilities for the program's administration back and forth between city and state agencies.[1]

Despite widespread criticism, the program has remained a permanent feature of the city's rental housing market through the 1990s.[2] Rent control's longevity in New York City stems in large part from the fertile seedbed in which it grew. The foundations for rent control were laid much earlier, during the tortured struggles between and among the city's landlords and tenants in the first four decades of the century. Between 1900 and 1943, the political, social, and ideological landscape for tenement operators had shifted in two critical ways, each of which contributed to the development and strength of this program. First, tenement landlords saw their authority to directly control their properties, influence their tenants, and discipline tenant activists greatly reduced. Within the larger history of corporate advocacy, New York's landlord associations in the early twentieth century stood on the fault lines between legal and legitimate lobbying practices such as those employed by REBNY on the one side and extra-legal, club-wielding, anti-labor intimidation practiced by the Brownsville Landlord's League on the other. Operating as it did in this gray area, GNYTA's experience foreshadowed the transition that many landlord groups would have to make in the 1930s.

Landlord advocates did not have to face this transition alone, however. Leaders from business organizations spanning the corporate spectrum routinely confronted similar choices as Progressive and New Deal reformers, Socialist activists and others challenged fundamental business practices in the first four decades of the twentieth century. Companies, both large and small, looked to their own local and national trade associations to quiet the protests of workers and consumers. For many of these organizations, like GNYTA, intimidation and occasional violence were standard tools. For these groups, adaptation and change became imperative following the passage of the Wagner Act in 1935, which gave workers some protections from corporate intimidation and terrorism. While tenant groups have remained the special bane of landlords and real estate associations, the links of GNYTA and similar organizations to anti-labor, union-busting groups should not be obscured. Indeed, through the twentieth century, such groups have often skirted the edge of legal and illegal behavior for the sake of their corporate clients. However, for most of these corporate advocates, their stories remain to be told.

The landlords' loss of authority emerges in large measure from a more fundamental change in landlord-tenant relations. In many ways, there was a political revolution among New York's consumers of rental housing. In 1900, well over 90 percent of Manhattan's population lived in rented apartments. By all demographic measures, New York was a city of tenants. While the quality of their accommodations differed widely, middle- and working-class tenants shared many fundamental experiences as tenants. Until the late 1910s, however, ethnic and class antagonisms had persuaded most middle-class New Yorkers that apartment dwelling was inherently different from tenement dwelling. Surrounded by modern amenities and the surface trappings of the private single-family home, middle-class apartment dwellers showed little sympathy for the tenant activists of 1904 and 1907–1908. Centered in the most squalid, overcrowded, and ethnically diverse areas of New York, these early uprisings came from the working class; they reflected the specific needs of the city's poorest renting families; and, for the most part, they stayed by, of, and for the working class. In general, middle-class New Yorkers looked on passively and let the landlords' traditional methods quickly stifle these modest protests.

This passivity disappeared during the housing shortage of the late 1910s and early 1920s. Beginning with the heat crisis of 1918, middle-class tenants became painfully aware of their status as tenants, and landlord-tenant reform gradually became part of the middle-class reform agenda. Despite significant successes early on by working-class tenant organizers, by the early 1920s, middle-class reformers had recast legal reform to suit their more conservative tastes, while middle-class tenant organizers had largely taken over the city's major tenant groups, either driving out their Socialist or working-class counterparts or watching as these individuals became victims of the Red Scare. Modest increases in wealth experienced by many residents in the Lower East Side and other working-class ethnic enclaves furthered middle-class co-option of the tenant agenda. In essence, the city's burgeoning middle class finally realized politically what they were demographically (and what they had been for many decades): they were tenants. Moreover, they were tenants in a city of tenants. This political realization led to the transformation of landlord-tenant laws in the 1920s, while it *permanently* altered landlord-tenant relations in the city. From the 1930s onward, tenant-based organizations exercised significant political influence—influence that came from the broadest economic and social spectrum. The housing shortage of the late 1910s helped mobilize a broad cross section of the city's tenant population, and since then, despite some periods of relative inaction, New York's tenant population has never fully "demobilized."

NOTES

Introduction

1. See, for example, Marc Weiss, *The Rise of the Community Builders: The American Real Estate Industry and Urban Land Planning* (New York: Columbia University Press, 1987); Sam Bass Warner, *Streetcar Suburbs: The Process of Growth in Boston, 1870–1900* (New York: Athenaeum, 1974); Gwendolyn Wright, *Building the Dream: A Social History of Housing in America* (New York: Pantheon, 1981); Michael Doucet and John Weaver, "The North American Shelter Business, 1860–1920: A Study of a Canadian Real Estate and Property Management Agency," *Business History Review* 58 (Summer 1984), pp. 234–262; Richard Plunz, *A History of Housing in New York City* (New York: Columbia University Press, 1990). For an excellent examination of the field of real estate history, see Marc Weiss, "Real Estate History: An Overview and Research Agenda," *Business History Review* 63 (Summer 1989), pp. 241–282.
2. See, for example, Thomas Kessner, *The Golden Door: Italian and Jewish Immigrant Mobility in New York City, 1880–1915* (New York: Oxford University Press, 1977); Matthew Edel, Elliot D. Sclar, and Daniel Luria, *Shaky Palaces: Homeownership and Social Mobility in Boston's Suburbanization* (New York: Columbia University Press, 1984); John E. Bodnar, Roger Simon, and Michael P. Weber, *Lives of Their Own: Blacks, Italians, and Poles in Pittsburgh, 1900–1960* (Urbana, IL: University of Illinois Press, 1982).
3. Donna Gabaccia "Little Italy's Decline; Immigrant Renters and Investors in a Changing City," in *The Landscape of Modernity*, ed. David Ward and Olivier Zunz (New York: Russell Sage Foundation, 1992), pp. 244–247.

1. The Growth of Tenement Districts in the Tenement Owners' City

1. New York State Tenement House Committee [NYSTHC], *Report* (1894), p. 540.
2. Milton Meltzer, *Taking Root: Jewish Immigrants in America* (New York: Farrar, Staus and Giroux, 1976), pp. 65–66.
3. Record and Guide, *A History of Real Estate Building and Architecture in New York City During the Last Quarter of a Century* (New York: Record and Guide, 1898), pp. 2–3; Isaac N. P. Stokes, *Iconography of Manhattan Island, 1498–1909* (New York: Robert H. Dodd, 1915) 1:16.
4. Michael Kammen, *Colonial New York: A History* (New York: Oxford University Press, 1975), p. 30.
5. Kammen, *Colonial New York*, p. 34.
6. Stokes, *Iconography*, 6: 6–13; Dingman Versteeg, *Manhattan in 1628*, p. 645. Landed patroons created a leasing system modeled after the Dutch land-owning patterns (although penalties for lease-breaking were more severe). Landowners also charged high rates, and nonpayment led to prompt eviction. This led to very tense relations between the tenants and the landowners, and the Hudson Valley experienced almost continuous until the Revolution. See Daniel M. Friedenberg, *Life, Liberty and the Pursuit of Land: The Plunder of Early America* (Buffalo, NY: Prometheus Books, 1992), p. 54; Sung Bok Kim, *Landlord and Tenant in Colonial New York: Manorial Society, 1664–1775* (Chapel Hill, NC: University of North Carolina Press, 1978), pp. 44–86, 281–415; Allan David Heskin, *Tenants and the American Dream: Ideology and the Tenant Movement* (New York: Praeger, 1983), pp. 3–15.
7. Elizabeth Blackmar, *Manhattan for Rent, 1785–1850* (Ithaca: Cornell University Press, 1989), pp. 15–16, 21.
8. Blackmar, *Manhattan for Rent*, p. 21; See also Kim, *Landlord and Tenant*, p. 138.
9. Blackmar, *Manhattan for Rent*, p. 25.
10. Kamman, *Colonial New York*, pp. 36–37.
11. Kammen, *Colonial New York*, p. 71; Freidenberg, *Life, Liberty and the Pursuit of Land*, p. 54.
12. Isaac Stokes, "Original Grants and Farms," *Iconography*, 6: 10–11, 78–79, 91–92, 141–143, cited from Blackmar, *Manhattan for Rent*, pp. 18–19, 283.
13. Kammen, *Colonial New York*, p. 279.
14. Ibid., p. 292
15. Blackmar, *Manhattan for Rent*, p. 28.
16. Ibid., pp. 26–27; Kim, *Landlord and Tenant*, p. 139.
17. Blackmar, *Manhattan for Rent*, p. 42.
18. Ibid., pp. 30, 37, 40; *Document of the Assembly of the State of New York*, Eighteenth Session (1857) 205: 1–3.

19. Sidney I. Pomeranz, *New York: An American City, 1783–1803, A Study of Urban Life* (Port Washington, NY: Ira J. Friedman, 1938), p. 180. See also John Denis Haeger, *John Jacob Astor, Business and Finance in the Early Republic* (Detroit: Wayne State University Press, 1991), pp. 244–279; Eugene Rachlis and John E. Marqusee, *The Landlords* (New York: Random House, 1963), pp. 3–30.
20. Sean Wilentz, *Chants Democratic: New York City and the Rise of the American Working Class, 1788–1850* (New York: Oxford University Press, 1984), pp. 107–8. See also Christine Stansell, *City of Women: Sex and Class in New York, 1789–1860* (New York: Knopf, 1986), pp. 120–129.
21. Pomeranz, *New York: An American City*, p. 196; Wilentz, *Chants Democratic*, pp. 107–117.
22. Edward Lubitz, "The Tenement Problem in New York City and the Movement for Its Reform, 1856–1867" (Ph.D. diss., New York University, 1970), p. 84.
23. Robert Ernst, *Immigrant Life in New York City, 1825–1863* (New York: Columbia University Press, 1949), pp. 41–43, 49; Pernicone, "Bloody Ould Sixth," p. 35.
24. Wilentz, *Chants Democratic*, pp. 132–133.
25. Blackmar, *Manhattan for Rent*, p. 188.
26. Document of the Assembly of the State of New York, Eighteenth Session (1857) 205: 18–19.
27. Ibid., pp. 1–13.
28. Philip Hone, *The Diary of Philip Hone* (New York: Dodd, Mead, 1927) 1: 245–246; 2: 896–897, 900.
29. Wilentz, *Chants Democratic*, p. 132.
30. Carol Groneman Pernicone, "'The Bloody Ould Sixth,' A Social Analysis of a New York City Working-Class Community in the Mid-Nineteenth Century" (Ph.D. diss., University of Rochester, 1973), p. 35. Groneman computed these figures from the New York State Census of 1865, doc. no. 13: 230–231, 241.
31. Citizens Association of New York, *Report of the Council of Hygiene and Public Health Upon the Sanitary Condition of the City* (New York: D. Appleton, 1866), p. 7.
32. "Report of the Select Committee Appointed to Examine into the Condition of Tenant Houses in New York and Brooklyn," in *Assembly Documents* 3 (205) (1857), p. 23, cited from Lubitz, "Tenement Problem," p. 76.
33. New York City, City Inspectors Department, *Annual Report* (1834), p. 16.
34. Select Committee Appointed to Examine Into the Condition of Tenant Houses in New York and Brooklyn, *Report* (1856), p. 23; Anthony Jackson, *A Place Called Home: A History of Low Cost Housing in Manhattan* (Cambridge: MIT Press, 1976), p. 17.
35. Blackmar, *Manhattan for Rent*, p. 217.

36. Thomas M. Quinn and Earl Phillips, "The Legal History of Landlord-Tenant Relations," in *Tenants and the Urban Housing Crisis*, ed. Stephen Burghardt (Dexter, MI: The New Press, 1972), pp. 91–93..
37. Tova Indritz, "The Tenants' Rights Movement," (MA Thesis, University of Pittsburgh, 1970), pp. 57–59.
38. Quinn and Phillips, "Legal History," pp. 92–95.
39. William P. McLoughlin, "Evictions in New York's Tenement Houses," *The Arena*, 7 (1893), p. 56.
40. Arlene K. Newman, "Ethnicity and Business Enterprise: A Study of the Jewish Mutual Insurance Companies of New York" (New York: City University of New York, Ph.D. diss., 1983), p. 49.
41. C.A. Kulp, *Casualty Insurance* (New York: Ronald Press 1928), p. 29, cited from Newman p. 50.
42. Robert H. Bremner, "The Big Flat: History of a New York Tenement House" *American Historical Review* 64 (1958–59), pp. 54–62; Richard Plunz, *A History of Housing in New York City* (New York: Columbia University Press, 1990), pp. 6–9; Jackson, *A Place Called Home*, pp. 12–17, 60.
43. Elizabeth Collins Cromely, *Home Alone: A History of New York's Early Apartments* (Ithaca: Cornell University Press, 1990), pp. 20–25. See also Lubitz, "Tenement Problem," 461–462.
44. Roy Lubove, "The New York Association for Improving the Condition of the Poor: The Formative Years" *New York Historical Society Quarterly* 43 (1959), p. 317.
45. John W. Cramer, "The Story of a Tenement House" *Frank Leslie's Sunday Magazine* 5 (6) (June 1879), p. 641. See also Samuel B. Halliday, *The Lost and Found; or Life Among the Poor* (New York: Blackman & Mason, 1859); Solon Robinson, *Hot Corn: Life Scenes in New York Illustrated* (New York: DeWitt and Davenport, 1854).
46. Lubitz, "Tenement Problem," pp. 313–349. See also Charles Rosenberg, *The Cholera Years: The United States in 1832, 1849, and 1866* (Chicago: University of Chicago Press, 1962).
47. Jackson, *A Place Called Home*, p. 32; Plunz, *History of Housing*, p. 22.
48. Plunz, *History of Housing*, p. 24.
49. "Report of the Committee," *Plumbing and Sanitary Engineer* 2 (March 1879), p. 90.
50. Jackson, *A Place Called Home*, p. 62.
51. Lubove, *Progressives and the Slums* (Pittsburgh: Univeristy of Pittsburgh Press), 1963, pp. 31, 97
52. Board of Health, *Annual Report* (1896), pp. 38–39, cited from Lubove, *Progressives and the Slums*, p. 93.
53. Lubove, *Progressives and the Slums*, pp. 27, 94.

54. Lubitz, "Tenement Problem," pp. 203, 208–210, 305–9.
55. Lubove, *Progressives and the Slums*, p. 3.
56. "The Tenement House Investigation," *New York Sun*, March 15, 1856.
57. Association for Improving the Conditions of the Poor, *Fourteenth Annual Report* (1857), pp. 37–38.

2. Tenement Ownership and Ethnic Enterprise in New York City

1. Concerning the methodology of this study, only those individuals with first and last names that were clearly Jewish were counted. Names which might or might not be Jewish, such as Hoffman, were counted as non-Jewish.
2. Leo Grebler, *Housing Market Behavior in a Declining Area* (New York: Columbia University Press, 1952), p. 96–101.
3. George Cohen, *The Jews in the Making of America* (Boston: Stratford Co., 1924), pp. 127–128.
4. Donna Gabaccia "Little Italy's Decline; Immigrant Renters and Investors in a Changing City," in *The Landscape of Modernity*, ed. David Ward and Olivier Zunz (New York: Russell Sage Foundation, 1992), p. 238
5. Jacob Rader Marcus, *United States Jewry, 1776–1985* (Detroit: Wayne State University Press, 1993) 3: 261–262.
6. Neil M. Cowan and Ruth Schwartz Cowan, *Our Parents' Lives: The Americanization of Eastern European Jews* (New York: Basic Books, 1989), p. 229.
7. Shelly Tenenbaum, *A Credit to Their Community: Jewish Loan Societies in the United States* (Detroit: Wayne State University Press, 1993), pp. 42–43.
8. Evan Clark, *Financing the Consumer* (New York: Harper, 1930), p. 5.
9. Tenenbaum, *A Credit*, pp. 38–39.
10. Thomas Kessner, *The Golden Door: Italian and Jewish Immigrant Mobility in New York City, 1880–1915* (New York: Oxford University Press, 1977), p. 64.
11. The reasons for this are not entirely clear. Little is known of the specific investment strategies of nineteenth-century institutional lenders. However, sources suggest that organizers of building and loan associations (also termed savings and loan associations) went through a period of intense real estate speculation after the passage of an act permitting their incorporation in 1851. These abuses severely tainted building and loans as proper lending institutions and forced legislators to pass strict restrictions on them. See Seymour Dexter, *A Treatise on Co-operative Savings and Loan Associations* (New York: D. Appleton, 1889), p. 53.
12. See, for example, Stephen G. Mostov, "Dun and Bradsteet Reports as a Source of Jewish Economic History: Cincinnati, 1840–1875," *American Jewish History* 72 (3) (March 1983), pp. 348–353.
13. Lawrence Veiller, "The Speculative Building of Tenement House," in *The*

Tenement House Problem, ed. Robert W. DeForest and Lawrence Veiller (New York: Macmillan, 1903) 1: 367–382. See also "Many Big Tenement Houses Built with Little Capital," *New York Times*, September 13, 1903. Historians face a complex problem of terminology when they look back at this era in the city's development. I have chosen to use the terms loan operator, builder, purchaser, and lessee. It should be noted, however, that contemporaries simply did not have commonly accepted terms for what these people did. Tenement owners were often called "landlords," or "property owners," while the loan operator was also called the "property owner." The term "lessee" might refer to the tenement owner, depending on the terms of his agreement, or it could refer to the person the owner leases the building to or the person the lessee sublets the building to. Thus, researchers should be cautious about taking these terms at face value when nineteenth-century landlords use them as self identifiers.

14. "Many Big Tenement Houses Built with Little Capital," *New York Times*, September 13, 1903.
15. Grebler, *Housing Market Behavior*, pp. 96–101; Joseph Platzker, "Who Owns the Lower East Side?" *East Side Chamber News* (July 1929), pp. 9–10.
16. Grebler, *Housing Market Behavior*, pp. 96–101; "Many Big Tenement Houses Built with Little Capital," *New York Times*, September 13, 1903.
17. Many Big Tenement Houses Built with Little Capital," *New York Times*, September 13, 1903.
18. Their relative obscurity is reflected in the historical sources where only two major studies have examined these ethnic capitalists. They are *Reports of the Immigration Commission: Immigrant Banks* [hereafter referred to as ICIB] 61st Congress, 3rd Session, 1911, Vol. 37, Senate Doc. 753; and *Report of the Commission of Immigration of the State of New York* [hereafter referred to as CISNY] Albany, NY: 1909. While these reports provide essential details of how immigrant banks worked and established their link with local real estate investment, they only begin to suggest the true scale of their operations and the larger economic importance of these institutions to local economic development.
19. *ICIB*, p. 212; Frederick M. Binder and David Reimers, *All the Nations Under Heaven: An Ethnic and Racial History of New York City* (New York: Columbia University Press, 1995), p. 156.
20. *ICIB*, pp. 212, 234.
21. *CISNY*, pp. 28–29, 38–41.
22. Ibid., pp. 39–40.
23. *ICIB*, p. 212.
24. Louis N. Robinson and Rolf Nugent, *Regulation of the Small Loan Business*

(New York: Russell Sage Foundation, 1935), p. 47, cited from Shelly Tenenbaum, "Immigrants and Capital: Jewish Loan Societies in the United States, 1880–1940," (Ph.D. diss., Brandeis University, 1986), p. 52.

25. John M. Glenn, Lilian Brandt and F. Emerson Andrews, *Russell Sage Foundation, 1907–1946* (New York: Russell Sage Foundation, 1947), p. 10, cited from Tenenbaum, "Immigrants and Capital," p. 54.
26. Ibid., pp. 210, 221.
27. *ICIB*, pp. 242–243.
28. *CISNY*, p. 30.
29. *ICIB*, p. 237.
30. Ibid., pp. 246, 249–251. Many bankers made considerably less. In a study of immigrant bank failures in New York conducted in 1907–1908, state officials noted that bankers' assets ranged from $200 to $400 at the lowest levels and went up to $151,397 with a majority controlling less than $6,000. See *CISNY*, pp. 27, 193.
31. *ICIB*, p. 207.
32. *CISNY*, p. 26.
33. *ICIB*, p. 244.
34. Rolf Nugent, Louis Robinson, and Evan Clark have conducted some of the few studies of unlicensed lenders. Unfortunately, their works, all done in the 1930s, reflect a strong bias toward credit unions, their promoters, and the Russell Sage Foundation in particular. Historians have largely ignored these capitalists and their role in local economic development.
35. Vincent P. Carosso, "A Financial Elite: New York's German-Jewish Investment Bankers," *American Jewish Historical Quarterly* 66 (1) (September 1976), pp. 74–75.
36. Clark, *Financing the Consumer*, p. 32.
37. Elizabeth Blackmar, *Manhattan for Rent* (Ithaca: Cornell University Press, 1989), pp. 185–187; Veiller, "Speculative Building," p. 370.
38. Jeffrey S. Gurrock, *When Harlem was Jewish, 1870–1930* (New York: Columbia University Press, 1979), p. 46.
39. Elgin R.L. Gould, "Financial Aspects of Recent Tenement House Operations in New York," in *The Tenement House Problem*, eds. Robert W. De Forest and Lawrence Veiller (New York: Macmillan, 1903) 1: 357–358.
40. Clarence Stein, "Housing Crisis," *The Survey* (September 1, 1920) p. 661.
41. "Many Big Tenement Houses Built with Little Capital," *New York Times*, September 13, 1903.
42. Gabaccia, "Little Italy's Decline," p. 238.
43. Veiller, "Speculative Building," pp. 370–373.
44. Arthur E. McFarlane, "The Inflammable Tenement," *McClure's Magazine*

(October 1911), pp. 694–695. See also Veiller, "Speculative Building," p. 375; *History of Architecture and the Building Trades of Greater New York* (New York: Union History Company, 1899) 2: 311–313.

45. "The Tribune's Account of the Tenement-House Inquiry," *Charities* 5 (29) (December 15, 1900), pp. 3–7. In 1900, Commissioner Brady sent 10,454 complaints of violations to department attorneys, but withdrew 8,042 before the cases came to trial. City officials and builders rarely considered the comfort and safety of the tenants or the long-term financial consequences for the ultimate buyer.

46. Luc Sante, *Low Life: Lures and Snares of Old New York* (New York: Vintage Books, 1991), p. 32; Philip Hone, *The Diary of Philip Hone* (New York: Dodd, Mead, 1927) 1: 245–246; 2: 896–897, 900.

47. Veiller, "Speculative Building," p. 372.

48. Charles H. Israels, "A Cure for Speculative Building," *Charities* 17 (1906–7), p. 347. See also Veiller, "Speculative Building," p. 371. These practices persisted through the early twentieth century. See, for example, Ignatz Reich, "Mortgage Moratorium," *Real Estate News* (August 1933), p. 266; Ignatz Reich, "The Quarter Annual Report," *Real Estate News* (October 1929), p. 10; E.T. Van Houten, "Likens Unorganized Landlords to Inert Cattle Awaiting Slaughter," *Real Estate News* (August 1933), p. 278.

49. See Gabaccia, "Little Italy's Decline," p. 245.

50. Hugo Rotheschild, *How to Invest and Protect Your Profits in Real Estate Syndicates*, ed. David Berman (New York: Doubleday, 1964), p. 6. See also Daniel Berman, *How to Reap Profits in Local Real Estate Syndicates* (Englewood Cliffs, NJ: Prentice-Hall, 1964), p. 2.

51. Leo Grebler, *Housing Market Behavior*, pp. 96–101. Grebler classified most of the large ground-leasing property owners, such as the Astors and Trinity Church, in the category of "estates" which accounted for 9.2 percent of the ownership in the Lower East Side, a figure that corresponded approximately with the figure (ten percent) in Platzker's study of the Lower East Side real estate owners in 1929. See Joseph Platzker, "Who Owns the Lower East Side?" *East Side Chamber News* (July 1929), pp. 9–10.

52. Jeffrey S. Gurrock, *When Harlem was Jewish, 1870–1930* (New York: Columbia University Press, 1979), p. 46.

53. Louis Winnick, "Long-Run Changes in the Valuation of Real Estate by Gross Rents," *The Appraisal Journal* 20 (October 1952), pp. 486–487, 496. See also Veiller, "Speculative Building," pp. 360–361; and Reginald P. Bolton, *Building for Profit: Principles Governing the Economic Improvement of Real Estate* (New York: Devinne Press, 1911), pp. 41–44.

54. Veiller, "Speculative Building," p. 373.

55. G. Richard Davis, "Importance of Proper Management," *Real Estate Record and Builders Guide* (January 18, 1913), p. 122.
56. "Free Rent in the Bronx," *New York Times*, July 29, 1900. See also "Bronx Flat Owners Unite,"*New York Times*, July 31, 1900; "To Abolish Free Rents," *New York Times*, August 7, 1900; "Real Estate Men at Odds," *New York Times*, August 12, 1900. Indeed, the problem did persist for tenement purchasers. See, for example, "The Free Rent or Concession Evil," *Real Estate News* (April 1933), p. 131.
57. "Free Rent in the Bronx," *New York Times*, July 29, 1900. See also "Bronx Flat Owners Unite,"*New York Times*, July 31, 1900; "To Abolish Free Rents," *New York Times*, August 7, 1900; "Real Estate Men at Odds," *New York Times*, August 12, 1900; Isidor Berger, "The Housing Emergency—Is it Fact or Fancy?" *Real Estate News* (October 1924), pp. 5.
58. Veiller, "Speculative Building," p. 374.
59. "The Real Estate Field," *New York Times*, December 9, 1894; Isidor Berger, "The Public and the Landlord," *Real Estate News* (August 1930), p. 270.
60. Ignatz Reich, "The Stability of the Tenement," *Real Estate News* (December 1921), p. 6.
61. Gabaccia, "Little Italy's Decline" p. 239.
62. Ibid.
63. I have chosen not to use "agent" in describing building lease holders, even though contemporaries often used the term, because professional property managers were beginning to emerge at this time, and they also called themselves "agents" on occasion. These professional agents usually managed more upscale property while the lessees referred to here managed exclusively tenement property and displayed very few "professional" attributes.
64. Irving Howe, *World of Our Fathers* (New York: Harcourt Brace, 1976), p. 164.
65. Blaustein, "Cockroach Landlords," 379–382. The lessee's reputation for poor tenement management dated back to the early nineteenth century. See, for example, John Griscom, *The Sanitary Conditions of the Laboring Population of New York* (New York: Harper, 1845), pp. 6–7; Edward Lubitz, "The Tenement Problem in New York City and the Movement for Its Reform, 1856–1867" (Ph.D. diss., New York University, 1970), pp. 128–137.
66. Richard Plunz , *A History of Housing in New York City* (New York: Columbia University Press), pp. 50-51; John Griscom, *The Sanitary Conditions of the Laboring Population of New York*, (New York: Harper and Brothers, 1845).
67. See, for example, Mary Sherman, "Manufacturing of Foods in the Tenements" *Charities and Commons* 15 (1906), pp. 669–673; and Elizabeth Fee and Steven H. Corey, *Garbage! The History and Politics of Trash in New York City* (New York: New York Public Library, 1994), pp. 13–20.

68. Gabaccia, "Little Italy's Decline," p. 240.
69. Hill, "Rental Agitation," p. 396. See also Blaustein, "Cockroach Landlords," p. 381.
70. Agnes Daley, "Life in a Tenement House," *Charities* 5 (28) (December 8, 1900), p. 2. This attitude among lessees went back to the early nineteenth century. See, for example, Griscom, *Sanitary Condition*, p. 6; Select Committee Appointed to Examine into the Condition of Tenement Houses in New York and Brooklyn, *Report* (Albany, NY: 1857), p. 29; and *New York Tribune*, March 29, 1856, cited from Lubitz, "The Tenement Problem," pp. 130–131.
71. William Mailly, "The New York Rent Strike" *Independent* 14 (3085) (January 16, 1908), pp. 152–153; Archibald A. Hill, "The Rental Agitation on the East Side," *Charities and Commons* (1904), p. 397.
72. Letter, Isadore Montifiore Levy to Governor Alfred Smith, April 21, 1919, Al Smith Papers, Box 260–46. State Archives, New York State Library, Albany.
73. According to a reporter for *Harper's Weekly*, during the rent strikes of 1907–8, most of the hardest hit landlords were "leasters." They were also the quickest to capitulate. See Victor Rousseau, "Low Rent or No Rent: The Tenement Dwellers' Rebellion in New York," *Harper's Weekly* (January 25, 1908), p. 17. See also Blaustein, "Cockroach Landlords," pp. 383–384.
74. Blackmar, *Manhattan for Rent*, pp. 30–32
75. NYSTHC, *Report* (1894), pp. 538–541.
76. "Death of S.V.R. Cruger," *New York Times*, June 24, 1898; "Col. Cruger's Funeral," *New York Times*, June 25, 1898.
77. NYSTHC, *Report* (1894), pp. 538–541.
78. "The Real Estate Field," *New York Times*, December 23, 1894.
79. NYSTHC, *Report* (1894), p. 538. Newspaper cites.
80. Blackmar, *Manhattan for Rent*, pp. 30–31.
81. NYSTHC, *Report* (1894), pp. 389–394.
82. Thomas M. Quinn and Earl Phillips, "The Legal History of the Landlord-Tenant Relations," from *Tenants and the Urban Housing Crisis*, ed. Stephen Burghardt (Dexter, MI: The New Press, 1972), pp. 89–108.
83. G. Richard Davis, "Importance of Proper Management," *Real Estate Record and Builders Guide* (January 18, 1913), p. 122.

3. Landlord Activism in the Early Twentieth Century

1. "Report of the Committee on the Incorporation of Cities and Villages, on the Bill Entitled 'An Act Concerning the Public Health of the Counties of New York, Kings, and Richmond, and the Waters Thereof'" in *Assembly Documents* (1861), Eighty-fourth Session, No. 59, p. 4; John H. Griscom,

Sanitary Legislation, Past and Future: The Value of Sanitary Reform and the Time Principles for Its Attainment (New York: Edmund Jones, 1862), p. 31, cited from Edward Lubitz, "The Tenement Problem in New York City and the Movement for Its Reform, 1856–1867" (Ph.D. diss., New York University, 1970), pp. 209, 306–7.

2. "Tenement Housing," *New York Sun*, April 13, 1870.
3. John W. Cramer, "The Story of a Tenement House," *Frank Leslie's Sunday Magazine* 5 (6) (June 1879), p. 642.
4. This simple examination used the Property Assessments for New York City, 1837 to 1853, to determine ownership and cross-referenced this list of owners with lists of city employees and elected officials in D. T. Valentine (compiler), *Manual of the Corporation of the City of New York* New York: 1837–1853 for approximately the same years. If anything, this analysis understates the actual number of property owners with political ties.
5. "The Tenement House Act" *New York Times*, May 25, 1879: 6. See also Richard Plunz, *A History of Housing in New York City* (New York: Columbia University Press, 1990), p. 27.
6. "Real Estate Owners' Association" *Real Estate Record and Builders Guide* (February 2, 1901), p. 181.
7. Arlene K. Newman, "Ethnicity and Business Enterprise: A Study of the Jewish Mutual Insurance Companies of New York" (Ph.D. diss., City University of New York, 1983), p. 67.
8. John I. Gilderbloom and Richard P. Applebaum, *Rethinking Rental Housing* (Philadelphia: Temple University Press, 1988), p. 84.
9. Michael A. Stegman, *Housing Investment in the Inner City: The Dynamics of Decline* (Cambridge: MIT Press, 1972), pp. 29–30.
10. Gilderbloom and Applebaum, *Rethinking*, pp. 86–87.
11. It should be clearly understood that the definitions used by these scholars and many others involve a much broader set of features than I have used here. Moreover, the basic separation between "amateurs" and "professionals" in the late twentieth century cuts between professional property managers, on the one hand, and people who own modest rental properties and run them part time, on the other. This separation is less relevant for the late nineteenth century when the field of property management did not exist and most landlords had little, if any, real estate experience. Moreover, given how little time and resources standing tenements required in the late nineteenth century, the range in the number of properties held by individual landlords is a much more problematic indicator of when owners must concentrate full time on their holdings. In many ways, this study lays the historical foundation for the development of the modern rental housing business which is the focus of these contemporary, empirical studies.

12. "Extent of the Real Estate Association" *Real Estate Record and Builders Guide* (February 9, 1901), p. 228; "Real Estate Owners' Association" *Real Estate Record and Builders Guide* (February 2, 1901), p. 181; "Wanted: A 'Napoleon' of Organization" *Real Estate Record and Builders Guide* (February 16, 1901), p. 280.
13. "Extent of the Real Estate Association" *Real Estate Record and Builders Guide* (February 9, 1901), p. 228.
14. "Building Code Attacked," *New York Times*, September 23, 1899.
15. "Building Code Attacked," *New York Time*, September 23, 1899.
16. "Hon. William J. Fryer," *Real Estate Record and Builders Guide* (June 8, 1907), p. 1109.
17. "Hon. William J. Fryer," *Real Estate Record and Builders Guide* (June 8, 1907), p. 1109; Death List of a Day: William J. Fryer," *New York Times*, June 5, 1907.
18. "The New Building Code," *Real Estate Record and Builders Guide* (September 9, 1899), p. 365.
19. "The Draft Building Code," *Real Estate Record and Builders Guide* (September 16, 1899), p. 399; "The Commission on Building Code," *Real Estate Record and Builders Guide* (March 11, 1899), p. 416–417.
20. "Building Code is Adopted," *New York Times*, September 13, 1899; "Building Code Attacked," *New York Times*, September 23, 1899; "Building Code Argument," *New York Times*, September 24, 1899.
21. "Building Code," *Real Estate Record and Builders Guide* (September 9, 1899), pp. 365–366.
22. "Building Code is Adopted," *New York Times*, September 13, 1899.
23. "The Draft Building Code," *Real Estate Record and Builders Guide* (September 16, 1899), p. 399.
24. "Building Code Signed," *New York Times*, October 26, 1899.
25. The Tenement House Committee had as members many of the biggest names in New York housing reform, including Felix Adler, member of the Tenement House Commission of 1884; Richard Watson Gilder; and well-known architects George B. Post; Ernest Flagg; and I.N. Phelps Stokes. See Roy Lubove, *The Progressives and the Slums: Tenement House Reform in New York City, 1890–1917* (Westport, CT: Greenwood Press, 1962), pp. 119–120.
26. "The Tenement House Commission," *Charities* 4 (20) (April 14, 1900), pp. 1–2; "A Tenement House Exhibition," *Charities Review* 9 (5) (July 1899), pp. 196–197; Lubove, *Progressives*, pp. 124–125; Anthony Jackson, *A Place Called Home: A History of Low-Cost Housing in Manhattan* (Cambridge: The MIT Press, 1976), pp. 117–118.
27. "The Tenement House Commission," *Charities* 4 (20) (April 14, 1900), pp. 1–2; "The Tenement House Commission," *Charities* 4 (21) (April 21, 1900); 1–5; Lubove, *Progressives*, p. 135; "Tenement Bills Signed," *New York Evening*

Post, April 11, 1901; "Tenement Bill Hearing," *New York Times*, April 11, 1901; "Plan to Change Tenement Code," *New York Herald*, April 10, 1901.

28. "The Tenement in Politics," *Charities* 5 (29) (October 12, 1901), p. 310; Charles Buek, "Opposed to the Building Law,"*Charities* 5 (29) (October 12, 1901), pp. 310–311; Jackson, *A Place Called Home*, pp. 123–125.
29. Lewis E. Palmer, "The Day's Work of a 'New Law' Tenement Inspector," *Charities and the Commons* (October 6, 1906), p. 80.
30. "The Appointment of Tenement House Commissioner," *Charities* 5 (29) (December 15, 1901), pp. 532–535; "Administration of the Tenement-House Law," *Charities* 9 (24) (December 13, 1902), pp. 606–616.
31. Richard Plunz and Janet Abu-Lughod, "The Tenement as a Built Form," in *From Urban Village to East Village: The Battle for New York's Lower East Side* ed. Janet L. Abu-Lughod (Cambridge, MA: Blackwell, 1994), p. 71.
32. "Free Renting," *Real Estate Record and Builders Guide* (September 25, 1900), p. 235.
33. "Extent of Real Estate Association," *Real Estate Record and Builders Guide* (February 9, 1901), p. 228.
34. "Real Estate Owners' Association," *Real Estate Record and Builders Guide* (February 2, 1901), p. 181. See also "Extent of Real Estate Association," *Real Estate Record and Builders Guide* (February 9, 1901), pp. 228–229; "Wanted: A 'Napoleon' of Real Estate," *Real Estate Record and Builders Guide* (February 16, 1901), pp. 280–281; "The United Property Owners' Association," *Real Estate Record and Builders Guide* (February 23, 1901), pp. 318–319.
35. "Real Estate Owners' Association," *Real Estate Record and Builders Guide* (February 2, 1901), p. 181. The original organizations that made up UREO's membership were the Tenth, Eleventh, and Seventeenth Ward Taxpayers' Association, the Twelfth and Nineteenth Ward Taxpayers Association, the West Side Taxpayers Association, the Twelfth and Twenty-Second Ward Real Estate Owners Protective Association, the West End Association, the Twenty-third Ward Property Owners Association and the Property Owners Union and Builders League. See "Extent of the Real Estate Association," *Real Estate Record and Builders Guide* (February 9, 1901), p. 228.
36. "What the United Does Free of Charge for Its Members," *The Citizen* (December 1924), p. 7.
37. "Opposition to the Tenement Law," *Charities* 7 (5) (August 3, 1901), p. 96; "Tenement Law Violently Attacked," *New York Times*, September 13, 1901; "Object to Changes in Building Laws," *New York Times*, October 12, 1901; "Will Fight to Repeal Tenement House Law," *New York Times*, October 13, 1901; "To Alter Old Tenement Houses," *New York Times*, October 20, 1901; "Opposition to the Tenement-House Law," *Charities* 7 (22) (November 30, 1901), pp. 459–461, 464–465.

38. "New Tenement Law," *Real Estate Record and Builders Guide* (June 29, 1901), p. 1136; "To Defeat the Tenement House Law," *Real Estate Record and Builders Guide* (September 7, 1901), p. 286; "Property Owners Protest," *Real Estate Record and Builders Guide* (September 14, 1901), pp. 315–316; "New Tenement Law," *Charities* 7 (12) (September 21, 1901), p. 239; "Ante-New Law Tenements," *Real Estate Record and Builders Guide* (October 5, 1901), pp. 403–4; "Ante-New Law Tenements," *Real Estate Record and Builders Guide* (October 26, 1901), pp. 530–532; "Ante-New Law Tenements," *Real Estate Record and Builders Guide* (November 9, 1901), pp. 611–612.
39. "Real Estate Owners Association," *Real Estate Record and Builders Guide* (February 2, 1901), p. 187.
40. "A Real Estate Curb Market," *The Menorah* 41 (3) (September 1906), pp. 117–118.
41. Grebler, *Housing Market Decline*, pp. 65–66, 79–80.
42. Gilderbloom and Applebaum, *Rethinking*, pp. 84–85. See also Stegman, *Housing Decline*, pp. 29–30; Roger Krohn, Fleming Berkeley, and Marilyn Manzer, *The Other Economy: The Internal Logic of Local Rental Housing*. Toronto: Peter Martin Associates, 1977.
43. Paula Hyman, "Immigrant Women and Consumer Protest: the New York City Kosher Meat Boycott of 1902," *American Jewish History* 70 (1) (September 1980), pp. 91–105. Jenna Joselit places this boycott within the larger context of tenant unrest that emerged in 1904. See Jenna Joselit "The Landlord as Czar: Pre-World War I Tenement Activity," in *The Tenement Movement in New York City, 1904–1984*, ed. Ronald Lawson with Mark Naison (New Brunswick, NJ: Rutgers University Press, 1986), pp. 41–42
44. "May Evict a Thousand," *New York Tribune*, April 5, 1904; "High Rents on East Side," *New York Tribune*, April 6, 1904; "Rack-Renting Landlords Fear Empty Houses," *The World*, April 7, 1904; "Evictions for 1,000 Families on Passover," *New York American*, April 5, 1904; "Bertha Liebson Tells How Landlords Grind and How Tenants Struggle," *The World*, April 17, 1904. For the lessee's role in precipitating the crisis, see Blaustein, "Cockroach Landlords," 379–382. For an overview of early 1900s tenant organization, their structure and ideological predecessors, see Joselit, "The Landlord as Czar," 39–50.
45. "Rents Fight to Courts," *New York Tribune*, April 8, 1904; "Organized Delay to Stop Rent Extortion," *The World*, April 8, 1904.
46. "Bertha Liebson . . . Tells How Landlords Grind and How Tenants Struggle," *The World*, April 17, 1904; "Justices Agree to Delay Fight of Landlords," *New York American*, April 11, 1904.
47. "Try to Mob a Landlord," *New York Tribune*, April 9, 1904; "To Evict Miss Liebson," *New York Tribune*, April 12, 1904; "Girl Leader in East Side Rent

Riot," *The World*, April 12, 1904; "Police Check Riot in East Side Hall,"*The World*, April 13, 1904.
48. "Mayor Says 'No' to Rent Parade," *The World*, April 10, 1904.
49. "High Rents on the East Side," *New York Tribune*, April 6, 1904.
50. "Police Check Riot in East Side Hall," *The World*, April 13, 1904; " 'Joan of Arc' of East Side Evicted," *The World*, April 15, 1904.
51. "Black Friday's Terror on East Side Over," *New York American*, April 9, 1904; "Justices Agree to Delay Fight of Landlord," *New York American*, April 11, 1904; Joselit, "Landlord as Czar," 43–44.
52. "Present Supply of Apartments," *New York Times*, November 10, 1907.
53. "Landlords Strike Back at Tenants," *New York Herald*, December 27, 1907.
54. "To Starve Out Landlords," *New York Times*, December 26, 1907.
55. "New Joan of Arc Leads Rent Strike," *New York Times*, December 27, 1907.
56. "Police Break Up Rent War Meeting," *New York Times*, December 29, 1907. The first of each month was a critical time for month-to month tenants who had to renew their leases.
57. "Rent Strike Spreads on the East Side," *New York Times*, December 28, 1907.
58. "Fire Threat by Tenants," *The Globe and Commercial Advertiser*, January 7, 1908.
59. "Rent Strike Spreads on the East Side," *New York Times*, December 28, 1907.
60. "30,000 Crusade to Cut Rents," *The Globe and Commercial Advertiser*, December 26, 1907; "Evictions Begin; 800 Landlords to Fight 70,000 Tenants," *New York Evening Journal*, December 27, 1907.
61. William Mailly, "The New York Rent Strike" *Independent* 14 no. 3085 (January 16, 1908), p. 152.
62. "Denounce Police in Lower Rent War," *New York Times*, December 30, 1907.
63. "Police Smash Heads in Rent Strike," *New York Evening Journal*, January 6, 1908; "100 Evicted in Big Rent Strike," *New York Evening Journal*, January 10, 1908.
64. "Tenants Declare Rent War Victory," *New York Herald*, December 28, 1907.
65. "Tenants Declare Rent War Victory," *New York Herald*, December 28, 1907.
66. "Landlords Organize the Rent War," *New York Times*, January 3, 1908; "History of the Greater New York Taxpayers Association," *Real Estate News* (February 1924), pp. 24–25.
67. "Landlords Pledge Cash to Organize Against Strike," *New York American*, January 4, 1908, "Plan a Black List of Rent Strikers," *New York Press*, January 5, 1908.
68. "Landlords Pledge Cash to Organize Against Strike," *New York American*, January 4, 1908; "Plan a Black List of Rent Strikers," *New York Press*, January 5, 1908.
69. "Rent Strike Crisis at Hand for 6,000," *New York Times*, January 8, 1908.

70. "Many Landlords Yield in Rent War," *New York Times*, January 5, 1908.
71. "Hundreds of Rent Strikers Facing Eviction To-Day," *New York American*, January 8, 1908; "Many East Side Landlords and Rent Strikers Settle Trouble," *New York Tribune*, January 9, 1908; "Rent Strikers are Paying Up," *The Globe and Commercial Advertiser*, January 9, 1908; Mailly, "New York Rent Strike," pp. 151–152.
72. "Both Sides See End to Rent War," *New York Times*, January 9, 1908.
73. "Rent Strikers Fight the Police," *New York Times*, January 6, 1908; "Rent Strike Crisis at Hand for 6,000," *New York Times*, January 8, 1908; Victor Rousseau, "Low Rent or No Rent: The Tenement Dwellers' Rebellion in New York," *Harper's Weekly* (January 25, 1908), p. 17.
74. "History of the Greater New York Taxpayers Association," *Real Estate News* (February 1924), p. 24.
75. "In Memoriam - Ignatz Reich," *Real Estate News* (June 1941), pp. 196–197; "Ignatz Reich, Head of Taxpayers' Group," *New York Times*, June 9, 1941.
76. Newman, "Ethnicity and Business Enterprise . . .," pp. 107–108; Isidor Berger, "The Governing Committees of the Greater New York Taxpayers Association," *Real Estate News* (February 1924), p. 23; "Report and Opening Remarks by President Reich at the Last General Meeting of the Greater New York Taxpayers Association, Sept. 27th, 1928," *Real Estate News* (October 1928), p. 21; "Vote for Isidor Berger for Councilman," *Real Estate News* (September 1937), p. 302; "Isidor Berger," *Real Estate News* (February 1924), p. 8; "Isidor Berger Elected Company President," *Real Estate News* (July 1941), pp. 228–230; Morris Kramer, "A Friend's Appraisal of Isidor Berger," *Real Estate News* (July 1941), pp. 238–239; "Isidor Berger, 85, Led Realty Groups," *New York Times*, April 19, 1954; "Isidor Berger Dead; Realty Field Expert," *New York Herald*, April 19, 1954.
77. For example, see "Report of the Committee to Albany on the 'Jesse Bill,'" *Real Estate News* (March 1920), p. 10; Commission on Housing and Regional Planning, *Report*, Leg. Doc. 43 (1924), p. 23; Senate and Assembly Committees on Cities, *Joint Hearing by the Senate and Assembly Committees on Cities*, March 23, 1920 (mimeograph) Al Smith Papers, File 260–46, pp. 121–127; Gertrude Male, "Throwing the Spotlight on our Officers at the Landlords Hearing Before the Housing Commission," *Real Estate News* (December 1925), p. 31.
78. "Report and Opening Remarks by President Reich at the Last General Meeting of the Greater New York Taxpayers Association, Sept. 27th, 1928," *Real Estate News* (October 1928), p. 21; "Vote for Isidor Berger for Councilman," *Real Estate News* (September 1937), p. 302; "Isidor Berger," *Real Estate News* (February 1924), p. 8; "Isidor Berger Elected Company President," *Real Estate News* (July 1941), pp. 228–230; Morris Kramer, "A Friend's Appraisal of Isidor

Berger," *Real Estate News* (July 1941), pp. 238–239; "Isidor Berger, 85, Led Realty Groups," *New York Times*, April 19, 1954; "Isidor Berger Dead; Realty Field Expert," *New York Herald*, April 19, 1954.

79. J. W. Burke, "Why is the Landlord Made the Goat?" *Real Estate News* (November 1924), pp. 22–23.
80. "Mrs. Stokes to Renters," *New York Tribune*, January 12, 1908.
81. J. J. Berger, "The League for the Protection of Property Rights," *Real Estate News* (April 1924), pp. 8–9. See also Ignatz Reich, "Report by President Reich," *Real Estate News* (June 1928), p. 9; "Second Test Case Hearing on Municipal Rent Law," *Real Estate News* (September 1929), p. 12.
82. Isidor Berger, "Housing Conditions Are Growing Better—Not Worse," *Real Estate News* (March 1925), p. 4.
83. Evers v. Davis, 86 *New Jersey Law Journal*, 90 Atl. 677 (1914), cited from Newman, "Ethnicity and Business Enterprise," pp. 52–53.
84. Newman, "Ethnicity and Business Enterprise," p. 100.
85. "Want Lower Insurance," *New York Times*, February 8, 1914; "The History of the Greater New York Taxpayers Association," *Real Estate News* (February 1924), p. 24–25; Ignatz Reich, "Greater New York Taxpayers Mutual Insurance Association Supersedes Unique Protective Organization," *Real Estate News* (September 1927), p. 11.
86. Simon Greenfield, "The Association and the Public," *Real Estate News* (December 1919), pp. 4–5.
87. Newman, "Ethnicity and Business Enterprise," pp. 106–107.
88. "Want Lower Insurance," *New York Times*, February 8, 1914.
89. Isidor Berger, "The Activities of the Protective and Defense Committee,"*Real Estate News* (May 1924), pp. 4–5; "Owners' Liability Rates due for Another Advance," *Real Estate News* (October 1924), pp. 8; "History of the Greater New York Taxpayers Association," *Real Estate News* (February 1924), p. 24.
90. Newman, "Ethnicity and Business Enterprise," pp. 107–108.
91. Newman, "Ethnicity and Business Enterprise," pp. 109–110.
92. Max Kahn, "The Two Fundamental Features of the Protective and Defense Committee Least Credited and Reasons Why," *Real Estate News* (January 1920), p. 8.
93. Elias Diamond, "Progress in Our Organization," *Real Estate News* (March 1922), p. 8. See also "The Dangers of the Wooden Stairway Remedied—Strong and Lasting Iron Plates to be Used," *Real Estate News* (March 1922), p. 37; "Stairway Accidents," *Real Estate News* (September 1927), p. 15. Other real estate organizations also tried to keep their members informed about the latest safety features to avoid liability cases. The Real Estate Board of New York, for example, promoted cast metal faucet handles over porcelain to avoid hand injuries when the porcelain broke.

94. Max Kahn, "We'll Get You Yet!" *Real Estate News* (December 1920), p. 19.
95. Simon Greenfield, "The Association and the Public," *Real Estate News* (December 1919), p. 5.
96. "Steps in the Growth of Our Membership," *Real Estate News* (February 1924), p. 23.
97. "History of the Greater New York Taxpayers Association," *Real Estate News* (February 1924), p. 25.
98. Max Kahn, "The Two Fundamental Features of the Protective and Defense Committee Least Credited and the Reasons Why," *Real Estate News* (January 1920), p. 8. It was a point of some mirth around the GNYTA offices how stymied tenants' attorneys were in making some claims stick. See Max Kahn, "We'll Get You Yet!" *Real Estate News* (December 1920), p. 19.
99. Newman, "Ethnicity and Business Enterprise," pp. 98–138.
100. Kahn, "The Two Fundamental Features of the Protective and Defense Committee," *Real Estate News* (January 1920), p. 8; "Reports of the P & D Committee Shelved," *Real Estate News* (March 1920), p. 11; "Buildings Registered with the Protective and Defense Committee, 1914–1923," *Real Estate News* (February 1924), p. 29.
101. Isidor Berger, "The Governing Committees of the Greater New York Taxpayers Association," *Real Estate News* (February 1924), p. 23. See also Ignatz Reich, "The Accomplishments of 1921," *Real Estate News* (February 1922), p. 8; Ignatz Reich, "Mortgage Moratorium," *Real Estate News* (August 1933), p. 266.
102. Ignatz Reich, "The Twentieth Anniversary of GNYTA," *Real Estate News* (January 1927), p. 8.
103. Ignatz Reich, "The Association and the Public," *Real Estate News* (August 1932), pp. 266–267. See also Ignatz Reich, "What the Greater New York Taxpayers Association Does for the Property Owner," *Real Estate News* (December 1928), pp. 11–12. Berger and other GNYTA members occasionally went on periodic campaigns to "educate the tenant" about the tax burden of landlords in the vain hope of mobilizing them against government waste and overtaxation. See, for example, Henry Goldschlag, "Educating the Tenant," *Real Estate News* (December 1921), p. 39.
104. The Allied Real Estate Interests Association followed UREO's organizational model. They became a confederation or an "association of associations." Rather than focusing on local taxpayers associations, however, the Allied became a confederation of mostly real estate boards, chambers of commerce, and so forth. Sources suggest that the Allied may have been largely a creature of the Real Estate Board of New York, however, its origins are somewhat obscure. See "New York Allied Property Owners Committee," *Real Estate News* (April 1928), pp. 327, 355–356.

105. See Gertrude Male, "Throwing the Spotlight on Our Officers at the Landlords Hearing Before the Housing Commission," *Real Estate News* (December 1925), p. 31.
106. J. J. Berger, "The League for the Protection of Property Rights," *Real Estate News* (June 1928), p. 9; "Second Test Case Hearing on Municipal Rent Law," *Real Estate News* (September 1929), p. 12. United action was important and yet often difficult to maintain. Each organization tended to have its own agenda in dealing with the city and the state, and often they were at cross purposes. See, for example, John Hylan Speech commending Mayor's Committee on Taxation and the Investigation of Mortgage Loans (1918), Hylan Papers, Box 22, Municipal Archives, New York City.
107. See Ignatz Reich, "Greater New York Taxpayers Mutual Insurance Association Supersedes Unique Protective Organization," *Real Estate News* (September 1927), p. 8.

4. Rent Strikes and the Landlord's "Reign of Terror"

1. Elizabeth Collins Cromley, *Alone Together: A History of New York's Early Apartments* (Ithaca: Cornell University Press, 1990), pp. 4, 11–31. See also Elizabeth Hawes, *New York, New York: How the Apartment House Transformed the Life in the City, 1869–1930* (New York: Henry Holt, 1993), pp. 35–52, 237–238.
2. Ibid.
3. "Government to Spend Millions in Building Here," *Real Estate Record and Builders' Guide* (April 20, 1918), p. 487.
4. Lauer and House, *The Tenant and His Landlord* (New York: Baker, Voorhis and Co., 1921), p. 17. See also "Cessation in Building Activity Causes Shortage of Rentable Space," *Real Estate Record and Builders Guide* (August 25, 1917), p. 231; "Shortage of Rentable Space in All Boroughs Found Through Survey Just Finished," *Real Estate Record and Builders Guide* (October 27, 1917), pp. 531–532.
5. Harold Platt provides a concise overview of this heat crisis, its causes and social impact in Chicago and to a lesser extent nationally in *The Electric City: Energy and the Growth of the Chicago Area, 1880–1930* (Chicago: University of Chicago Press, 1991), pp. 204–208.
6. "Coal Situation Grave; Suffering is Intense," *New York Herald*, February 6, 1918. See also "Duty of Every Citizen is to Conserve Coal," *Real Estate Record and Builders Guide* (October 27, 1917), p. 537.
7. "Coal Situation Grave; Suffering is Intense," *New York Herald*, February 6, 1918.
8. Housing Committee of the Reconstruction Commission of the State of New

York (abbreviated to RC), *Housing Conditions: Report of the Housing Committee of the Reconstruction Commission of the State of New York*, (March 26, 1920), p. 30; "Tenants Seek Heat in Court," *New York Call*, January 4, 1918; "Bronx Tenants Hold Protest at Cold Flats," *New York Call*, January 17, 1918.

9. "Thirty Dispossess Cases Grow Out of No Heat, No Rent Policy," *Bronx Home News* (West Harlem and Washington Heights Edition), January 9, 1918. See also "Irate Tenants Denounce Some Landlords for the Lack of Heat," *Bronx Home News*, January 2, 1918; "Tenants Win 'No Heat, No Rent' Cases; Court Order Reduction," *Bronx Home News*, January 13, 1918.
10. "Thirty Dispossess Cases Grow Out of No Heat, No Rent Policy," *Bronx Home News* (West Harlem and Washington Heights Edition), January 9, 1918.
11. "Bronx Women Organize New Tenants League," *New York Call*, January 20, 1918; "Women Unite to Fight Rent," *New York Call*, January 23, 1918; "Bronx Tenants Organize New Rent League," *New York Call*, January 25, 1918.
12. "Thirty Dispossess Cases Grow Out of No Heat, No Rent Policy," *Bronx Home News*, January 9, 1918.
13. "Forty-Nine Tenants Go on 'Rent Strike' Because of Lack of Heat," *Bronx Home News*, December 19, 1917.
14. "Tenants Win 'No Heat, No Rent' Cases; Court Order Reduction," *Bronx Home News* (West Harlem & Washington Heights Edition), January 13, 1918; "Bronx Tenants Win Heat Strike," *New York Call*, February 10, 1918; "Bronx Tenants Refuse to Pay Month's Rent," *New York Call*, February 15, 1918; "Court Upholds Bronx Tenants," *New York Call*, February 17, 1918.
15. "Assemblyman Introduces Bill for Fair Adjustment of Landlord vs. Tenant," *Bronx Home News*, February 10, 1918.
16. "Supreme Court Now Rules in Favor of Shivering Tenants," *Bronx Home News* (West Harlem & Washington Heights Edition), January 16, 1918.
17. "Heights Tenants Ask Legislature to Insure Heat," *New York Tribune*, March 12, 1918.
18. "Bronx Tenants Win Heat Strike," *New York Call*, February 10, 1918.
19. "Would Force Landlords to Give Heat," *New York Herald*, February 5, 1918.
20. "Court Upholds Bronx Tenants," *New York Call*, February 17, 1918; "Bronx Landlord Ousts Tenants Who Asked Heat," *New York Call*, February 22, 1918. At times, tenants' threats to organize were enough to draw concessions from landlords. For example, thirty tenants at 64 East 97th Street withheld rent for lack of heat and hot water. They threatened to form a tenants' league, and, to head this off, the lessee, an agent for Emordus Holding Company, offered to reduce the rent. The tenants rejected the offer, choosing instead to take their chances in the municipal courts with the assistance of legal counsel provided by the Socialist Party. Ultimately they settled for a fifteen percent reduction in rents for all tenants, not just those with written leases. "Bronx Tenants

Refuse to Pay Month's Rent," *New York Call*, February 15, 1918; "Landlord Tries Hard to Oust Tenants," *New York Call*, February 16, 1918.
21. "Heights Tenants Form League," *Bronx Home News*, February 17, 1918.
22. Ibid.; "Heights Tenants' League Organize and Elect Officers; To Hold Rally To-night," *Bronx Home News*, February 27, 1918.
23. "Bronx Tenants to Meet Tomorrow," *New York Call*, February 16, 1918; "Tenants Will Meet Tonight," *New York Call*, August 17, 1918; "Evicted Bownsville Tenants Win Strike," *New York Call*, August 20, 1918; "Tenants Excited by More Increases," *New York Call*, September 17, 1918.
24. "Ordinance is Introduced to Protect Monthly Rent Payers," *Bronx Home News*, January 23, 1918.
25. "Delegation Representing 10,000 Tenants Appeals to Mayor," *Bronx Home News*, February 3, 1918.
26. "Bronx Landlords to Define Their Position Through Publicity Campaign," *New York Times*, February 10, 1918; RC, *Report* (March 26, 1920), p. 30.
27. "Tenants to be Trained," *Real Estate Record and Builders Guide* (January 26, 1918), p. 106.
28. "Tenants to be Trained," *Real Estate Record and Builders Guide* (January 26, 1918), p. 106.
29. "Bronx Squires Issue Heat Ultimatum to the Tenantry," *New York Herald*, January 30, 1918.
30. "Bronx Landlords Plan Spring Drive on Non-Paying Tenants," *New York Herald*, January 28, 1918.
31. "Bronx Squires Issue Heat Ultimatum to the Tenantry," *New York Herald*, January 30, 1918.
32. "Bronx Landlord Ousts Tenants Who Asked Heat," *New York Call*, February 22, 1918.
33. JLC, *Report*, 1920, p.10. See also Edith Berger Drellich and Andree Emery, *Rent Control in War and Peace*. (New York: National Municipal League, 1939), p. 28.
34. RC, *Report*, March 23, 1920, pp. 6–8.
35. State Board of Housing, *Report*, Leg. Doc. 112 (1928), p. 29; "Propose Building as Rent Solution," *New York Times*, April 18, 1919.
36. "Propose Building as Rent Solution," *New York Times*, April 18, 1919.
37. "4,000 Brownsville Tenants Unanimously Vote to Strike Against Exorbitant Rents," *New York Call*, May 6, 1919.
38. "Outrages Rampant Against Tenants," *New York Call*, May 31, 1918.
39. "Brownsville Tenants Strike at Rent Raise," *New York Call*, April 26, 1918.
40. "Evicted Brownsville Rent Strikers Make Their Homes in the Streets," *New York Call*, May 22, 1918; "Landlords Try to Justify Rent Piracy as City's Anger Mounts," *New York Call*, April 20, 1919.

41. "Tenants and Landlords in Test of Power," *New York Call*, March 20, 1920.
42. "All Landlords Asked to Join Defense Union" *New York Call*, September 27, 1919.
43. "This Week Will Decide Big Rent Strike in Bklyn," *New York Call*, May 21, 1918.
44. "Outrages Rampant Against Tenants," *New York Call*, May 31, 1918.
45. "Brownsville Landlords Arrest Rent Strikers They Couldn't Conquer," *New York Call*, May 26, 1918; "Brownsville Rent Strikers in Police Court," *New York Call*, May 30, 1918; "Outrages Rampant Against Tenants," *New York Call*, May 31, 1918.
46. "Outrages Rampant Against Tenants," *New York Call*, May 31, 1918.
47. "Leader of Thugs held for Hearing - Owners Find Ally in Judge Who Refuses Stays," *New York Call*, July 1, 1919.
48. MCRP, *Report, 1918–1919*, p. 46.
49. "Landlord Puts Dozen Families Out on Street," *New York Call*, February 21, 1919; "Profits Above Lives, Answer of Landlords to Rent Payers," *New York Call*, May 5, 1919; "Leader of Thugs held for Hearing—Owners Find Ally in Judge Who Refuses Stays," *New York Call*, July 1, 1919.
50. "Landlord Puts Dozen Families Out on Street," *New York Call*, February 21, 1919.
51. "Leader of Thugs held for Hearing—Owners Find Ally in Judge Who Refuses Stays," *New York Call*, July 1, 1919.
52. "Owners Juggle Real Estate in Rent Boosting," *New York Call*, April 18, 1919; "Landlords Try to Justify Rent Piracy as City's Anger Mounts," *New York Call*, April 20, 1919.
53. "Say Higher Costs Force Up Rentals," *New York Times*, April 19, 1919.
54. "Landlord Puts Dozen Families Out on Street," *New York Call*, February 21, 1919.
55. "Rent Strikes Empty Houses in Brownsville," *New York Call*, April 30, 1918.
56. "Brooklyn Rent Strikers Win Out," *New York Call*, March 31, 1918.
57. "Rent Strikes Empty Houses in Brownsville," *New York Call*, April 30, 1918.
58. "Brooklyn Rent Strikers Win Out," *New York Call*, May 30, 1918; "Tenants Rally to Hear of Land Hog's Methods," *New York Call*, July 15, 1918.
59. "300 Tenants to be Evicted; Refused to Pay Increased Rent," *Bronx Home News*, August 8, 1918; "Landlords Get More Than 500 Dispossess Notices in Bronx Court," *Bronx Home News*, September 19, 1918.
60. "300 Tenants to be Evicted; Refused to Pay Increased Rent," *Bronx Home News*, August 8, 1918.
61. "Panken's Rent Verdict Upset," *New York Call*, August 9, 1918.
62. "300 Tenants to be Evicted; Refused to Pay Increased Rent," *Bronx Home News*, August 8, 1918.

63. "Will Back Rent Bill," *New York Call*, July 5, 1918.
64. "Nine Families Evicted as Rent Strikes Spread in Brownsville Again," *New York Call*, August 16, 1918.
65. "Tenants Rebel at Higher Rents; Will Fight Lessee by Appeal to Governor," *Bronx Home News*, August 20, 1918.
66. "Many Bronx Landlords Don't Want Families with Children," *Bronx Home News*, August 27, 1918; "Greed of Landlords and Movers Increases Moving Day Misery," *Bronx Home News*, September 10, 1918; "Bronx Tenants to Ask President to Investigate Profiteering Landlords," *Bronx Home News*, September 12, 1918.
67. "Bronx Tenants to Ask President to Investigate Profiteering Landlords," Bronx Home News, September 12, 1918.
68. MCRP, *Report, 1918–1919*, p. 48.
69. "State Investigates High Rents," *New York Call*, April 10, 1919.
70. "Uses Law of Common Sense," *New York Times*, April 11, 1919.
71. See Randolph E. Bergstrom, *Courting Danger: Injury and Law in New York City, 1870–1910* (Ithaca: Cornell University Press, 1992), pp. 4, 115–143.
72. "Landlords Must Heat Flats, New City Law," *New York Call*, December 1, 1918.
73. "Rent-Striking Tenants Threaten to Use Tents for Summer Months," *New York Call*, April 9, 1919.
74. Joint Legislative Committee on Housing (abbreviated to JLC), *Report of the Joint Legislative Committee on Housing*, September 20, 1920, Leg. Doc. 11 (Extraordinary Session), p. 6.
75. "Housing Guidebook," p. 33, Works Projects Administration, Historical Records Survey, Federal Writers Project, Box 3603, Municipal Archives, New York City; JLC, *Report* (1920), p. 6.
76. "Complaints of Rent Robbery Display Greed of Landlords," *New York Call*, April 17, 1919; Frank Mann, "The Remodeling of Private Homes for Tenements," *Real Estate Magazine* (1919–1920), p. 66; "Rehabilitation of Greenwich Village: Reclamation of Century-old Houses as an Aid to the Housing Problem," *Real Estate Magazine* (1919–1920), p. 176; "Landlords Raise Their Rents Whenever Labor Wage is Raised," *Bronx Home News*, October 24, 1918.
77. "Uses Law of Common Sense," *New York Times*, April 11, 1919.
78. "Bronx Tenants Have a Real Day in Court," *New York Call*, April 9, 1919; "Rent-Striking Tenants Threaten to Use Tents for Summer Months," *New York Call*, April 9, 1919; "Rent Victims to Demand Evil be Remedied at City Hall Rally," *New York Call*, May 13, 1919; "Judge Blames 400 for Rent Gouging," *New York Times*, December 3, 1919.
79. "Rack Rent Brings on Tenants' Strike," *New York Call*, April 15, 1919.
80. RC, *Report*, March 26, 1920, p. 31; Committee Appointed to Investigate Hous-

ing and Ice Conditions, *Preliminary Report*, 1920, p. 11; "Propose Building as Rent Solution," *New York Times*, April 18, 1919; "Agree to Arbitrate with Their Tenants," *New York Times*, May 10, 1919; "Offers Plan to Aid Housing Situation," *New York Times*, May 26, 1919; "Sees Change Needed in Building Loans," *New York Times*, May 28, 1919; "Bronx Tenants Give Rent Figures," *New York Times*, May 30, 1919; "How the New Rent Laws Protect the Tenant," *New York Times*, April 11, 1920.

81. Committee Appointed to Investigate Housing and Ice Conditions, *Preliminary Report*, 1920, p. 31.
82. JLC, *Report*, 1920, p. 6. See also "Profiteering Landlord Called Breeder of 'Bolshevism' at Hearing on Rents," *New York Call*, August 2, 1919; "2,000 Families Move in Rain," *Bronx Home News*, October 2, 1919; "Investigate Rent Strike Organizers," *New York Times*, October 4, 1919; "So Many Families Are Being Evicted, Health of Borough is Menaced," *Bronx Home News*, October 5, 1919.
83. "Marshal Beats Rent Strikers, Says League," *New York Call*, September 5, 1919; "Rent Robbery Main Campaign Issue to Toiling Voters of City," *New York Call*, October 16, 1919.
84. "Propose Building as Rent Solution," *New York Times*, April 18, 1919.
85. "Realty Men Warned Against Rent Rises," *New York Times*, November 16, 1919.
86. "Landlords to Demand Another Increase in Rental Next October," *New York Times*, February 23, 1919; "Recent Rent Legislation in New York and Its Nation-Wide Significance," *Real Estate Magazine* (July 1920), pp. 576–577.
87. "City Heads Confer on Famine in Flats," *New York Times*, April 25, 1919.
88. Letter from Nathan Hirsch to Mayor John Hylan, February 13, 1919, pp. 2–3, Hylan Papers, Box 42—"Mayor's Committee on Taxation."
89. "Moral Suasion With a Punch Brings Rent Profiteers to Book," *The Sun*, July 13, 1919; "East Side Renters on Strike Against Insanitary Rooms," *New York Call*, September 10, 1919; "Investigate Rent Strike Organizers," *New York Times*, October 4, 1919; "Start Inquiry Into Rent Agitators," *New York Times*, October 16, 1919; "Thousands in Fees Paid Tenant League," *New York Times*, October 18, 1919; "1,500 East Side Rentpayers Hit Back at Press 'Extortion' Lies," *New York Call*, October 20, 1919; "Swann's Aide Attacks East Harlem Tenants' League Before Judge," *New York Call*, October 22, 1919; "Witness' Story Against Tenant League Refuted," *New York Call*, October 22, 1919; "Tenants League Under Fire," *New York Tribune*, October 31, 1919.
90. MCRP, *Report, 1918–1919*, p. 51; "Rent Complaints on the Increase," *New York Times*, April 27, 1919.
91. "Moral Suasion With a Punch Brings Rent Profiteers to Book," *The Sun*, July 13, 1919.

92. MCRP, *Report, 1918–1919*, p. 39.
93. "The Mayor and the Tenants," *New York Call*, October 18, 1919.
94. "Moral Suasion With a Punch Brings Rent Profiteers to Book," *The Sun*, July 13, 1919.
95. "East Side Renters on Strike Against Insanitary Rooms," *New York Call*, September 10, 1919; " Investigate Rent Strike Organizers," *New York Times*, October 4, 1919; "Start Inquiry Into Rent Agitators," *New York Times*, October 16, 1919; "Thousands in Fees Paid Tenant League," *New York Times*, October 18, 1919; "1,500 East Side Rentpayers Hit Back at Press 'Extortion' Lies," *New York Call*, October 20, 1919; "Swann's Aide Attacks East Harlem Tenants' League Before Judge," *New York Call*, October 22, 1919; "Witness' Story Against Tenant League Refuted," *New York Call*, October 22, 1919; "Radicals Use Rent Problem to Make Socialist Voters," *New York Tribune*, October 31, 1919.
96. "Jailing Women is Blow at Tenants," *New York Call*, November 30, 1919.
97. "Police Called to Quell Near Riot at Bronx Meeting of Mayor's Committee," *Bronx Homes News*, September 25, 1919; "Tenants Threaten Landlord Scored as Hypocrite by Mayor's Committee," *Bronx Home News*, October 16, 1919.
98. "Mayor's Committee to Continue Fight on Rent Profiteering; May Open Bronx Branch," *Bronx Home News*, January 8, 1920.
99. Isidor Berger, "Rent Adjustment vs. Rent Profiteering," *Real Estate News* (January 1920), p. 3.
100. "Little Wonder," *Real Estate Magazine* (May 1920), p. 485.
101. "Landlord Defies Mayor's Rent Profiteering Committee, Says He does Not Fear Investigation," *Bronx Home News*, January 15, 1920.
102. "Tenants Act to End Evils While Officials Talk," *New York Call*, April 26, 1919;"Marshal Beats Rent Strikers, Says League," *New York Call*, September 5, 1919.
103. "City Investigator to Hear Landlord," *New York Times*, April 24, 1919; "City Heads Confer on Famine in Flats," *New York Times*, April 25, 1919; "Tenants to Call on Mayor Hylan to Ask Remedy," *New York Call*, May 15, 1919;"Moral Suasion With a Punch Brings Rent Profiteers to Book," *The Sun*, July 13, 1919; "Tenants Battle with Landlords," *New York Times*, September 24, 1919; "Misguided Zeal — or Plain Bullying?" *Real Estate Magazine* (1919–1920), p. 26.
104. "Cases of Rent Profiteering to be Heard in Borough Hall To-Morrow Night," *Bronx Home News*, September 21, 1919.
105. "The Mayor and the Tenants," *New York Call*, October 18, 1919.
106. "Cases of Rent Profiteering to be Heard in Borough Hall To-Morrow Night," *Bronx Home News*, September 21, 1919.
107. Committee Appointed to Investigate Housing and Ice Conditions of the State, *Preliminary Report*, 1920, p. 10; RC, *Report*, March 26, 1920, p. 21.
108. MCRP, *Report, 1918–1919*, p. 42.

109. "Band Plays 'Homesick Blues' While Bronx Tenants Protest Rent Increases," *Bronx Home News*, September 11, 1919.
110. "Landlord Defies Mayor's Rent Profiteering Committee, Says He does Not Fear Investigation," *Bronx Home News*, January 15, 1920.
111. "Mayor's Committee to Continue Fight on Rent Profiteering; May Open Bronx Branch," *Bronx Home News*, January 8, 1920.
112. "The Mayor and the Tenants," *New York Call*, October 18, 1919.
113. "Municipal Judge Asks New Law to Curb Rent Profiteering," *New York Call*, April 15, 1919.

5. Shades of Activism During the Red Scare

1. Julian Jaffe, *Crusade Against Radicalism: New York During the Red Scare, 1914–1924* (Port Washington, NY: Kennikat Press, 1972), pp. 3–4.
2. M. J. Heale, *American Anticommunism: Combating the Enemy Within, 1830–1970* (Baltimore: Johns Hopkins University Press, 1990), p. 65.
3. Robert Justin Goldstein, *Political Repression in Modern America*. (Cambridge, MA: Schenkman Pub. Co., 1978), pp. 139–141.
4. See Christopher Lasch, *The American Liberals and the Russian Revolution*. (New York: Columbia University Press, 1962), pp. 127–157, 190–222.
5. M. J. Heale, *American Anticommunism*, pp. 60–67; "Agents Beat Radicals; Force False Avowals" *New York Call*, February 2, 1920; Stanley Coben, *A. Mitchell Palmer: Politician* (New York: DaCapo Press, 1972), pp. 196–246; Curt Gentry, *J. Edgar Hoover: The Man and the Secrets* (New York: Penguin Books, 1992), pp. 95–98.
6. Harold Josephson, "The Dynamics of Repression: New York During the Red Scare," *Mid-America: An Historical Review* 59 (3) (October 1977), pp. 133–135.
7. "No Rent Relief Seen in Old Party Plans Maturing at Albany," *New York Call*, March 26, 1920.
8. Jaffe, *Crusade*, pp. 169–198; Zosa Szajkowski, *Jews, Wars, and Communism* (New York: KTAV, 1972), pp. 1, 123, cited in Richard Plunz, *A History of Housing in New York City* (New York: Columbia University Press, 1990), pp. 126, 352, 394.
9. Along with the sources already cited, for a decent examination of certain aspects of the Red Scare's impact in New York, see also Thomas E. Vadney, "The Politics of Repression, A Case Study of the Red Scare in New York," *New York History* 49 (1968), pp. 56–75; David R. Coburn, "Governor Alfred E. Smith and the Red Scare, 1919–1920," *Political Science Quarterly* 88 (3) (September 1973), pp. 423–444; Robert K. Murray, *Red Scare: A Study in National Hysteria, 1919–1920*. New York: McGraw-Hill, 1955) More general works on the Red Scare include David H. Bennett, *The Party of Fear: From*

Nativist Movements to the New Right in America (Chapel Hill, NC: University of North Carolina Press, 1988), pp. 183–198; Robert Justin Goldstein, *Political Repression in Modern America* (Cambridge, MA: Schenkman Publishing Company, 1978), pp. 139–191; John Higham, *Strangers in the Land: Patterns of American Nativism, 1860–1925* New Brunswick, NJ: Rutgers University Press, 1955.

10. "Bronx Landlords to Define Their Position Through Publicity Campaign," *New York Times*, February 10, 1918; "Bolshevism Here and Abroad," *Real Estate Record and Builders' Guide* (April 12, 1919), p. 460. See also "Rent Strikes Largely Due to Bolshevik Propaganda," *Real Estate Record and Builders' Guide* (December 20, 1919), pp. 625–626.
11. "Rent Strike Leaders Investigated," *New York Tribune*, October 31, 1919;"1,500 East Side Rentpayers Hit Back at Press 'Extortion' Lies," *New York Call*, October 20, 1919; "Swann Aide Attacks East Harlem Tenants' League Before Judge," *New York Call*, October 22, 1919; "Witness' Story Against Tenant League Refuted," *New York Call*, October 22, 1919; "Radicals Use Rent Problem to Win Votes," Real Estate News (November 1919), pp. 2–4.
12. Oscar L. Meyerson, "The View of the Real Estate Owner," *Real Estate News* (March 1920), p. 15.
13. "Bolshevism Here and Abroad," *Real Estate Record and Builders Guide* (April 12, 1919), p. 455; See also Max Wolff, "Why There is More Need for 'Organization' Now Than Ever Before," *Real Estate News* (February 1920), pp. 8–9.
14. "Urges Speed to Curb Reds," *New York Times*, April 10, 1919.
15. Isidor Berger, "The Effects of Housing Legislation," *Real Estate News* (December 1920), pp. 4–5.
16. Simon Greenfield, "The Association and the Public," *Real Estate News* (December 1919), p. 4.
17. Isidor Berger, "Watch Your Step," *Real Estate News* (December 1920), p. 22.
18. Isidor Berger, "Rent Adjustment vs. Rent Profiteering," *Real Estate News* (January 1920), p. 3; Isidor Berger, "The New Rent Laws," *Real Estate News* (April 1920), p. 2.
19. Isidor Berger, "The Effects of Housing Legislation," *Real Estate News* (December 1920), pp. 4–5; Simon Greenfield, "The Association and the Public," *Real Estate News* (December 1919), p. 4.
20. "Vote for Isidor Berger for Councilman," Real Estate News (September 1937), p. 302; "Isidor Berger Elected Insurance Company President," *Real Estate News* (July 1941), pp. 229–230, 238–239; "Isidor Berger, 85, Led Realty Groups," *New York Times*, April 19, 1954; "Isidor Berger Dead; Realty Field Expert," *New York Herald Tribune*, April 19, 1954.
21. Meyer Goldberg, "The President's Farewell," *Real Estate News* (December 1920), pp. 6–7.

22. "Say Building is Only Way to Ease Renting Situation," *Real Estate Record and Builders' Guide* (May 3, 1919), p. 580; "Legislators Who will Investigate Rentals Organize," *Real Estate Record and Builders' Guide* (May 10, 1919), p. 622; "Brownsville has Local Rent Parley in Lyceum Tonight," *New York Call*, April 24, 1919. On the flaws of GNYTA's reports, see *The Public Papers of Alfred E. Smith* (1924), p. 89.

23. "Hilly Rent Board Head," *New York Times*, January 7, 1920; "Rent Board Asks $4,950," *New York Times*, January 8, 1920; "Nominated Candidates," *Real Estate News* (November 1919), p. 6; "Hilly Says Reds Plan Red Revolt," *New York Times*, April 18, 1920.

24. "Isidor Berger, Manager," *Real Estate News* (February 1924), p. 8; "Vote for Isidor Berger for Councilman," *Real Estate News* (September 1937), p. 302; "Isidor Berger Elected Insurance Company President," *Real Estate News* (July 1941), pp. 229–230, 238–239; "Isidor Berger, 85, Led Realty Groups," *New York Times*, April 19, 1954; "Isidor Berger Dead; Realty Field Expert," *New York Herald*, April 19, 1954.

25. "Realty Exploiters, in Thin Disguise, Support Nominees Who Look Friendly," *New York Call*, October 30, 1919.

26. "Landlords' O.K. of Tammany in 2nd Court District Unites Tenants Behind Socialists," *New York Call*, November 3, 1919.

27. Simon Greenfield, "The Association and the Public," *Real Estate News* (December 1919), p. 4.

28. Letter from Stewart Browne to Governor Al Smith: 1–3, Al Smith Papers, Box 200–51–1, Housing and Regional Commission File, State Archives, State Library of New York, Albany.

29. "Stewart Brown, Civic Leader, 84," *New York Times*, August 5, 1938.

30. See New York City Board of Estimate, *Minutes*, May 19, 22, 1914; cited from S. J. Makielski, Jr. *The Politics of Zoning: The New York Experience* (New York: Columbia University Press, 1966), pp. 24–25, 201.

31. "Owner Sees City Housing as Only Solution," *New York Call*, September 4, 1920.

32. "Want Lower Insurance," *New York Times*, February 8, 1914.

33. "New Officers Elected for the United Real Estate Owners Association," *Real Estate News* (November 1919), pp. 5–6. Although the actual extent of this kind of interconnected or networked management is unclear, a cursory view of other organizations suggests a similar pattern. For example, just as UREO's treasurer, Thomas Krekeler, sat on GNYTA's board of directors, he was also president of the Taxpayers' Association of the 10th, 11th, and 17th Wards. John Hylan Papers, Box 192, Taxpayers' Association of the 10th, 11th, and 17th Wards newsletter, dated March 3rd, 1919. Isaac Hyman was legal counsel for UREO at the same time that he represented the Harlem Proper-

ty Owners Association. Senate and Assembly Committees on Cities, Joint Hearing by the Senate and Assembly Committees on Cities, March 23, 1920: 3, 140–142, Al Smith Papers, Box 260–46; "New Officers Elected for the United Real Estate Owners Association," *Real Estate News* (November 1919), p. 5.

34. "Delegates and Committees Appointed for the Year 1921," *Real Estate News* (January 1921), p. 12. While this approach may have been UREO's standard arrangement, it is unclear how exceptional UREO's arrangement with GNYTA was.

35. "Delegates and Committees Appointed for the Year 1921" *Real Estate News* (January 1921), p. 12; Stewart Browne, "Legislation at Albany," Real Estate News (April 1921), p. 11. For some sense of GNYTA's immediate priorities concerning the rent laws and the activities of their Law and Legislative Committee, see S. Shelinsky, "Report of Law and Legislative Committee," *Real Estate News* (April 1921), pp. 18–19.

36. Charles A. Riesner, "The History of the Real Estate Board of New York, Inc.," *Real Estate Magazine* (February 1931), pp. 66–69.

37. "Lectures on Real Estate," *Real Estate Magazine* (December 1921), p. 185; "Courses in Real Estate," *Real Estate Magazine* (January 1922), p. 210. REBNY published some of the real estate course lectures in Real Estate Magazine and Real Estate Record and Builders' Guide. For a general overview of the material covered, see Harry Hall, et al., *Real Estate Manual for Brokers, Owners, and Operators*. New York: Doubleday, 1925.

38. Riesner, "History of the Real Estate Board," 70–75, 81. One of these real estate editors, Richard O. Chittick of the Globe and Commercial Advertiser, eventually became REBNY's executive secretary and managing editor of Real Estate Magazine in 1914.

39. "Importance of the Building Manager," *Real Estate Magazine* (February 1915), p. 32.

40. "For Licensing Brokers," *Real Estate Magazine* (March 1921), p. 320; "New Rent Legislation Awaits Court of Appeals Decision," *Real Estate Record and Builders' Guide* (March 5, 1921), p. 299; "Bills to License Realty Brokers and Salesmen Passed," *Real Estate Record and Builders' Guide* (April 23, 1921), pp. 521, 532; "For Licensing Brokers," *Real Estate Magazine* (March 21, 1921), p. 320.

41. See "Alderman Pass Ordinance to License Lessees," *Real Estate News* (December 1919), p. 11; Max Wolff, "Where Politics Works Against the Constituency," *Real Estate News* (January 1920), p. 14.

42. See, for example, Isidor Berger, "Effects of Housing Legislation," *Real Estate News* (December 1920), pp. 3–5;" Deprecates Lack of Concerted Action," *Real Estate Magazine* (July 1920), p. 582; see also "Legislation Complicates Housing Situation," *Real Estate Magazine* (October 1920), pp. 66, 77; "Disap-

proves 'Roving' Commission for Lockwood-Untermyer Committee," *Real Estate Magazine* (February 1921), p. 259.

43. "Realty Folk Going to Albany Hearing," *Sun and New York Herald*, March 21, 1920.
44. "More than 2,000 at Albany Attend Hearing in Rent War," *Evening Post*, March 23, 1920; Senate and Assembly Committees on Cities, Joint Hearing by the Senate and Assembly Committees on Cities, March 23, 1920 (mimeograph), pp. 52–56, Al Smith Papers, Box 260-46. Through the early 1920s, Browne continued to deviate from the views of many UREO landlords and other landlord leaders by reluctantly supporting rent control on the grounds that many landlords would vengefully evict activist tenants. See Stewart Browne, "Rent Control Laws: The Landlord's Side," *Housing Betterment* 13 (3) (August 1924), p. 257.
45. Elisabeth Israels Perry, *Belle Moskowitz: Feminine Politics and the Exercise of Power in the Age of Alfred E. Smith*. (New York: Oxford University Press, 1987), pp. 124–125.
46. Anthony Jackson, *A Place Called Home: A History of Low-Cost Housing in Manhattan* (Cambridge, MA: MIT Press, 1976), pp. 168–169.
47. State of New York, Housing Conditions: Report of the Housing Committee of the Reconstruction Commission of the State of New York, March 26, 1920: 64. For a concise summary of the findings of the Reconstruction Commission's Housing Committee, see "How Tax Exemption Broke the Housing Deadlock in New York City," (May 1920), pp. 2–46 to 2–48.
48. RC, *Report* (1920), pp. 1–7.
49. Perry, *Belle Moskowitz*, p. 131.
50. Richard O. Chittick, "A Strenuous Legislative Session," *Real Estate Magazine* (May 1920), pp. 477–479; "Asks Unrestricted Rent on New Homes," *New York Times*, August 23, 1920.
51. "Elkus Housing Plan Attacked by Hirsch," *New York Times*, May 18, 1920.
52. Perry, *Belle Moskowitz*, pp. 132–4.
53. Ibid.; Jackson, *A Place Called Home*, pp. 172–173.
54. Committee Appointed to Investigate Housing and Ice Conditions of the State (abbreviated to CIHIC), *Preliminary Report of the Committee Appointed to Investigate Housing and Ice Conditions of the State*, 1920, Leg. Doc. 14 (1920), p. 3.
55. Edith Berger Drellich and Andree Emery, *Rent Control in War and Peace*, pp. 31–32; "All City's Unions Threaten Strike on Rent Gougers," *New York Times*, March 7, 1920; "Labor Declines to be Goat for Rent Raisers," *New York Call*, March 15, 1920; "Tenants and Landlords in Test of Power," *New York Call*, March 20, 1920; "Tenants and Landlords in Test of Power," *New York Call*, March 22, 1920; "Organize Revolt Against High Rents," *New York Times*,

March 30, 1920; "Strike of Tenants Planned for May," *Sun and New York Herald*, March 27, 1920.

56. "Find Housing Problem Remedy of U.S. Troops Will Be Needed in 90 Days, Says Stonebridge," *Bronx Home News*, March 18, 1920.
57. "Mayor Ready to Adopt Home News Rent Profiteering Plan," *Bronx Home News*, March 11, 1920; "$100,000,000 in Plan to Solve Rent problem," *Sun and New York Herald*, March 13, 1920; "Says Profiteers Threatened Death," *Evening Post*, March 13, 1920; "Labor Declines to be Goat for Rent Raisers," *New York Call*, March 15, 1920; "Tax Exemption is Housing Remedy," *Evening Post*, March 15, 1920.
58. "Advocate Rent Strike for 700,000," *Sun and New York Herald*, March 30, 1920.
59. "Members Column," *Real Estate News* (May 1920), p. 13.
60. "Capital Quits Hylan in Rent Profiteer War," *Sun and New York Herald*, March 21, 1920.
61. CIHIC, *Preliminary Report*, pp. 3–7.
62. Jackson, *A Place Called Home*, p. 161; "Joint Legislative Committee Inquires into Cement," *Real Estate Record and Builders' Guide* (January 8, 1921), pp. 51–53.
63. "Untermyer Asks More Power for Lockwood Committee," *Real Estate Record and Builders' Guide* (January 22, 1921), p. 103; JLC, *Final Report of the Joint Legislative Committee on Housing*, Leg. Doc. 48 (1923), pp. 60–62.
64. JLC, *Report of the Joint Legislative Committee on Housing* Leg. Doc. 11 (1920), pp. 4–6.
65. "Deprecates Lack of Concerted Action," *Real Estate Magazine* (July 1920), p. 582. See also "Legislation Complicates Housing Situation," *Real Estate Magazine* (October 1920), pp. 66, 77; "Disapproves 'Roving' Commission for Lockwood-Untermyer Committee," *Real Estate Magazine* (February 1921), p. 259.
66. James Ford, *The Slums and Housing* (Cambridge: Harvard University Press, 1936) 1: 234.
67. The MCRP, for example, advocated laws that would have mandated a standard written lease. MCRP, *Report* (1918–1919), p. 50. See also Frederick Spiegelberg, "Recent Emergency Rent Legislation," *Real Estate Magazine* (May 1920), p. 465.
68. Lauer and House, *The Tenant and His Landlord*, pp. 38–39; Frederick Spiegelberg, "Recent Emergency Rent Legislation," *Real Estate Magazine* (May 1920), pp. 465–468, 501; "Legislature Enacts Eleven Landlord and Tenant Laws," *Real Estate Record and Builders Guide*, April 3, 1920: 439; CIHIC, *Preliminary Report*, p. 10.
69. Lauer and House, *The Tenant and His Landlord*, pp. 38–42. Chapter 138 also

reduced landlords' ability to punish tenants by doing away with laws dating back to 1774 which had demanded double rent and damages from tenants who willfully held over after receiving a dispossess notice. This change was largely symbolic since it had not been enforced for decades.

70. Lauer and House, *The Tenant and His Landlord*, p. 40.
71. The Lockwood Committee first pushed to require landlords to give ten days' notice if they wanted to terminate a monthly tenancy (where the tenant had secured a lease for the definite period of one month). In June 1919, lawmakers lengthened the time for month-to-month tenancies (where a tenant secured a lease for an indefinite period of time) from five to thirty days.
72. Lauer and House, *The Tenant and His Landlord*, pp. 42–43. Chapters 209 and 210 of the new laws also eliminated the differences between month-to-month tenancies and monthly tenancies in regard to the length of time allowed in a notice to vacate. With this new law, all tenants received thirty days notice to vacate.
73. Frederick Spiegelberg, "Recent Emergency Rent Legislation," *Real Estate Magazine* (May 1920), p. 465.
74. Harold G. Aron, "The New York Landlord and Tenant Laws of 1920," *Cornell Law Quarterly* (November 1920), pp. 1–7.
75. This provision created a great deal of confusion as 25 percent increases were not necessarily disallowed. They simply had to be justified to municipal court judges.
76. Frederick Spiegelberg, "Recent Emergency Rent Legislation," *Real Estate Magazine* (May 1920), pp. 465–468. The laws put some teeth into these provisions by barring landlords' access to summary proceedings in cases involving 25 percent or greater increases in rent.
77. Judges varied in what they considered evidence but none of the various criteria acted as serious obstacles to tenants.
78. "Tenant's Rights and Obligations," *The Citizen* 17 (68) (August 1923), p. 7.
79. Clarence S. Stein, "The Housing Crisis in New York," *The Survey* 44 (September 1920), pp. 659–661; Edith Berger Drellich and Andrée Emery, *Rent Control in War and Peace* (New York: National Municipal League, 1939), p. 60. See also Edith Elmer Wood, *Recent Trends in American Housing*. New York: Macmillan, 1931.
80. "Says Anti-Profiteering Laws Enacted at Albany Hold Out False Hope of Low Rents," *Sun and New York Herald*, April 4, 1920; "Real Estate Board Attacks Rent Bills," *New York Times*, April 19, 1920; "Housing Shortage Laid to Lockwood," *Sun and New York Herald*, July 12, 1920; "Legislation Complicates Housing Situation," *Real Estate Magazine* (October 1920), pp. 66, 77; "Laws Do Not Relieve Emergency," *Real Estate Magazine* (December 1920),

p. 177; Walter C. Wyckoff, "A Rational View of the Housing Shortage," *Real Estate Magazine* (February 1921), p. 256.
81. "Rent Gouging Laws Halt Realty Deals," *New York Times*, April 3, 1920.
82. Charles G. Edwards, "Why Real Estate Should be Organized," *Real Estate Magazine* (July 1922), p. 504.
83. Isidor Berger, "Proposed Radical Legislation and Possible Effects," *Real Estate News* (March 1920), p. 2.
84. "No Rent Relief Seen in Old Party Plans Maturing at Albany," *New York Call*, March 26, 1920.
85. "All City's Unions Threaten Strike On Rent Gougers," *New York Times*, March 7, 1920; "Socialist Rent Plan, Rejected, Now City's Hope," *New York Call*, March 11, 1920; "Labor Declines to be Goat for Rent Raisers," *New York Call*, March 15, 1920; "Organize Revolt Against High Rents," *New York Times*, March 30, 1920.
86. "Coercion Issue in Court," *New York Times*, March 31, 1920.
87. "Real Estate Board Attacks Rent Bills," *New York Times*, April 19, 1920; "Tenants Will Call Big Strike Despite Mayor," *New York Call*, April 19, 1920.
88. "Hilly Says Reds Plan Rent Revolt," *New York Times*, April 20, 1920; "Tenants Strike Bogey Derided," *New York Call*, April 25, 1920.
89. "Pay Raised Rent and Keep Still," *New York Call*, October 9, 1918; "Harlem Lessee Threatens to Evict Tenants," *New York Call*, January 15, 1919; "No Rent Relief Seen in Old Party Plans Maturing At Albany," *New York Call*, March 26, 1920; "Landlords Get Nervous About Rent Agitation," *New York Call*, April 28, 1920; "U.S. Agents Take Up Rent Riot Threats," *New York Times*, April 28, 1920; "Says Rent Revolt was Loose Talk," *New York Times*, May 1, 1920.
90. "Tenants Strike in Brownsville," *New York Call*, March 5, 1920.
91. "Socialists Appeal to Working Classes," *Sun and New York Herald*, April 6, 1920.
92. "Says Rent Revolt was Loose Talk," *New York Times*, May 1, 1920; "Palmer Warns of Nation-Wide Plot—Government Agents Directed to Curb May Day Demonstrations," *Evening Post*, April 30, 1920.
93. "Tenants' May Day Strike a Failure," *Evening Post*, May 2, 1920.
94. "Tenants Will Call Big Strike Despite Mayor," *New York Call*, April 19, 1920; "Hilly Says Reds Plan Rent Revolt," *New York Times*, April 20, 1920; "United Tenants Assail Report of Rent Strike," *New York Call*, April 21, 1920.
95. "Tenant Strike Bogey Derided," *New York Call*, April 25, 1920; "Tenant Soviet is Ridiculed as Owners' Bogey" *New York Call*, April 28, 1920.
96. Curt Gentry, *J. Edgar Hoover: The Man and the Secrets* (New York: Penguin Books, 1992), pp. 96–97.
97. "Moving Van Men Threaten Strike," *New York Times*, April 29, 1920; "To Quiz Hilly on Rent Strike," *New York Call*, April 29, 1920.

98. "City Under Guard Against Red Plot Threatened Today," *New York Times*, May 1, 1920; " "Says Rent Revolt was Loose Talk," *New York Times*, May 1, 1920; "Plot for Red May Day Revolt Fails," *New York Times*, May 2, 1920; "Tenants' May Day Strike a Failure," *New York Times*, May 2, 1920.
99. "Calls Rent Laws Merely Makeshift," *New York Times*, July 4, 1920.
100. "Court Attacks Undated Warrants," *New York Times*, August 4, 1920; "Justice Robitzek Informs Landlords They Cannot Use Warrants as Clubs on Tenants," *Bronx Home News*, August 5, 1920; "Landlords Staging Colossal Bluff in Attempting to Nullify Rent Laws," *Bronx Home News*, September 2, 1920.
101. "300 Landlord-Tenant Cases to be Heard in Bronx Municipal Court Today," *Bronx Home News*, July 6, 1920; "The Tenants Win Little by the New Rent Laws; Landlords Gain, Says O'Sullivan," *Bronx Home News*, July 11, 1920.
102. "Sees 40,000 in Bronx Homeless in April," *New York Times*, July 31, 1920; "Predicts Riots and Martial Law if Legislature Don't Change Conditions," *Bronx Home News*, August 12, 1920; "Call Conferences on Housing Relief," *New York Times*, September 11, 1920; "Riot and Bloodshed May be Averted by the Enactment of Effective Rent Laws," *Bronx Home News*, September 19, 1920; "New Rent Laws Signed; 100,000 Evictions Voided," *New York Times*, September 28, 1920.
103. "Would Bar Eviction During Rent Crisis," *New York Times*, August 27, 1920; "Would Stay Eviction Orders Until Appeal Can be Taken; Oppose Rotation of Judges," *Bronx Home News*, September 5, 1920;"5,000 Bronx Tenants Plan to Attend Hearing as Housing Session Opens," *Bronx Home News*, September 21, 1920.
104. Lauer and House, *The Tenant and His Landlord*, pp. 43–45.
105. The laws prescribed that dispossess proceedings were in order in only four instances: (1) when the tenant was objectionable, as defined by chapter 131 (2) when the landlord owned the tenement and required possession for himself or his family to live in (3) when the building was scheduled for demolition and plans were set for constructing a new building, and (4) where the tenement was owned on a cooperative basis. In all other cases, courts were to deny landlords access to dispossess proceedings. See "New Rent Law Signed; 100,000 Evictions Voided," *New York Times*, September 28, 1920; Lauer and House, *The Tenant and His Landlord*, pp. 51–52. The legislature also passed the Strauss Bill in 1921 that made discriminating against families with children a misdemeanor. There is no evidence that officials enforced the law or that it significantly altered landlord practices. See "No Discrimination Against Children in Apartment Houses," *Real Estate Record and Builders Guide* (April 30, 1921), p. 552.

6. Landlords in the Tenants' Court

1. "Victory Parade Held by Tenants," *Sun and New York Herald*, April 13, 1920. See also "700 Rent Disputes Heard by Judges," *New York Times*, April 9, 1920.
2. "Landlord-Tenant Cases Drop Off Now that Justice Wm. E. Morris is Back; 100 for Today," *Bronx Home News*, August 12, 1920; "Fearing Justice Morris, Landlords Refuse to Bring Cases Before Him," *Bronx Home News*, August 15, 1920; "Justice Morris Gets Ovation in Speaking at Meeting of Fair Play Rent Association," *Bronx Home News*, August 15, 1920; "Justice Wm. Morris Gets Poison Pen Letters from Disgruntled Landlords," *Bronx Home News*, August 17, 1920; "Tenants Romp Home Winners When Justice Morris Returns to Municipal Court Bench," *Bronx Home News*, September 21, 1920; "Justice Morris Jockeyes Rent Case Out of Court," *Bronx Home News*, February 6, 1921; "Landlords Taboo Fireworks, Fearing Publicity; One Speaker Ignores Rule," *Bronx Home News*, March 31, 1921.
3. "Trials Under Emergency Rent Laws Clog Municipal Courts," *Real Estate Record and Builders Guide* (April 15, 1922), p. 454.
4. "Summary Proceedings—As It Effects the Tenement," *Real Estate News* (February 1921), p. 26; "Landlords and Tenants Stand Pat as May 1 Approaches," *Real Estate Record and Builders Guide* (April 16, 1921), p. 489; "May 1 Strikes Threatened," *New York Times*, July 26, 1921; "Tenants Must Pay Costs in Dispossess Proceedings for Non-payment of Rent," *Real Estate News* (June 1921), p. 25; "Owners Are Absolutely Entitled to Legal Disbursements in Dispossess Proceedings for Non-payment," *Real Estate News* (September 1921), p. 37; Reuben J. Wittstein, "Landlord and Tenant Information," *Real Estate News* (March 1922), p. 36.
5. "Over Three Hundred Landlord-Tenant Cases to be Heard in Municipal Court Today," *Bronx Home News*, July 13, 1920.
6. "New Rent Gouging Laws Fill Courts; Evaders Exposed," *New York Times*, April 6, 1920; "City Marshals Resent Home News Expose; 150 Tenant Cases Mondays," *Bronx Home News*, August 26, 1920; "City Marshals Violate Law Appearing for Landlords in Municipal Courts," *Bronx Home News*, August 22, 1920.
7. "Justices Plan Joint Action in Rent Decisions," *New York Sun and Herald*, April 6, 1920; "Tenants Will Knit Leagues Into One Body," *New York Call*, April 7, 1920.
8. "City Marshals Resent Home News Expose; 150 Tenant Cases Mondays," *Bronx Home News*, August 26, 1920; "City Marshals Violate Law Appearing for Landlords in Municipal Courts," *Bronx Home News*, August 22, 1920.
9. "Amendment to Rent Legislation Increases Fees by $3 Per Ouster," *New York Times*, May 11, 1920; Abraham J. Dworsky, "Summary Proceedings—As It Effects the Tenement," *Real Estate News* (February 1921), p. 26.

10. "New Rent Gouging Evasions Exposed," *New York Times*, June 22, 1920.
11. "Tenants Will Call Big Strike Despite Mayor," *New York Call*, April 19, 1920.
12. "Landlords Make Ridiculous Charges Against Tenants They Want Evicted," *Bronx Home News*, July 26, 1921; "Landlord Seeks to Oust Accused Owner of 'Ice Cream Saloon,' " *Bronx Home News*, July 26, 1921; Commission of Housing and Regional Planning (abbreviated to CHRP), *Report of Commission of Housing and Regional Planning*, Leg. Doc. 40 (1926), pp. 67–68.
13. "Landlords Staging Colossal Bluff in Attempting to Nullify Rent Laws" *Bronx Home News*, September 2, 1920; "40,000 Notified to Move on Oct. 1," *New York Times*, September 4, 1920.
14. "Landlords Taboo Fireworks, Fearing Publicity, One Speaker Ignores Rule," *Bronx Home News*, March 31, 1921.
15. "40,000 Notified to Move on Oct. 1," *New York Times*, September 4, 1920.
16. "Landlord and Tenant Legislation," *Real Estate Magazine* (February 1921), p. 260.
17. "Votes to Restrict Lockwood Inquiry," *New York Times*, January 27, 1921; "M'Whinney Denies Lobby Reached Him," *New York Times*, January 30, 1921; "Serious Omissions in the New Rent Laws," *Real Estate Magazine* (May 1920), p. 469.
18. "Legislature Flooded with Landlord and Tenant Bills," *Real Estate Record and Builders Guide* (September 25, 1920), p. 415; "Rent Law Amendments," *Real Estate Magazine* (January 1921), p. 207; "Flood of Housing Bills Continues Unabated at Albany," *Real Estate Record and Builders Guide* (January 19, 1924), p. 7; "Storming of Capital Hill," *Real Estate Magazine* (May 1924), p. 870; "Many Drastic Measures Aimed at Landlords Met Defeat," *Real Estate Record and Builders Guide* (May 10, 1924), p. 7; "Drastic Housing Measures at Albany Arouse Opposition," *Real Estate Record and Builders Guide* (February 7, 1925), p. 10; "Marshaling the Tenant Army Again," *Real Estate Record and Builders Guide* (March 14, 1925), p. 7; "Many Bills Aimed at Property Owners Presented at Albany," *Real Estate Record and Builders Guide* (January 22, 1927), p. 9.
19. "Court of Appeals Will Pass on the Validity of the New Rent Laws," *Real Estate Record and Builders Guide* (January 22, 1921), p. 102; "Storming of Capital Hill," *Real Estate Magazine* (May 1924), p. 870; "Many Drastic Measures Aimed at Landlords Met Defeat," *Real Estate Record and Builders Guide* (May 10, 1924), p. 7; "Fate of Real Estate Legislation Now Clear," *Real Estate Record and Builders Guide* (March 14, 1925), p. 7; "Legislative Majority Openly Oppose State Housing Aid," *Real Estate Record and Builders Guide* (January 23, 1926), p. 10.
20. "An Overworked 'Emergency,' " *Real Estate Record and Builders Guide* (April 1, 1922), p. 389; "Further Extension of Emergency Rent Laws Rejected," *Real*

Estate Record and Builders Guide (March 24, 1923), p. 360; "New Stage Reached in Rent Legislation," Real Estate Record and Builders Guide (January 16, 1926), p. 5; "New Phase of Rent Law Agitation," Real Estate Record and Builders Guide (February 13, 1926), p. 5.

21. Tenement House Department (abbreviated to THD), Tenth Report of the Tenement House Department of the City of New York—Report of the Years 1918–1929, pp. 6–7. See also J. M. Lonergan, "The Housing Situation in the City of New York," Monthly Bulletin of the Department of Health 9 (2) (February 1921), p. 27.
22. J.M. Lonergan, "The Housing Situation in the City of New York," Monthly Bulletin of the Department of Health 9 (2) (February 1921), p. 27.
23. The number of cases in Manhattan went from 366 in 1919 to 790 in 1921 to 1,224 in 1924. Complaints to the Tenement House department jumped from 36,129 in 1919 to 79,054 in 1920 to 89,025 in 1921 with actual violations increasing from 13,469 in 1919 to 43,290 in 1921. THD, Tenth Report, pp. 7, 154.
24. "Refractory Landlords Must Face Court on Repairs; Magistrates Abolish Board of Review," Bronx Home News, April 19, 1921; "25 Landlords Fined, 1 Jailed for Failure to Make Repairs," New York Times, September 6, 1923; "Law and Order," Real Estate News (November 1923), p. 13; "Antiquated Law Clogging the Courts," Real Estate Record and Builders Guide (June 25, 1927), p. 5.
25. "Summonses Issued by Commissioner Mann," Real Estate News (December 1921), p. 7.
26. "Landlords Deny Blame for City Showing Decay—Tenants Accused of Deliberate Vandalism," Real Estate News (January 1922), p. 48. See also Reuben J. Wittstein, "What Are the Rent Laws?" Real Estate News (March 1923), p. 16; "Law and Order," Real Estate News (November 1923), p. 13; Isidor Berger, "Rent Beater's Cure," Real Estate News (July 1925), p. 4.
27. "The Steam Heat and Hot Water Problem," Real Estate News (March 1921), p. 32; "A Check on Malicious Mischief," Real Estate Magazine (January 1922), p. 218; Isidor Berger, "Tenants' Treatment of Tenement Property," Real Estate Magazine (April 1922), p. 368; Isidor Berger, "The Real Causes for Rent Increases," Real Estate News (October 1921), pp. 3–4.
28. THD, Tenth Report, p. 154.
29. "Summonses Issued by Commissioner Mann," Real Estate News (December 1921), p. 7, "Disgusted Court Attendant," Real Estate News (December 1921), p. 50; "A Check on Malicious Mischief," Real Estate Magazine (January 1922), p. 218.
30. "Municipal Rent Laws Declared Void," Real Estate News (November 1929), p. 8.
31. Alter F. Landesmaan, Brownsville: The Birth, Development and Passing of a

Jewish Community in New York (New York: Bloch, 1971), pp. 302–303. See also Robert Justine Goldstein, *Political Repression in Modern America From 1870 to the Present* (Cambridge, MA: Schenkman, 1978), pp. 161–163; Julian Jaffe, *Crusade Against Radicalism: New York During the Red Scare, 1914–1924* (Port Washington, NY: Kennikat Press, 1972), pp. 7–75.

32. "Tenants Combine; Ask Court Inquiry," *New York Times*, February 8, 1921.
33. Katherine Meyer, "A Study of Tenant Associations in New York City with Particular Reference to the Bronx, 1920–1927," (M.A. Thesis, Columbia University, 1929), pp. 3–4, 11.
34. Meyer, "A Study of Tenant Associations," pp. 34–35.
35. "Presents Housing Bill," *New York Times* February 8, 1921; "Orr Offers Bill for City Housing," *New York Call*, February 8, 1921; "Rally to Start Co-operative Housing Drive," *New York Call*, April 18, 1921; "Charles Solomon, Unorthodox Magistrate, Dies," *New York Times*, December 10, 1963.
36. Meyer, "A Study of Tenants Associations," pp. 22–24, 26–28.
37. Ibid., pp. 5, 11,15–17.
38. "Commission Takes Up Housing Conditions in New York," *Real Estate Record and Builders Guide* (October 20, 1923), p. 487; "Storming of Capital Hill," *Real Estate Magazine* (May 1924), p. 870; "Marshaling the Tenant Army Again," *Real Estate Record and Builders Guide* (October 17, 1925), p. 5; "Marshaling the Tenant Army Again," *Real Estate Record and Builders Guide* (March 14, 1925), p. 7.
39. Isidor Berger, "The Activities of the Protective and Defense Committee," *Real Estate News* (May 1924), pp. 4–5; "Owners' Liability Rates due for Another Advance," *Real Estate News* (October 1924), p. 8; "History of the Greater New York Taxpayers Association," *Real Estate News* (February 1924), p. 24.
40. Simon Greenfield, "The Association and The Public," *Real Estate News* (December 1919), p. 5.
41. Ignatz Reich, "What the Greater New York Taxpayers Association Does for the Property Owner," *Real Estate News* (December 1928), p. 22.
42. Randolph E. Bergstrom, *Courting Danger: Injury and Law in New York City, 1870–1910* (Ithaca: Cornell University Press, 1992), pp. 4, 115–143.
43. Max Kahn, "Constructive Liability Legislation," *Real Estate News* (February 1921), p. 11; Elias Diamond, "Progress in Our Organization" *Real Estate News* (March 1922), p. 8; John J. Berger, "The Ounce of Prevention," *Real Estate News* (April 1922), p. 20; J. W. Burke, "How the Landlord Can Beat the Crooked Lawyer," *Real Estate News* (January 1925), p. 24; "Are You Just a Landlord?" *Real Estate News* (January 1925), p. 44.
44. "Revises Public Liability Rates for Owners', Landlords' and Tenants' Risks," *Real Estate Record and Builders Guide* (February 9, 1918), p. 163.

45. Isidor Berger, "Housing Conditions are Growing Better—Not 'Worse,'" *Real Estate News* (March 25, 1925), pp. 4–5. These are Berger's own figures, and they should be taken as rough approximations. While Berger was known for a certain degree of exaggeration in his political writings, his deep involvement with GNYTA's insurance programs would clearly classify him as an expert.
46. *Altz v. Lieberson.* 233 N.Y. 16, 134 N.E., 703 (1922), cited from Newman, "Ethnicity and Business Enterprise," p. 130.
47. "New Court Decision," *Real Estate News* (October 1924), p. 5, cited from Newman, "Ethnicity and Business Enterprise," pp. 130–132.
48. The [Rhode Island Insurance Company] Spectator (May 23, 1946), p. 38, cited from Newman, "Ethnicity and Business Enterprise," p. 164.
49. Ignatz Reich, "Greater New York Taxpayers' Mutual Insurance Association Supersedes Unique Protective Organization," *Real Estate News* (September 1927), pp. 4–7; "The Association's Twenty-fifth Anniversary," *Real Estate News* (August 1932), p. 260; "GNYTA's Mutual Insurance Program," *Real Estate News* (July 1941), p. 239.
50. Newman, "Ethnicity and Business Enterprise," pp. 144–146.
51. "Our Bronx Office," *Real Estate News* (January 1928), p. 14; Isidor Berger, "The Success of an Ideal," *Real Estate News* (August 1939), p. 264.
52. "Our Bronx Home?" *Real Estate News* (January 1928), pp. 14–15; In 1936, for example, when, according to Berger, accident claims were dramatically increasing in number, GNYTA was instrumental in petitioning the Appellate Division for an official investigation into accident frauds and so-called "ambulance chasing." Its activities led to the appointment of a Manhattan assistant district attorney as chief of the Accident Fraud Bureau. See Isidor Berger, "The Success of an Ideal," *Real Estate News* (August 1939), p. 264; Isidor Berger, "Doing One Thing Well," *Real Estate News* (July 1941), p. 226.
53. Newman, "Ethnicity and Business Enterprise," p. 148.
54. Isidor Berger, "Still Pounding Them Out," *Real Estate News* (March 1923), p. 5; "Door Knob Polishing and How to Stop It," *Real Estate Magazine* (April 1924), p. 812; "Housing Situation Changes as Moving Day Approaches," *Real Estate Record and Builders Guide* (September 20, 1924), p. 8; "Housing Situation This Fall," *Real Estate Record and Builders Guide* (September 27, 1924), p. 5; Isidor Berger, "Why—The Rent Laws Extension?" *Real Estate News* (October 1925), p. 4; "Housing Situation Changes as Moving Day Approaches," *Real Estate Record and Builders Guide* (September 20, 1924), p. 8.
55. Leo Grebler, *Housing Market Behavior in a Declining Area: Long-Term Changes in Inventory and Utilization of Housing in New York's Lower East Side* (New York: Columbia University Press, 1952), p. 118; J. J. Berger, "March," *Real Estate News* (March 1924), p. 13; Isidor Berger, "The Housing Emergency—Is it Fact

of Fancy?" *Real Estate News* (October 1924), pp. 4–5; "Are You Just a Landlord?" *Real Estate News* (January 1925), p. 44; Isidor Berger, "Housing Conditions are Growing Better—Not 'Worse,' " *Real Estate News* (March 1925), p. 4; "The Battle of the Buildings," *Real Estate News* (March 1925), p. 25.

56. THD, *First Report*, (1902/3), p. 49.
57. Clarence Kahn, "Modern Property Management Versus Individual Landlordism," *Real Estate News* (March 1931), pp. 90, 102.
58. The annual rates of turnover were staggering. "Offers Plans to Aid Housing Situation" *New York Times*, May 26, 1919; "Kaplan Introduces Bill to Force Landlords to Keep Oral Leases Made with Tenants," *Bronx Home News*, January 18, 1920.
59. CHRP, *Report*, Leg. Doc. 40 (1926), pp. 77–82; CHRP, *Report*, Leg. Doc. 66 (1926), p. 19; "Tenants Ask Hylan to Remove Mann," *New York Times*, July 29, 1923.
60. Maria Jastrow, *A Time to Remember: Growing Up in New York Before the Great War* (New York: W. W. Norton, 1979), pp. 13–14, 62–69.
61. Isidor Berger, "Rent Beater's Cure," *Real Estate News* (July 1925), p. 4; Isidor Berger, "Beware the Rent Thief—How to Detect and Treat Him—Collect Delinquent Rents," *Real Estate News* (October 1925), p. 16.
62. David McAdam, *The Rights, Duties, Remedies and Incidents Belonging to and Growing Out of the Relations of Landlord and Tenant* (New York: Remick, Schilling & Co., 1900) 2: 1469.
63. "Bronx Tenants to Ask President to Investigate Profiteering Landlords," *Bronx Home News*, September 12, 1918; Frederick Spiegelberg, "The Recent Housing Legislation," *Legal Aid Review* 19 (2) (April 1921), pp. 1–7.
64. "Kaplan Introduces Bill to Force Landlords to Keep Oral Leases Made with Tenants," *Bronx Home News*, January 18, 1920.
65. ''1,372 Rent Cases Settled in Week," *New York Call*, July 14, 1919; "Tenants' League Demands State Use $50,000,000 on Building Homes," *New York Call*, July 17, 1919; "Advise Prospective October Lessees," *New York Times*, April 11, 1920; "Monthly Tenants Aided by New Law," *New York Times*, April 16, 1920.
66. "Landlords to Fight Unions of Tenants," *New York Times*, September 23, 1919.
67. "Browne Defends Lease," *New York Times*, July 16, 1923.
68. "Shows Landlords How to Raise Rents," *New York Times*, July 17, 1921.
69. Ibid.; "Lawyer Advises Tenants," *New York Times*, July 19, 1921. For other examples, see "Landlords Staging Colossal Bluff in Attempting to Nullify Rent Laws," *Bronx Home News*, September 2, 1920; ''40,000 Notified to Move on Oct. 1," *New York Times*, September 4, 1920; "Lockwood Scores New Trick Leases," *New York Times*, July 27, 1921.
70. "Landlords Adopt 'Ironclad' Lease," *New York Times*, July 10, 1923. For the full text of a slightly modified version of UREO's lease, see Appendix B.

71. See for example "Irate Tenants Denounce Some Landlords for the Lack of Heat," *Bronx Home News*, January 2, 1918.
72. Stewart Chaplin, *A Treatise on the Law of Landlord and Tenant as It Exists in the State of New York*. (New York: Baker, Voorhis & Company, 1899), pp. 677–679, 688. See also David McAdam, *The Rights, Duties, Remedies and Incidents Belonging to and Growing Out of the Relations of Landlord and Tenant* . (New York: Remick, Schilling & Company, 1900) 2: 1468–1470.
73. "Landlords Adopt 'Ironclad' Lease," *New York Times*, July 10, 1923.
74. " 'Ironclad Lease' Declared Ridiculous by Leading Realtors," *Real Estate Record and Builders Guide* (July 21, 1923), p. 71.
75. "Nathan Hirsch Quits Realty Association," *New York Times*, July 17, 1923; "Iron Clad Lease Assailed by Hirsch," *New York Evening Post*, July 17, 1923; "Taxpayers' Association Protests," *New York Times*, July 20, 1923; "Nathan Hirsch, 81, Rent-Gougers' Foe," *New York Times*, May 20, 1947.
76. "Iron Clad Lease Assailed by Hirsch," *New York Evening Post*, July 17, 1923; " 'Ironclad' Lease Dies Under Fire," *New York Times*, July 20, 1923; "Tenants Would Ask Extra Bus Session to Extend Rent Law," *New York Times*, July 24, 1923.
77. "Untermeyer to Lead Fight on New Lease," *New York Times*, July 15, 1923; "Browne Defends Lease," *New York Times*, July 16, 1923; "Browne is Willing to Test New Lease," *New York Times*, July 17, 1923.
78. "Would Bar Eviction During Rent Crisis," *New York Times*, August 27, 1920. CHRP reports, other sources on standardized leases.
79. CHRP, *Report of Commission of Housing and Regional Planning* (1924), pp. 27–28.
80. G. L. Genung, "Landlord and Tenant," in *Real Estate Manual for Brokers, Owners, and Operators*, ed. Harry Hall et al. (Garden City, NY: Doubleday, Page, 1925), pp. 125–128.
81. "Rent Strikers Win Victory in Eviction Case," *Bronx Home News*, November 5, 1918.
82. "Landlord Demands Extra Month's Rent From Tenants and Threatens Evictions," *Bronx Home News*, July 25, 1920. See also CHRP, *Report*, Leg. Doc. 43 (1923) pp. 27–28.
83. "Schemes of Greedy Landlords Who Demand Cash Deposits; How One Room Was Rented," *Bronx Home News*, September 28, 1920.
84. "Landlord Demands Extra Month's Rent From Tenants and Threatens Evictions," *Bronx Home News*, July 25, 1920.
85. "Rent Losses," *Real Estate News* (May 1931), p. 153; "Floaters," *Real Estate News* (June 1932), p. 191; "Tenants Demand Lower Rentals and More Luxuries," *Real Estate News* (January 1932), p. 15.
86. J.J. Berger, "Beating the 'Rent-Beat,' " *Real Estate News* (August 1931), pp.

268–269; "Beating the "Rent Beat,' " *Real Estate News* (September 1931), p. 296; "Association Starts Campaign to Curb 'Skipping Tenant Evil,' " *Real Estate News* (January 1932), pp. 16–17; "The 'Skipping Tenant Evil,' " *Real Estate News* (February 1932), p. 44; "Proposed Anti-skip Law Making Progress," *Real Estate News* (November 1932), pp. 380, 390; "The Free Rent or Concession Evil," *Real Estate News* (April 1933), pp. 128, 141; "When Your Tenants Move Out Owing Rent," *Real Estate News* (January 1940), p. 371; "The Skipping-Tenant Evil," *Real Estate News* (July 1940), p. 226; Daniel Eisenberg, "The Habits and Habitats of Rent 'Skips,' " *Real Estate News* (July 1940), pp. 238–239.
87. Ignatz Reich, "What Renting Means Today" *Real Estate News* (June 1923), pp. 194, 205.

7. The Depression and the Decline of Amatuer Tenement Operators

1. "Rent Laws to Expire June First," *Real Estate News* (May 1929), p. 25.
2. "Another Step in De-Control," *Real Estate Record and Builders Guide* (Dec. 15, 1928), p. 5; "Another Step Nearer Normalcy," *Real Estate Record and Builders Guide* (March 30, 1929), p. 5; "Again Urges That Rent Laws be Allowed to Die," *Real Estate Record and Builders Guide* (March 30, 1929), p. 7; "Emergency Rent Laws Expiring," *Real Estate Record and Builders Guide* (May 18, 1929), p. 5; "Explains the Status of Tenancies After May 31," *Real Estate Record and Builders Guide* (May 18, 1929), p. 7.
3. For a brief overview of some of the new legal complexities, see Reuben Wittstein, "The Law and the Landlord," *Real Estate News* (December 1930), pp. 416–417. See also J.J. Berger, "Colored Rent Facts Colored," *Real Estate Magazine* (September 1930), pp. 308–309.
4. Isaac Goldberg, "The Mortgage Situation," *Real Estate News* (September 1927), p. 22.
5. Isidor Berger, "The Partnership of Mortgagees and Landlords," *Real Estate News* (March 1932), pp. 86–87.
6. State Board of Housing (abbreviated to SBH), *Report of the State Board of Housing* (1929), pp. 65–66. See also "Vacancies Constantly Increase in Low-Priced Tenements," *Real Estate Record and Builders Guide* (February 26, 1927), p. 7.
7. "General History Limited Dividend Movement," Housing Guide Book, WPA Historical Records Survey, Federal Writers Project, Box 3634, Municipal Archives, New York City, pp. 9–10, 13; SBH, *Report*, (1928), pp. 17–18.
8. SBH, *Report* (1929), p. 71.
9. Deborah Dash Moore, *At Home in America: Second Generation New York Jews* (New York: Colombia University Press, 1981), p. 72; Zalmen Yoffeh, "The

Passing of the East Side," *Menorah Journal* 15 (December 1929), pp. 265–275; "Rent Laws and Slums," *Real Estate Magazine* (April 1930), p. 23. See also Nancy L. Green, "Sweatshop Migrations: The Garment Industry Between Home and Shop," in *The Landscape of Modernity: Essays on New York City, 1900–1940*, ed. David Ward and Olivier Zunz (New York: Russell Sage Foundation, 1992), pp. 222–223; SBH, *Report* (1929), p. 55.

10. Frederick M. Binder and David Reimers, *All the Nations Under Heaven: An Ethnic and Racial History of New York City* (New York: Columbia University Press, 1995), p. 156–157.
11. Between 1909 and 1940 in the Lower East Side, the highest average annual rate of decline in the used-housing inventory occurred between 1928 and 1934. The number of occupied units dropped 4.4 percent a year, even as the total number of units standing dropped 2.4 percent a year. These figures were consistently higher than for Manhattan as a whole. Leo Grebler, *Housing Market Behavior in a Declining Area: Long-Term Changes in Inventory and Utilization of Housing in New York's Lower East Side* (New York: Columbia University Press, 1952), pp. 35–36, 123–125; "Moving This Fall is Most Extensive Since 1920," *Real Estate Record and Builders Guide* (September 29, 1929), p. 7.
12. SBH, *Report* (1929), p. 55.
13. Richard Plunz, *A History of Housing in New York City* (New York: Columbia University Press, 1990), pp. 151–153, 161, 165–167.
14. SBH, *Report* (1928), pp. 40–41.
15. Tenement House Department (abbreviated to THD), *Tenth Report of the Tenement House Department of the City of New York—Report for the Years 1918–1929* p. 24.
16. Ignatz Reich, "Vacant Apartments that can be Filled," *Real Estate News* (January 1929), p. 11.
17. "Many Bills Aimed at Property Owners Presented at Albany," *Real Estate Record and Builders Guide* (January 22, 1927), p. 9; "New Crop of Rent Bills Introduced," *Real Estate News* (January 1928), p. 10; "Denounces Bills at Albany to Bait Landlords," *Real Estate Record and Builders Guide* (January 28, 1928), p. 9; "Denounces Bills at Albany to Bait Landlords," *Real Estate Record and Builders Guide* (January 28, 1928), p. 9; "Legislature Not to Extend Emergency Rent Laws," *Real Estate Record and Builders Guide* (March 10, 1928), p. 7.
18. "General History Limited Dividend Movement," 5–6, Housing Guide Book, WPA Historical Records Survey, Federal Writers Project, Box 3634, Municipal Archives, New York City; "Report and Opening Remarks by President Reich at the General Meeting of the Greater New York Taxpayers Association," *Real Estate News* (October 1928), p. 7.

19. "Recommended Important Changes in Emergency Rent Law," *Real Estate Record and Builders Guide* (January 16, 1926), pp. 7–8; "Rent Laws to be Continued," *Real Estate Record and Builders Guide* (February 6, 1926), p. 5; "Legislation Plans Extension of Rent Laws to June 1, 1927," *Real Estate Record and Builders Guide* (February 6, 1926), p. 10; SBH, *Report* (1928), pp. 9–10, 58–59.
20. Edith Berger Drellich and Andrée Emery, *Rent Control in War and Peace* (New York: National Municipal Review, 1939), p. 60–61; CHRP, *Report* Leg. Doc. 66 (1926), pp. 48–49.
21. A. J. Simberg, "Modernizing Old Tenements," *Real Estate News* (November 1929), pp. 17–19.
22. Donna Gabaccia, "Little Italy's Decline: Immigrant Renters and Investors in a Changing City" in *The Landscape of Modernity: Essays on New York City, 1900–1940*, ed. David Ward and Olivier Zunz (New York: Russell Sage Foundation, 1992), pp. 245–246.
23. Leo Grebler, *Experience in Urban Real Estate Investment: An Interim Report Based on New York City Properties* (New York: Columbia University Press, 1955), pp. 82–87.
24. Grebler, *Housing Market Behavior*, pp. 40–44.
25. See, for example, James B. Stewart, "Prophets of 'Inevitable Slump' Jolted by Current Trading," *Real Estate Magazine* (December 1928), p. 13; E. T. Scowcroft, "1928 a Pageant of Spectacular Real Estate Transactions," *Real Estate Magazine* (January 1929), pp. 10–12.
26. Isidor Berger, "The Partnership of Mortgagees and Landlords," *Real Estate News* (March 1932), pp. 86–87.
27. Anton L. Trunk, "The Attitude of Lending Institutions Toward Mortgagors," *Real Estate Record and Builders Guide* (November 26, 1932), p. 6.
28. Philip K. Kniskern, "Kniskern Speaks on Mortgages at Convention," *Real Estate Record and Builders Guide* (October 12, 1929), p. 7; "Real Estate Benefit Seen in Stock Depression," *Real Estate Record and Builders Guide* (November 2, 1929), pp. 7, 33; Michael Casey, "Wall Street's Debacle Should Be an Impetus to Real Estate," *Real Estate Magazine* (November 1929), p. 7.
29. "Exchange Formed to Sell Real Estate Securities," *Real Estate Record and Builders Guide* (November 24, 1928), pp. 7, 9; "Creation of Real Estate Board of New York Exchange," *Real Estate Magazine* (December 1928), pp. 9–10; "Those Who Developed the Exchange Plan," *Real Estate Magazine* (December 1928), pp. 11–12; "Many Seeking Seats on New Real Estate Exchange," *Real Estate Record and Builders Guide* (May 11, 1929), p. 8; "Will Stabilize Real Estate Securities," *Real Estate Record and Builders Guide* (August 10, 1929), p. 5; "Many Notables Witness Opening of Securities Exchange," *Real Estate Magazine* (January 1930), pp. 9–10; Peter Grimm, "Destined to Quicken the Pulse of Real Estate," *Real Estate Magazine* (January 1930), pp. 11, 44.

30. Isidor Berger, "The Partnership of Mortgagees and Landlords," *Real Estate News* (March 1932), pp. 86–87.
31. Grebler, *Housing Market Behavior*, p. 97.
32. New York City Housing Authority, *Report of the New York City Housing Authority Hearings* (January 25, 1937), pp. 21–26, 45–46; "Harrying the Landlord," *Real Estate News* (February 1932), p. 45.
33. Joseph C. Lombardi, "Can Mortgage Interest Rates be Uniformly Readjusted?" *Real Estate Record and Builders Guide* 131 (2) (January 1933), p. 1; R.M. Hurd, "The Mortgage Situation in New York City," *Real Estate Record and Builders Guide* 131 (4) (February 1933), p. 1.
34. See, for example, Ignatz Reich, "Mortgage Moratorium Defeated," *Real Estate News* (April 1933), pp. 122–123.
35. See, for example, Lyman Brewster Ives, "A Consideration of Apartment House Operating Problems," *Real Estate Record and Builders Guide* (December 31, 1932), pp. 8–11; George Edgecomb, "Agency Management Prestige Gains Through Depression," *Real Estate Magazine* (December 1932), pp. 11–12, 38–39.
36. Grebler, *Housing Market Behavior*, pp. 96–101.
37. George Edgecomb, "Agency Management Prestige Gains Through Depression," *Real Estate Magazine* (December 1932), p. 11; see also Clarence Kahn, "Modern Property Management versus Individual Landlordism," *Real Estate News* (March 1931), p. 90; Ignatz Reich, "What Renting Means Today," *Real Estate News* (June 1932), p. 194.
38. Ignatz Reich, "Our Quarter Annual Report," *Real Estate News* (October 1929), pp. 10–11; "Among Our Friends and Allies," *Real Estate Magazine* (April 1929), pp. 38, 60; I. Montifiore Levy, "Lower East Side Destined for Epochal Housing Projects," *Real Estate Magazine* (May 1929), pp. 24–25, 53. The involvement of GNYTA representatives was prompted in part by vocal criticism of the plan by Lower East Side landowners. Mayor Walker combined landlord-involvement in the project with threats of higher tax assessments to overcome their opposition. See Anthony Jackson, *A Place Called Home: A History of Low-Income Housing in Manhattan* (Cambridge: MIT Press, 1976), pp. 188–189.
39. Robert Caro, *The Power Broker: Robert Moses and the Fall of New York* (New York: Vintage Books, 1974), pp. 375–376, 378. See also Plunz, *History of Housing*, pp. 208–209; and Jackson, *A Place Called Home*, pp. 188–189, 193–194.
40. See especially Lyman Brewster Ives, "A Consideration of Apartment House Operating Problems," *Real Estate Record and Builders Guide* (December 31, 1932), pp. 8–11. See also "Peter Grimm Discusses Poorly Built Buildings," *Real Estate Record and Builders Guide* (June 30, 1928), p. 6; "Describes Need of Real Estate Profession," *Real Estate Record and Builders Guide* (Nov. 9,

1929), p. 7; "Standard Apartment House Lease Object of Group," *Real Estate Record and Builders Guide* (Dec. 7, 1929), p. 6; E. R. Munn, "Reciprocal Relationship Between Renting and Managing," *Real Estate Magazine* (March 1930), pp. 27–28; Charles G. Edwards, "High Ideals Have Practical Value in Real Estate Profession," *Real Estate Magazine* (January 1931), pp. 23–26; William E. Barton, "Going Back to First Principles of Management Economics," *Real Estate Magazine* (April 1931), pp. 22–25, 51–55; "Defects of Concession System in Apartment Renting Bared," *Real Estate Magazine* (June 1931), pp. 5, 40; "J. Irving Walsh Sees Hope in Construction Decline," *Real Estate Record and Builders Guide* (June 13, 1931), pp. 9–10; Charles W. Lange, "Defects of Concession System in Apartment Renting Bared," *Real Estate Magazine* (June 1931), pp. 5–6, 40; Freeman Crowell, "Standard Practices in Apartment House Management," *Real Estate Record and Builders Guide* (November 12, 1932), pp. 3–4. A similar trend may have occurred in commercial property as well. See Lee Thompson Smith, "Some of the Broader Phases of Building Management," *Real Estate Magazine* (March 1930), pp. 39–41, 60.

41. Freeman Crowell, "Standard Practices in Apartment House Management" *Real Estate Record and Builders Guide* (November 12, 1932), p. 3.
42. Caro, *The Power Broker*, pp. 323–325.
43. Ignatz Reich, "Kind and Unkind Words About Landlords" *Real Estate News* (January 1932), p. 18; "Dispossess Proceedings" *Real Estate News* (February 1933), p. 45.
44. Mark Naison, "From Resistance to Rent Control: Tenant Activism in the Great Depression," in *The Tenant Movement in New York City*, eds. Ronald Lawson with Mark Naison (New Brunswick: Rutgers University Press), pp. 99–100.
45. "Rent Strikes—A Challenge to Organized Landlords" *Real Estate News* (February 1932), p. 54; "Association Seeks Injunction Against Picketing Tenants" *Real Estate News* (March 1932), p. 90; Igantz Reich, "Rent Picketing Injunction Granted" *Real Estate News* (April 1932), p. 124; "Fighting Owners' Battles" *Real Estate News* (May 1932), p. 152; "Socialist Party Instigates Lower rent Agitation" *Real Estate News* (May 1932), p. 166; Ignatz Reich, "The Association at Work" *Real Estate News* (August 1932), p. 266; Isidor Berger, "The Rent Strike Racket" *Real Estate News* (January 1933), p. 12; Ignatz Reich, "The Rent Strike Menace" *Real Estate News* (February 1933), p. 50; Sidney Smith, "The Legal Aspect of Rent Strikes" *Real Estate News* (February 1933), p. 53; "Rent Picketing Held Illegal" *Real Estate News* (March 1933), p. 83.
46. "A Brief History of the Tenants' Movements in New York City" typescript in Heinz Norden Collection, Taniment Library, New York University, pp. 4–6.
47. Naison, "From Eviction Resistance," pp. 100–101.

48. "Reds Fight Police in Bronx Evictions," *New York Times*, February 2, 1932, cited from Peter Marcuse, "The Beginning of Public Housing in New York," *Journal of Urban History* 12 (4) (August 1986), p. 356.
49. Naison, "From Eviction Resistance," pp. 102–104.
50. Mayor's Order Stays Evictions" *Real Estate News* (December 1930), p. 410; "High Court Rules on Evictions" *Real Estate News* (January 1931), p. 9; "Letters to Mayor Walker and Chief Marshal Jacobs" *Real Estate News* (January 1931), p. 12; "Legislation" *Real Estate News* (March 1933), p. 79; "The Marshal's Bill Dies" *Real Estate News* (April 1933), p. 115.
51. Katherine Meyer, "A Study of Tenement Associations in New York City with Particular Reference to the Bronx, 1920–1927" (M.A. Thesis, Columbia University, 1929), pp. 34–35.
52. Joel Schwartz, "Tenant Unions in New York City's Low-Rent Housing, 1933–1949" *Journal of Urban History* 12 (4) (August 1986), pp. 416–417; Plunz, *History of Housing*, pp. 151–158, 210–212.
53. Schwartz, "Tenant Unions in New York City's Low-Rent Housing, 1933–1949," pp. 416–417.
54. Ibid., 417–418; Norden, "A Brief History of the Tenants' Movements in New York City," 5–6, typescript in Heinz Norden Collection, Taniment Library, New York University; Ira S. Robbins, "Tenant Management Conflict in Housing Project," *Real Estate Record and Builders Guide* (November 16, 1935), pp. 15–18.
55. Norden, "A Brief History of the Tenants' Movements in New York City," pp. 7–8.
56. Schwartz, "Tenant Unions in New York City's Low-Rent Housing," pp. 420–421; Mark Naison, "From Eviction Resistance," pp. 120–122.
57. Citizens' Housing and Planning Council, *How Tax Exemption Broke the Housing Deadlock in New York City* (May 1960), pp. 3–63, 3–68, 3–69. For comments by REBNY and GNYTA officials see "Governor's Plans Stir Some Dissent," *New York Times*, January 7, 1926; "Assails Smith Plan for Housing Relief," *New York Times*, February 25, 1926; "Berger Criticizes Gov. Smith's Plan," *New York Times*, March 7, 1926; Ignatz Reich, "The Sham Behind the 'First Houses,'" *Real Estate Magazine* (February 1936), p. 26; Ignatz Reich, "Housing the Poor—A Hypocrisy!" *Real Estate News* (March 1936), p. 23.
58. "Assails Smith Plan for Housing Relief," *New York Times*, February 25, 1926; "Berger Criticizes Gov. Smith's Plan," *New York Times*, March 7, 1926.
59. "Stewart Browne, Civic Leader, 84," *New York Times*, August 5, 1938; I. Hirschell Phillips, "Moratorium Bill, Aimed at Halting Foreclosures, Becomes Law," *Real Estate Magazine* (September 1933), p. 4; "J. Irving Walsh," *Real Estate Magazine* (July 1933), p. 23.
60. Naison, "From Eviction Resistance," pp. 95, 120–122.

61. Ibid., pp. 127–129.
62. Schwartz, "Tenant Unions in New York City's Low-Rent Housing," p. 437.
63. "Peter Grimm, Former President of Board, Honored by Columbia University" *Real Estate Magazine* (July 1934), p. 28.
64. Naison, "From Eviction Resistance," p. 127.
65. By 1947, Congress had discontinued most federally-mandated rent control programs with the exception of New York City's. In New York, lawmakers replaced the war-time emergency programs with more permanent rent controls to be run by state and municipal authorities and applied to pre-1947 multi-family dwellings.
66. Ronald Lawson, "The Political Face of New York's Real Estate Industry" *New York Affairs* 6 (2) (1980), p. 91.

Conclusion. The Tenant City

1. See, for example, Michael A. Stegman, "The Model: Rent Control in New York City," in *The Rent Control Debate*, ed. Paul L. Niebanck (Chapel Hill, NC: University of North Carolina Press, 1985), pp. 30–32.
2. For a review of some of the criticism directed against rent control in New York, see William Tucker, *The Excluded Americans: Homelessness and Housing Policies* (Washington DC: Regnery Gateway, 1990), pp. 268–277.

SELECTED BIBLIOGRAPHY

Part I: New York Real Estate Periodicals

American Architect and Building News.
Annual Record of Assessed Valuations. (1904–1944).
Apartment Building Construction, Manhattan, 1902–1953. [by] Gordon Macdonald.
Bronx Real Estate and Building News. Real Estate Board of the Bronx. (1927–).
Building Age and National Builder. (1879–1930).
Building Developer. (1927–1929).
Building Investment in Metropolitan New York (1925–1932).
Building Operation; the Realty Authority of Metropolitan New York. (1932–1936).
Building Reporter and Realty News (1944–).
Citizen. United Real Estate Owners Association. (1923–1931).
Citizens Housing Council of New York. (1940–41).
Diary and Manual. [Real Estate Board of the Bronx Annual]. (1929–).
Diary and Manual. [Real Estate Board of New York Annual]. (1915–1945).
House and Real Estate Owners' Association of the Twelfth and Nineteenth Wards Bulletin. (1914–1922).
National Association of Real Estate Boards, *Annual Reports of the President.*
———. *Constitution and By-laws.* 1924.
———. *News Service.* (1924–1951).
———. *Semi-annual Survey of Real Estate Markets.* (1924–1951).
New York Realty Journal [weekly] (1905–1911).
Office Building Construction, Manhattan, 1901–1953. [by] Gordon MacDonald. 1952.
Pease and Elliman's Real Estate Indicator. (1912–).
Property; The National Realty Mart. (1931–).

Real Estate and Building Management Digest. The Real Estate Board of New York. (1934–1937).
Real Estate Board of New York, *Tenement House Series.* (1943–1944?).
Real Estate Daily News; the Metropolitan Builder. (1928–1929).
Real Estate Magazine. The Real Estate Board of New York. (1920–1934).
Real Estate Magazine: A National Monthly for Owners, Brokers, Builders, Investors. (1912–1915).
Real Estate News. Greater New York Taxpayers' Association. (1919–1944).
Real Estate Record and Builders Guide. (1866–present).
Real Estate Views. (1938–1942).
Reference, Diary and Yearbook. [Brooklyn Board of Realtors].
Some Economic Aspects of the Recent Emergency Housing Legislation in New York. [by Samuel McLure Lindsay] 1924.
Technical Information for Real Estate Experts. [by] William E. Davies. 1915.

Part II: Newspapers

American Hebrew.
Bronx Home News. (1906–1924)
Brooklyn Eagle. (1841–)
Daily North Side News. (1897–1936?)
Daily Worker. (1922–)
Daily People.
East Side Chamber News. (1928–1943)
Evening Post.
Globe and Commercial Advertiser.
Harlem Home News.
Harper's Weekly.
Jewish Daily Forward.
New York Age. (1910–)
New York American.
New York Amsterdam News.
New York Call. (1908–1923)
New York Evening Journal.
New York Herald. (1841–)
New York Sun.
New York Times. (1851–)
New York Tribune.
New York World.
Weekly Tenant.

Part III: Legislative Reports, Hearings, Collections, and Governmental Papers

Al Smith Papers, State Archives, State Library of New York, Albany, New York.
Commission of Housing and Regional Planning Hearings, (1923–1927)—"Stein Commission"
Hearings of the Senate and Assembly Committees on Cities, Mar. 23, 1920. Transcript in Smith Papers, Box 260–46 II.
Heinz Norden Collection, Taniment Library, New York University.
Hylan Papers, Municipal Archives, New York.
Jacob Riis Papers, The New York Public Library.
Joint Legislative Committee on Housing, Hearings, 1919–1920, 7 vols., unpublished.
New York City Board of Aldermen, *Public Hearings Held by the Committee on Buildings*. June 2, 1909.
New York City Department of Health, *Monthly Bulletins* (1910–1922).
New York City Housing Authority Hearings on Living and Housing Conditions in the City of New York, June 25, 1937.
New York State Commission on Housing and Regional Planning Hearings, 1925.
"Report of the Mayor's Committee on Taxation and Investigation of Mortgage Loans and the Mayor's Committee on Rent Profiteering," (New York, 1919).
"Report of the Mayor's Committee on Housing," New York: February 29, 1924.
Report of the Commission of Immigration of the State of New York. Albany, NY: 1909.
Reports of the Immigration Commission: Immigrant Banks, 61st Congress, 3rd Session, 1911, Vol. 37, Senate Doc. 753
Reports of the State Board of Housing, L.D. (1928–1930).
Reports of the Tenement House Department. (1901–1929).
Richard Watson Gilder Papers, The New York Public Library.
Tenement House Department Print Collection, Local History and Genealogy Division, New York Public Library.
WPA Survey—e.g. "Housing Guidebook for New York City" & "Housing in New York" Municipal Archives, New York.

Part IV: Primary Sources on Landlord-Tenant Law

Aron, Harold G. "The New York Landlord and Tenant Law of 1920" *Cornell Law Quarterly* (November 1920): pp. 1–35.
Attorney-at-law. *Practical Instruction on the Law of Landlords and Tenants and of Purchasers and Sellers of Real Estate*. New York: William M. Perkins, 1872.

Chaplin, Stewart. *A Treatise on the Law of Landlord and Tenant as it Exists in the State of New York*. New York: Baker, Voorhis and Co., 1899.

George, William. *The Law of Apartments, Flats and Tenements*. New York: Fallon Law Book Company, 1908.

Lauer, Edgar, and Victor House. *The Tenant and his Landlord*. New York: Baker, Voorhis and Co., 1921.

Levine, Abraham Lincoln. *Handy Manual on Landlord and Tenant*. Brooklyn, New York: Tandard Text press, 1932.

McAdam, David. *The Rights, Duties, Remedies and Incidents Belonging to and Growing Out of the Relation of Landlord and Tenant* (3 vols). New York: Remick, Schilling and Co., 1900.

Member of the New York Bar. *Walker's Landlords' and Tenants' Guide for New York*. New York: Walker and Co., 1885.

Sloane, Charles W. *A Treatise on the Law of landlord and Tenant with Special Reference to the Law of the State of New York*. New York: S.S. Peloubet and Co., 1884.

Townshend, John. *The Law and Practice on Proceedings by Landlords to recover Possession of Demised Premises on the Non-Payment of Rent or Expiration of the Term*. New York: Baker, Voorhis and Co., 1866.

Underhill, H. C. *A Treatise on the Law of Landlord and Tenant* (2 vols). Chicago: T.H. Flood and Co., 1909.

Part V: Primary Sources, Books and Articles

American Face Brick Association. *Industrial Buildings and Housing; Valuable Information for the Designers and Prospective Owner of Factories and Homes.* 1926.

Arner, G. B. L. "Land Values in New York City" *The Quarterly Journal of Economics* 36 (August 1922): 545–580.

"Attack on the Tenement House Laws" *Catholic World* 76 (1902–3): 851.

Bacon, Albion Fellows. *What Bad Housing Means to the Community*. Boston: American Unitarian Association, 1910–12.

Bede, John W. *O.K., It's A Deal; Odd Tales about Real Estate*. 1946.

Blaustein, David. "Cockroach Landlords" *New Era Illustrated Magazine* 4 (6) (May 1904): 379–383.

Bolton, R.P. *Building for Profit: Principles Governing the Economic Improvements of Real Estate*. New York: Devinne, 1911.

Boyd, John Taylor. "A Step Towards Slum Clearance" *Architectural Record* 57 (1925): 205–216.

Brown, Frank Chouteau. "The Low-Rental Apartment—An Economic Fallacy, Part I" *Architectural Record* 55 (5) (May 1924): 405–415.

———. "The Low-Rental Apartment—An Economic Fallacy, Part II" *Architectural Record* 55 (6) (June 1924): 588–597.

Campbell, Helen. "Studies in the Slums II—Water Street and Its Works" *Lippincott's Magazine* 25 (May 1880): 568–573.

———. "Studies in the Slums II—Jerry" *Lippincott's Magazine* 25 (June 1880): 740–745.

Campbell, Mrs. Helen et al. *Darkness and Daylight in New York, or Lights and Shadows of New York Life*. Hartford, CT: Hartford Publishing, 1897.

Carey, W.A. *How to Buy and Sell Real Estate at a Profit; a Handbook*. 1905.

Charities. [later called *The Survey and Charities and Commons*] Charity Organization Society, (1899–1925)

Citizens' Association of New York. *Report of the Council of Hygiene and Public Health Upon the Sanitary Condition of the City*. New York: D. Appleton, 1866.

Citizens' Housing Council of New York. *Housing Agencies in the City of New York; An Analysis of the Powers and Activities of the Four Public Agencies...* 1941.

———. *How Tax Exemption Broke the Housing Deadlock in New York City*. New York: Citizens' Housing Council, 1960.

City of New York Vacancy and Rent Survey, January 1938. WPA.

Collins, Ellen. "Housing Reform Through Enlightened Management" *Municipal Affairs* 6 (3) (Fall 1902): 458–461.

Cramer, John W. "The Story of a Tenement House" *Frank Leslie's Sunday Magazine* 5 (6) (June 1879): 641–645.

———. "Recent Progress in Tenement House Reform" *Annals: American Academy of Political and Social Sciences* (March 1904): 297–310.

———. "The Truth About Trinity's Tenements" *The Survey* (February 26 1910): 797–808.

Cross and Brown Company; Fifty Years of Real Estate Service, 1910–1960.

DeForest, Robert W., and Lawrence Veiller. *The Tenement House Problem*. [2 vols] New York: MacMillan, 1903.

Dinwiddie, Emily W. *The Tenants' Manual*. New York: 26 Jones Street, 1903.

Drellich, Edith Berger, and Andree Emery. *Rent Control in War and Peace*, for the Citizen's Housing and Planning Council of New York, 1939.

Foster, George. *New York by Gas Light, and Other Urban Sketches*. New York: 1850.

Gage, Daniel D. "Wartime Experiments in Federal Rent Control" *Journal of Land and Public Utility Economics* 23 (1947).

Gries, John, and James Ford, (eds.). *Slums, Large-scale Housing and Decentralization*. Washington, D.C.: National Capitol Press, 1932.

Griscom, John, The Sanitary Conditions of the Laboring Population of New York. New York: Harper and Brothers, 1845.

Gross, Arthur. "The New Multiple Dwelling Dwellings Law of New York" *Archi-

tectural Forum 53 (3) (September 1930): 273–276.

Hall, Harry, et al. (eds.). *Real Estate Manual for Brokers, Owners, and Operators.* Garden City, New York: Doubleday, Page and Co., 1925.

History of Architecture and the Building Trades of Greater New York. [2 vols] New York: Union History Company, 1899.

"Housing Standards in Brooklyn: An Intensive Study of the Housing record of 3227 Working-men's Families." Brooklyn, (October 1918).

How To Care for Property; Outlining a Safe Course for the Landlord to Pursue in the Conduct of his Property. 1906.

Hurd, Richard. *Principles of City Land Values.* New York: Real Estate Record and Guide, 1903.

King, Albert B. *The Tenement Houses of New York City.* New York: Albert B. King, 1891.

Mailly, William. "The New York Rent Strike" *Independent* 14 (3085) (January 16, 1908): 148–152.

McFarlane, Arthur E. "The Inflammable Tenement" *McClure's Magazine* (October 1911): 690–701.

Meyer, Katherine J. "A Study of Tenant Associations in New York City with Particular reference to the Bronx" Master's Thesis, Columbia University, Department of Sociology, 1928.

Murphy, J.R. *Pointers on Real Estate...* Lectures by J.R. Murphy. J.R. Murphy Real Estate School. 1926.

National Housing Association Publications Series (1911–1919).

National Urban League. "Housing Conditions Among Negroes in Harlem, New York City" *Publication of the National Urban League*, 4 (2) (January 1915).

Nevins, Richard, History of Horace S. Ely & Co. of New York. 1955.

New York City Housing Authority. *The Failure of Housing Regulation.* New York: 1936.

New York Housing Authority. *Studies of Physical Occupancy and Financial Condition of Properties in New York City.* 1936. WPA.

New York Urban League. *Urban Housing Management Association, Inc.* 1943,—Arthur C. Holden Papers, Cornell University

Norden, Heinz. "the Relationship between Landlords and Tenants in Low Rent Housing,"—report submitted to Citizen's Housing Council, Feb. 17, 1938,—Norden Papers.

"Opening Gun of a Slum War" Literary Digest (November 6, 1926): 12–13.

Oppenheim, Beatrice, Look Before You Lease: The Tenants Home Companion. New York: Vanguard Press, 1940.

Pellew, H. E., et al. "New York Tenement Houses" *The Sanitarian* (March 1879): 107–111.

Pink, Louis H. *The New Day in Housing.* New York: John Day Company, 1926?.

President's Conference on Home Building and Home Ownership. Washington D.C., 1931.

Rawson, Jonathan A., Jr. "Modern Tenement Houses" *Popular Science Monthly* (February, 1912, pp. 191–196.

Record and Guide. *A History of Real Estate Building and Architecture in New York City.* New York: Record and Guide, 1898.

Roberts, Isaac. *Rent Reduction and Home Ownership Through Co-operation.* New York: White Oak Publishing Co., 1922.

Sanitary Condition of the Tenements of Trinity Church. New York: The Evening Post Printing House, 1895.

Schaffter, Dorothy. *State Housing Agencies.* New York: Columbia University Press, 1942.

Schaub, Edward L. "The Regulation of Rentals During the War Period" *The Journal of Political Economy* 18 no. 1 (January, 1920, pp. 1–36.

Smith, John Cotton. *Improvement of the Tenement House System of New York.* New York: American Church Press, 1879.

Speigelberg, Frederick. "The Recent Housing Legislation," *Legal Aid Review* 19 (2) (April 1921).Stein, Clarence. "The Housing Crisis in New York," *The Survey* (September 1, 1920): 659–661.

Sutton, Charles. *The New York Tombs: Its Secrets and Its Mysteries.* San Francisco: A. Roman & Co., 1874.

Swan, Herbert S. *The Housing Market in New York City.* Made for the Inst. of Public Admins. in New York, 1944.

Tenement House Administration. New York: Bureau of Municipal Research, 1909.

Tenement Housing System in New York. New York: n.p., 1878.

Veiller, Lawrence. *Housing Reform: A Handbook for Practical Use in American Cities.* New York: Charities Publications, 1910.

Welfare Council of New York City, Housing Information Bureau Publications. (1930–).

Welfare Council of New York City. *Homes by Tenure and Value by Monthly Rental by Healthy Areas.* 1930.

What the Law requires of Old Law Tenements. New York: Multiple Dwellings Law Committee, 1935.

Whitaker, Charles Harris, et al. *The Housing Problem in War and in Peace.* New York: Octagon, 1918.

Wood, Edith Elmer. *The Housing of the Unskilled Wage Earner: America's Next Problem.* New York: Macmillan, 1919.

———. *Slums and Blighted Areas in the Untied States.* Housing Division Bulletin No. 1, 1935.

Part VI: Secondary Sources

Albion, Robert Greenhalgh. *The Rise of New York Port: 1815–1860*. New York: Scribner, 1939.

Barrows, Robert G. "Beyond the Tenement: Patterns of American urban Housing, 1870–1930" *Journal of Urban History* 9 (August 1983):395–420.

Beito, david T. *Taxpayers in Revolt: Tax Resistance During the Great Depression*. Chapel Hill: University of North Carolina Press, 1989.

Berghstrom, Randolph E. *Courting Danger: Injury and Law in New York City, 1870–1910* Ithaca, New York: Cornell University Press, 1992.

Blackmar, Elizabeth. *Manhattan for Rent, 1785–1850*. Ithaca, New York: Cornell University Press, 1989.

Bouma, Donald. "Analysis of the Social Power Position of a Real Estate Board," *Social Problems* 10 (1) (1962): 121–132.

Bremner, Robert H. "The Big Flat—History of a New York Tenement House." *American Historical Review* 64 (1954): 55–62.

Caro, Robert. *The Power Broker: Robert Moses and the Fall of New York*. New York: Vintage Books, 1974.

Chandler, Alfred D. *The Visible Hand: The Managerial Revolution in American Business*. Cambridge, MA: 1977.

Chauncey, George. *Gay New York: Gender, Urban Culture, and the Making of the Gay Male World, 1890–1940*. New York: Basic Books, 1994.

Cowan, Neil M. and Ruth Schwartz Cowan. *Our Parents' Lives: The Americanization of Eastern European Jews*. New York: Basic Books, 1989.

Cromley, Elizabeth Collins. *Alone Together: A History of New York's Early Apartments*. Ithaca, New York: Cornell University Press, 1990.

Davies, Pearl J. *Real Estate in American History*. Washington, D.C.: 1958.

Domosh, Mona. "The Symbolism of the Skyscraper: Case Studies of New York's Tallest Buildings," *Journal of Urban History* 14 (May 1988): 321–345.

Doucet, Michael, and John Weaver. "The North American Shelter Business, 1860–1920: A Study of a Canadian Real Estate and Property Management Agency," *Business History Review* 58 (Summer 1984): 234–262.

———. "Urban Land Development in Nineteenth Century North America: Themes in the Literature," *Journal of Urban History* 8 (May 1982): 299–342.

Dreier, Peter. "The Tenant Movement," in *Marxism and the Metropolis: New Perspectives in Urban Political Economy*. eds. William K. Tabb and Larry Sawyer. New York: Oxford University press, 1984.

Edel, Matthew, and Elliot D. Sclar and Daniel Luria. *Shaky Palaces: Homeownership and Social Mobility in Boston's Suburbanization*. New York: Columbia University Press, 1984.

Ernst, Robert. *Immigrant Life in New York City, 1825–1863*. New York: Columbia University Press, 1949.

Fee, Elizabeth, and Steven Corey, Garbage! The History and Politics of Trash in New York City. New York: The New York Public Library, 1994.

Feagin, Joe R., and Robert Parker. *Building American Cities: The Urban Real Estate Game*. Englewood Cliffs, NJ: 1990.

Fitzgerald, Gerald E. "History of Zoning in New York City." (Thesis). 1955.

Foglesong, Richard E. *Planning the Capitalist City: The Colonial Era to the 1920s*. Princeton, NJ: 1986.

Friedenberg, Daniel M. *Life, Liberty and the Pursuit of Land: The Plunder of Early New York*. Buffalo, New York: Prometheus Books, 1992.

Gabaccia, Donna, *From Sicily to Elizabeth Street: Housing and Social Change Among Italian Immigrants, 1880–1930*. Albany, New York: SUNY, 1984.

———. "Little Italy's Decline: Immigrant Renters and Investors in a Changing City," from Olivier Zunz and David Ward (eds.). *The Landscape of Modernity: New York's Built Environment, 1880–1940*. New York: Russell Sage Foundation, 1992.

Genevro, Rosalie. "Site Selection and the New York City Housing Authority," *Journal of Urban History* 12 (August 1986): 334–352.

Gilderbloom, John I., and Richard P. Applebaum. *Rethinking Rental Policy*. Philadelphia: Temple University Press, 1988.

Gilfoyle, Timothy J. *City of Eros: New York City, Prostitution, and the Commercialization of Sex, 1790–1920*. New York: Norton, 1992.

Goren, Arthur A. *New York Jews and the Quest for Community: The Kehillah Experiment, 1908–1922*. New York: Columbia University Press, 1970.

Grebler, Leo, *Experience in Urban Real Estate Development*. New York: Columbia University Press, 1955.

———. *Real Estate Markets in a Declining Area* New York: Columbia University Press, 1952.

Greenberg, Cheryl Lynn. *"Or Does it Explode?" Black Harlem in the Great Depression*. New York: Russell Sage Foundation, 1982.

Gurock, Jeffrey S. *When Harlem was Jewish, 1870–1930*. New York: Columbia University Press, 1979.

Harris, Richard. "Working-Class Home Ownership in the American Metropolis" *Journal of Urban History* 17 (Nov. 1990): 46–69.

Hartog, Hendrik. *Public Property and Private Power: The Corporation of the City of New York in American Law, 1730–1870*. Chapel Hill: University of North Carolina Press, 1983.

Heskin, Allen David. *Tenants and the American Dream: Ideology and the Tenant Movement*. New York: Praeger, 1983.

Hirsch, Arnold. *Making the Second Ghetto: Race and Housing in Chicago, 1940–1960*. New York: Cambridge University Press, 1983.

Howe, Irving. *World of Our Fathers: The Journey of the East European Jews to America and the Life They Found and Made*. New York: Bantam Books, 1976.

Hughes, Everett C. *The Chicago Real Estate Board: The Growth of an Institution*. Chicago: 1931.

Indritz, Tova. *The Tenants' Rights Movement*. MA Thesis: Pittsburgh: University of Pittsburgh, 1970.

Jackson, Anthony. *A Place Called Home: A History of Low-Cost Housing in Manhattan*. Cambridge: MIT Press, 1976.

Jackson, Kenneth T. *Crabgrass Frontier: The Suburbanization of the Untied States*. New York: 1985.

Jaher, Frederick Cople. "Style and Status: High Society in Late Nineteenth Century New York," from F.C. Jaher (ed.). *The Rich, Wellborn and the Powerful* Urbana: University of Illinois Press, 1973.

———. "Nineteenth Century Elites in New York and Boston," *Journal of Social History* 6 (1972–1973): 32–3.

Kammen, Michael. *Colonial New York: A History*. New York: Oxford University Press, 1975.

Keller, Molly. "How New York's Developers reshaped the Metropolis," from *The Working Papers Series*. Denver: Society for American City and Regional Planning History, 1990.

Kessner, Thomas. *The Golden Door: Italian and Jewish Immigrant Mobility in New York City, 1880–1915*. New York: Oxford University Press, 1977.

———. *Fiorello H. LaGuardia and the Making of Modern New York City*. New York: Penguin Books, 1989.

Kim, Sung Bok. *Landlord and Tenant in Colonial New York: Manorial Society, 1664–1775*. Chapel Hill: University of North Carolina Press, 1978.

Kirk, Carolyn, and Gordon Kirk Jr. "The Impact of the City on Home Ownership: A Comparison of Immigrants and Native Whites at the Turn of the Century." *Journal of Urban History* 7 (August 1981): 471–498.

Lawson, Ronald. "The Political Face of New York's Real Estate Industry." *New York Affairs* 6 (2) (1980): 88–109.

———. with Mark Naison. *The Tenant Movement in New York City*. New Brunswick, NJ: Rutgers University Press, 1986.

Lipskey, Michael. "Rent Strikes in New York City: Protest Politics and the Power of the Poor." Ph.D. diss., Princeton University, 1967.

Lubitz, Edward. "The Tenement Problem in New York City and the Movement for Its Reform, 1856–1867." Ph.D. diss., : New York University, 1871.

Lubove, Roy. "The New York Association for Improving the Condition of the Poor: The Formative Years," *New York Historical Society Quarterly* 43 (1959).

———. *The Progressives and the Slums*. Pittsburgh: University of Pittsburgh, 1963.

———. *Twentieth-Century Pittsburgh: Government, Business, and Environmental Change*. New York: 1969.

Mandelbaum, Seymour. *Boss Tweed's New York*. New York: Wiley, 1965.

Marcuse, Peter. "The Beginnings of Public Housing in New York," *Journal of Urban History* 12 (August 1986): 353–390.

———. "Housing in Early City Planning" *Journal of Urban History* 6 (Feb. 1980): 153–176.

Marsh, Benjamin C. *Lobbyist for the People: A Record of Fifty Years*. Washington, D.C.: Public Affairs Press, 1953.

Miles, Michael, et al. *Real Estate Development: Principles and Process*. Urban Land Institute, 1991.

Moore, Deborah Dash. *At Home in America: Second Generation New York Jews*. New York: Columbia University Press, 1981.

Naison, Mark, Communists in Harlem During the Depression. New York: Grove Press, 1983.

Neibanck, Paul L. (ed.). *The Rent Control Debate*. Chapel Hill: University of North Carolina Press, 1985.

Osofsky, Gilbert. *Harlem: The Making of a Negro Ghetto, 1880–1930*. New York: Harper Torchbooks, 1966.

Pegg, Betsy. *Dreams, Money and Ambition: A History of Real Estate in Chicago*. Ph.D. diss.: University of Rochester, 1973.

Philpott, Richard A. *A Social History of Housing in New York City*. New York: Columbia University Press, 1990/

Pomeranz, Sidney I. *New York: An American City, 1783–1803, A Study of Urban Life*. Port Washington, New York: Ira J. Friedman, Inc., 1938.

Quinn, Thomas M., and Earl Phillips. "The Legal History of Landlord-Tenant Relations," in *Tenants and the Urban Housing Crisis*, ed. Stephen Burghardt. Dexter, MI: The New Press, 1972.

Rabinowitz, Alan. *The Real Estate Gamble: Lessons from Fifty Years of Boom and Bust*. New York: Amacom, 1980.

Rachlis, Eugene, and John E. Marqusee. *The Landlords*. New York: Random House, 1963.

Schwartz, Joel. *The New York Approach: Robert Moses, Urban Liberals, and Redevelopment in the Inner City*. Columbus, OH: Ohio University Press, 1993.

———. "Tenant Unions in New York City's Low-Rent Housing, 1933–1949" *Journal of Urban History* 12 (4) (August 1986, pp. 414–443.

Schachtman, Tom. *Skyscraper Dreams: The Great Real Estate Dynasties of New York*. Boston: Little, Brown and Company, 1991.

Stach, Patricia B. "Deed Restriction and Subdivision Development in Columbus, Ohio, 1900–1970," *Journal of Urban History* 15 (Nov. 1988): 42–68.

Stansell, Christine. *City of Women: Sex and Class in New York, 1789–1860*. New York: Knopf, 1986.

Stegman, Michael. "Slumlords and Public Policy" *The Appraisal Journal* 36 (April 1968): 201–211.

Stern, Robert A., et al. New York 1930: Architecture and Urbanism Between the Two World Wars. New York: 1987.

———. *New York 1900: Metropolitan Architecture and Urbanism* New York: Rizzoli, 1983.

Sternlieb, George. *The Tenement Landlord*. New Brunswick, NJ: Rutgers University Press, 1966.

Stokes, Isaac, N.P. *Iconography of Manhattan Island, 1498–1909*. New York: Richard H. Dodd, 1915.

Tenenbaum, Shelly. *A Credit to Their Community: Jewish Loan Societies in the United States*. Detroit: Wayne State University Press, 1993.

Tucker, William. *The Excluded Americans: Homelessness and Housing Policies*. Washington, D.C.: Regnery Gateway, 1990.

Ward, David, Poverty, Ethnicity and the American City, 1840–1925: Changing Conceptions of the Slum and the Ghetto. New York: Cambridge University Press, 1989.

———. and Olivier Zunz (eds.). *The Landscape of Modernity: Essays on New York City, 1900–1940*. New York: Russell Sage Foundation, 1992.

Warner, Sam Bass, Jr. *The Private City: Philadelphia in Three Periods of Growth*. Philadelphia: University of Pennsylvania Press, 1968.

———. *Streetcar Suburbs: The Process of Growth in Boston, 1870–1900*. New York: Athenaeum, 1962.

Weiss, Marc A. "Developing and Financing the Garden Metropolis: Urban Planning and Housing Policy in the early Twentieth Century," in *The Working Papers Series*. Denver: Society for American City and Regional Planning History, 1990.

———. "Real Estate History: An Overview and Research Agenda," *Business History Review* 63 (Summer 1989): 241–282.

———. *The Rise of the Community Builders: The American real Estate Industry and Urban Land Planning*. New York: New York University Press, 1986.

Wilentz, Sean. *Chants Democratic: New York City and the Rise of the American Working Class, 1788–1850*. New York: Oxford University Press, 1984.

Winnick, Loius. "Long-Run Changes in the Valuation of Real Estate by Gross Rents," *The Appraisal Journal* 20 (October 1952): 485–497.

Wright, Gwendolyn. *Moralism and the Model Home*. Chicago: University of Chicago Press, 1981.

———. *Building The Dream: A Social History of Housing in America*. New York: 1981.

INDEX

Academy Housing Project, Bronx, 182
Advisory Council of Real Estate Interests, 137
Agents, *see* Tenement House, lessees and leasing agents
Albany, 9, 58, 59, 60
Altz v. Lieberson, 154
Amalgamated Clothing Workers and International Ladies Garment Workers Union, 172
American Defense Society, 121
American Federation of Labor, 120
American Legion [Centralia, WA], 121
American Protective League, 121
Apartments and apartment living, 93–94
Ashforth, Edward, 127
Association for Improving the Conditions of the Poor, 22, 28
Astor, John Jacob, 13,
Astor, William W., 53
Astors, The, 36

Bache and Company, 41
Bayards, The, 11, 13
Beckerman, Abraham, 151
Beekmans, The, 11
Berger, Isador: background, 82–83; and GNYTA programs, 83–89, 123–124, 153; and insurance programs, 155–157; and mortgages, 176–177; and renovation, 174; and rent laws, 137, 147, 173–174, ties to other organizations, 126
Bingham, Police Commissioner, 79
Boston, 9
Bowery, 62
Brady, Thomas J., 66
British Council of Foreign Plantations, 10–11
Bronx, The, 47, 96, 97, 98, 106, 107, 109–110, 116–117, 138, 171
Bronx Council of Tenants Leagues, 151
Bronx Federation of Property Owners, 122, 146, 147
The Bronx Home News, 96, 97, 110, 114, 117, 165
Bronx Tenants League, 98–99, 102
Brooklyn, 171
Brooklyn Central Labor Union, 132
Brooklyn Real Estate Board, 128
Browne, Stewart: background, 125–126; and insurance, 86; and "Ironclad" lease, 157–166; and other organizations, 90, 146; and rent laws, 111, 136–137; and security

deposits, 157–159; and tenant vandalism, 149–150; and UREO, 128–129, death, 186
Brownsville, 97, 106, 107, 138
Brownsville Landlords' League, 103, 105–106, 118, 124, 192
Brownsville Tenants' League, 113, 132, 137, 139, 151
Buffalo, N.Y., 173
Builders League, 67
Building Trades, 58–70

Cabot, John, 11
Cahan, Abraham, 75
Cardozo, Benjamin, 154
Central Federated Union, 132, 138
Chandler, Charles F., 25
Charity Organization Society, 44, 64, 67–69, 152, 184
Charleston, South Carolina, 9
Christie-Forsythe Project, 178
Christie-Forsythe Project Property Owners Association, 83
Citizen Association of New York, 24
Citizens Budget Commission in 1929, 187
Citizens Housing Council, 184
Citizens' Protective Housing League, 150
Citizen's Union, 67
City and Suburban Homes Company, 139, 182
City Marshals, 76, 78, 79, 98, 144–145, 180, 189
City-wide Tenants Council (CWTC), 184–188
Columbia University, 151
Communist Party, 150, 179–184
Consolidated Tenants League, 179, 183
Continental Conference, 38

Copeland, Royal, 109,
Croker, Benjamin, 68
Cruger, Stephen Van Rensselaer, 7–8, 51–54
Cruickshank, E.A., 71

Daily North Side News, 114
Davies, J. Clarence, 127, 176
Day, Joseph P., 127
De Forest, Robert, 25, 67
DeLancey, James, 12
DeLanceys, The, 13
The Depression, *see* Tenement House, during the Great Depression
Deutsch, Bernard, 146
Diamond, Elias, 132, 160
Dix, Morgan, 7–8
Doyle, Edward P., 128, 137, 147
Dunbar Apartments, Harlem, 182
Dutch West Indies Company, 8–11

East Harlem, 46
East River, 11
East Side Tenants League, 104, 113, 122, 150
Edwards, Charles G., 147
Elkus, Abram, 129–130
Elliman, Douglas, 111
Ellman, A., 105
Ely, Horace S., 127
Ely, John A., 62
Emergency Relief Bureau, 187
Emergency rent laws, *see* Landlord-tenant laws, rent laws
England, 17–18
Espionage Act of 1917, 121
Esterbrook, William, 65–66
Etna Iron Works, 65

Fair Play Rent Association, 150, 151, 152
Federal Food Board, 95

256

Federal Fuel Administration, 95, 96
Federation of Architects, Engineers, Chemists, and Technicians, 186
Federation of Bronx Property Owners, 100
Feinstone, Morris, 139
Fifth Ward, 49
Five Points, 16, 49, 59
Fort Amsterdam, 9
Frank, Isaac, 104, 105, 106
French, Fred F., 182, 183
The Freiheit, 150
Fryer, William J., 64–70, 72–73

Garfield, Harry A., 95
Gengung, Judge, 97, 101
Gilder, James Watson, 26, 27, 51–54, 67
Gisnet, Morris, 99
Gitlin, Leo, 132, 139, 151
Goldsmith, Captain, 114, 117
Gompers, Samuel, 120
Gotham Court, 22–23,
Gould, Elgin R.L., 42
The Great Depression, *see* Tenement House; during the Great Depression
Greater New York Taxpayers Association (GNYTA): alliances, 100, 122, 125–129, 150; and arbitration, 122–124; and elections, 124–125; and eviction resistance, 180–181; Inspection Department, 153; and insurance, 153, 155–156; Law and Legislative Committee, 82; and lobbying, 147, 150, 167, 173; and programs, 81–91, 104–105, 153; promoting development, 178; Protection and Defense Committee, 83, 86–88, 153, 156; Rent Adjustment Committee, 123–124; and rent laws, 141; violence and detectives, 102–107, 118, 125, 180, 192; and decline, 185–186, 192
Greater New York Tenants League, 102, 104, 107–113, 117, 122, 139, 143, 150–151
Greater New York Mutual Insurance Association, 83
Grimm, Peter, 187
Griscom, John, 49
Grunfeld, Julius, 158–159

Hannah, Edward, 132, 138, 139
Harlem, 32, 42, 71, 107, 171, 179
Harlem Tenants' League, 114, 179
Harper's Weekly, 59
Hechscher, August, 178, 182
Heidelbach, Ickelheimer and Company, 41
Henry, William, 99
Hilly, Arthur: and MCRP, 124, 129, 138, 144–145, 180; and "Red Scare," 124, 139–140, 143,
Hirsch, Nathan, 111–116, 129, 132, 137–138, 143, 163
Hirshfield, David, 115
Homewood Gardens, Brooklyn, 182
Hone, Philip, 15,
Hoover, J. Edgar, 121, 139
Horace S. Ely and Company, 62
Hylan, John, 99–100, 111–113, 129, 132

Illinois Central Railroad, 53
"Immigrant banks," 36–40, 144
Immigration, 11, 37, English, 10–11, Jewish, 16, 32–33, Italian, 49
Immigration Act of 1918, 121
Industrial Workers of the World (IWW), 121
Insurance, *see* Tenement House,

INDEX 257

insurance; and Greater New York Taxpayers Association, and insurance
"Ironclad" lease, 157–166

James II, King of England, 11
Janeways, The, 13
Jenks, Edmund, 173
Jewish Charities in New York, 75
Jewish Daily Forward, 150
Jewish loan societies, 34
Joint Committee on the Affairs of Boroughs, 67
Joshnoff, Morris, 97, 107
Judges, *see* Municipal Court Judges

Knickerbocker Village, 182–183, 189
Knickerbocker Village Tenants Association (KVTA), 183

Ladies Anti-Beef Trust Association, 75
LaGuardia, Fiorello, 178
Landlord-tenant laws, 17–21, 56, 96–98, 99, 107–109, 111, 114, 129–133; dispossess proceedings and evictions, 109–111, 134–136, 139–140, 143–145, 179; rent laws, 133–141, 144–150, 169–170, 173, 189
Landlords, *see* Tenement House, landlords
Landlord associations, 61, 91, 146
Landlords' League, *see* Brownsville Landlords' League
Landlords' Protective Association, 103
Lawyers' Guild, 184
Lawyers' Title Insurance Company, 59, 62
Leases, *see* Tenement House; written and oral leases; and "Ironclad" lease
Lehman Brothers, 41

Lessees, *see* Tenement House, lessees and leasing agents
Lewinson, Judge, 117
Liability, *see* Tenement house; liability and lawsuits
Liebson, Bertha, 75, 76
Leitner, Jacob, 101
Lending, *see* Tenement House, loans and lenders; and "immigrant banks"
Limited Dividend Act of 1926, 172
Limited Dividend housing, 182
Little Italy, 32, 43
Livingstons, The, 65
Lockwood, Charles, 129, 131, 133
"Lockwood Committee," *see* New York (State), Joint Legislative Committee on Housing, "Lockwood Committee"
Lower East Side, 8, 16, 22, 32, 35–36, 38, 46, 60, 62, 73, 77, 79, 81–82, 124; and evictions, 143; and tenement property, 169, 171, 177
Lower East Side Public Housing Conference, 183–184
Luce, Robert, 113,
"Lumping," 43
Lusk, Clayton R., 122

MacNulty, Alexander, 147
Mann, Frank, 103, 148, 150
Markus, Henry, 71–72
"Marshal Row," 145
Marshals, *see* City Marshals
Mayor's Committee on Rent Profiteering, *see* New York (City), Mayor's Committee on Rent Profiteering
McClure's Magazine, 44
McVickar and Cruger, 51
Mediterranean Conference, 38

258

Metropolitan Fair Rent Committee, 188
Meyer, Katherine, 151, 152
Minkoff Bill of 1939, 186–187
Model Tenements, 1, 22–26, 182, 184
Morganstern, Morris, 100–101, 122
Morris, William E., 143
Mortgage, see Tenement House, loans and lenders; and "immigrant banks"
Moskowitz, Belle, 130
Moses, Robert, 130, 178
Multiple Dwellings Law, 154, 174–175, 187
Multiple Dwellings Law Revision Committee, 83
Municipal Court Judges, 76, 109–110, 139–140, 143, 146
Murray Hill, 11
Mutual Life Insurance Company, 53

Netherlands, The, 17
Neuman, Pauline, 77–78, 80
New Amsterdam, 9–10, 19,
New England, 10
New Netherland, 10–11
New York (City): 11; Board of Aldermen, 116, 123; Board of Examiners, 66; Board of Estimate, 126; Board of Health, 27, 53, 59, 72, 78, 99, 109; Buildings Department, 27, 64, 65, 66, 67, 69, 115; City Hall, 60; Committee on the Revision of the Building Code, 66–67; Fire Department, 115; Health Department, 115, 117, 148; Mayor's Committee on Rent Profiteering (MCRP), 111–118, 120, 123–124, 129, 132, 138, 144, 145, 160, 180; Mayor's Committee on Unemployment, 180; Municipal Housing Authority, 187; New York City Housing Authority, 184; Police Department, 115; property, 12–13; Tenement House Department, 69–70, 78, 115, 148, 156, 182; Water Supply, Gas, and Electricity Department, 115
New York (State): Assembly Judiciary Committee, 173; Board of Housing, 131, 171–172, 182, 183; Commission of Housing and Regional Planning, 164; Insurance Department, 153, 155, 156; Joint Committee to Investigate Seditious Activities, 122; Joint Legislative Committee on Housing "Lockwood Committee," 129, 131–133; Reconstruction Commission, 129–132, 133, 137; Supreme Court, 140
New York, Colonial, see New Amsterdam
New York Call, 103, 108, 110
New York City Housing Authority, see New York (City), New York City Housing Authority
New York Globe, 38
New York Herald, 77, 80, 114
New York Life Insurance and Trust Company, 53
New York Real Estate Exchange, 127
New York Real Estate Securities Exchange, 127
New York Rent Protective Association, 75
New York State Association of Real Estate Boards, 128
New York Sun, 28, 58, 114
New York Times, 43, 52, 53, 59, 114, 145, 162, 180
New York Tribune, 76

INDEX 259

New York World, 38
Newton, Charles D., 122
Niles, W. W., 71
Norden, Heinz, 183, 184
North Atlantic Conference, 38

Ogden, David, 53, 59, 62, 71
Orr, Samuel, 98, 99, 122, 152
Ottinger Law, 134
Owners' Syndicate Company, 98

Palmer, A. Mitchell, 121, 138, 139, 152
Philadelphia, 11
Phillips, Harold: and coal shortage, 100–101; and creation of GNYTA, 80–82; and elections, 124–125; and insurance, 86; in municipal court, 83, 87; and other organizations, 122, 124, 126, 160; and programs, 123, 124
The Plumber and Sanitary Engineer, 25
Post, Langdon, 182
"Profiteering," *see* World War I; and profiteering
Protective Association of Harlem Property Owners, 70–71
Public housing, 131, 173, 181, 187, 189

Queens, 171
Queensbridge Houses, 187

Rafter, Edward, 55
Real estate agents, *see* Tenement House, lessees and leasing agents
Real estate associations, 61–63, 73, 91, 100, 136, 178
Real Estate Board of Brokers, *see* Real Estate Board of New York (REBNY)
Real Estate Board of New York (REBNY), background, 127–129; and the "concession evil," 178; and leasing, 163; and lobbying, 132, 147–148, 167, 184, 185, 187; and other organizations, 90, 124, 126; and professionalization, 178; and "profiteering," 115; and public housing, 131, 184–185; and real estate securities, 176; and rent laws, 137, 141, 147, 157; and YMCA, 164
The Real Estate News, 90, 149, 169, 177
Real Estate Owners Association, 111
The Real Estate Record and Builders' Guide, 33, 56, 62, 66, 67, 68, 123
Reconstruction Commission, *see* New York (State), Reconstruction Commission
Reconstruction Finance Corporation, 182, 183
"Red Scare," 118–125, 183, 193
Reich, Ignatz, 82–84, 89, 155, 166, 172–174
Rent Controls, 187–189, 191–193
Rent Strikes, *see also* Tenant groups
Rent Strikes, of 1904, 74–77, 93–94, 193
Rent Strikes of 1907–1908, 77–82, 93–94, 193
Rent Strikes of 1918–1922, 95–108, 110, 112
Rent Strikes of the 1930s, 179–186
Republican Party, 53
Riis, Jacob, 23, 182
Robinson, Aaron, 139
Robitzek, Judge, 97, 101
Rochester, N.Y., 173
Roosevelts, The, 12
Roosevelt, Theodore, 68
Russell Sage Foundation, 35
Russian Revolution, 120, 121
Rutgers, Henry, 12

Saint Louis, Missouri, 40
Scholem Aleichem Cooperatives, Bronx, 182
Schwab, Joseph, 111
Sedition Act of 1918, 121
Settlement House Movement, 152
"Skinning," 43
Smith, Al, 129–130, 131
Socialist Party, *see* The Socialists
Socialists, The, 76, 93; Anti-Rent Agitation Bureau, 78; and city officials, 79–80, 82, 112–113, 119–121; and the Communist Party, 150, 180; and landlord organizations, 106, 125; and tenant organizations, 98, 100, 150, 180, 182; and the U.S. Justice Department, 138; and decline, 151
Society of Architectural Iron Manufacturers, 67
Sokolski, Albert, 124
Solomon, Charles, 122, 151
Somerstein, Michael, 115
South Bronx Tenants League, 152
Speculative builders, *see* Tenement House, speculative building
Stabler, Walter, 127
Stein, Clarence, 42, 137, 173, 182
Stokes, I. N. Phelps, 67
Strauss, Nathan, 184
Stuyvesant, Peter, 9, 12
Suburban growth, 172–173, 188

Tammany Hall, 68–69, 113
Tax Commission, 90
Taxpayers Alliance, 71
Tenant groups: and arbitration, 113, 116–117, 123; Brownsville, 103, 107–108, 179–180; and Eviction Resistance, 180; in Hell's Kitchen, 179–180; the South Bronx, 179–180 (*See also* Rent Strikes; and names of individual organizations)
Tenants Defense Union, 138
Tenement House: abandonment, 110; construction, 14, 15, 16, 17, 25, 41–45, 102–103, 171; conversions, 110, 174; during the Great Depression, 175–179; entrepreneurs and small-scale operators, 33–35, 45–47, 55–56, 169, 175, 188–190; health and safety, 7–8, 24–25, 44, 53, 55–56, 68, 85, 107 134, 148; inspection, 58–59, 64, 68, 79, 115–116, 149; insurance, 153, 189; landlords, 15, 17, 20–21, 28, 54, 60, 74, 77–78, 80–82, 107–108; laws and reform, 21–28, 56, 64–71, 74–75; lessees and leasing agents, 8, 15, 32–34, 47–54, 77, 80–82, 101, 108, 110, 189–190; liability and lawsuits, 84–87, 134–135, 153, 154–155, 174–175; loans and lenders, 34–42, 44–46, 89, 144, 170–171, 175–177; lobbying and lobbyists, 57–91, 100; maintenance and repairs, 174–175, 189; management, 31–32, 51–54, 60–61, 178; ownership, 32–34, 37, 40–41, 60–61, 173; population, 14; security deposits, 157–159; speculative building, 14–15, 16, 32, 35–36, 41–46; vacancies, 110, 124, 170–172, 175; written and oral leases, 134, 145–146, 157–166, 178
Tenement House Commission of 1900, 64–70
Tenement House Committee of 1894, 26–27, 51–54
Tenement House Law of 1867, 25, 27, 58
Tenement House Law of 1879, 26
Tenement House Law of 1894, 22

Tenement House Law of 1901, 56, 64, 69–71, 74, 85, 88, 93, 154
Thomas Garden Apartments, Bronx, 182
Tremont and Melrose Tenants Association, 150, 151, 152, 182
Trinity Church, 7–8, 12, 36, 50–55
Trinity Corporation, *see* Trinity Church
Trunk, Anton, 175
Trustees of Canandaigua v. Foster, 21

Union Insurance Company, 53
United Hebrew Trades, 132
United Neighborhood Homes Housing Committee, 184
United Real Estate Owners Association (UREO): formation, 64, 70, 71–72; and GNYTA, 86, 90, 125–127, 160–161; and lobbying, 128, 129, 141, 146, 167; and MCRP, 124; and rent laws, 111; and decline, 185–186
Untermeyer, Samuel, 129, 133
Upper West Side, 62, 171

Van Rensselaers, The, 11
Veiller, Lawrence, 43, 47, 64–70, 137
Vladeck, Benjamin, 132
Vladeck Houses, 187

Wagner Act, 192
Walker, Jimmy, 178, 180
Wall, Austin, 97–98, 107
Wall Street, 9
Ware, James, 25–26

Warren, Peter, 12
Washington Heights, 61–62, 97
Washington Heights Progressive Association, 61
Washington Heights Taxpayers Association, 61, 70
Washington Heights Tenants League, 99, 102
Welfare Council, Housing Section, 184
West Harlem, 97
West Side, 44
West Side Taxpayers Association, 147
Williamsburg Houses, 187
Williamsburg Tenants League, 102
Wilson, Woodrow, 120
Wingate, Charles, 25
Wood, Edith Elmer, 173
Workers' Alliance, WPA, 184
Workers' Cooperative Colony, 172
Workingmen's Home, "The Big Flat," 22–23
Workmen's Consumers League, 103
Works Progress Administration, 184
World War I: and profiteering, 111, 114–115, 118, 128; shortages caused by, 95–100

Yiddish Cooperative Heimgesellschaft, 172
Yorkville, 171
Young Mens Christian Association (YMCA), 164

Zeltner, Louis "Wireless Louie," 125